The
MANDALA
WORKBOOK

161

Also by Susanne F. Fincher

Coloring Mandalas 1: For Insight, Healing, and Self-Expression
Coloring Mandalas 2: For Balance, Harmony, and Spiritual Well-Being
Coloring Mandalas 3: Circles of the Sacred Feminine
Creating Mandalas: For Insight, Healing, and Self-Expression

The
MANDALA
WORKBOOK

Susanne F. Fincher

A Creative Guide for Self-Exploration,

Balance, and Well-Being

SHAMBHALA BOSTON & LONDON 2009

Shambhala Publications, Inc.
Horticultural Hall
300 Massachusetts Avenue
Boston, Massachusetts 02115
www.shambhala.com

9 8 7 6 5 4

Printed in the United States of America

⊗ This edition is printed on acid-free paper that meets
the American National Standards Institute Z39.48 Standard.

♻ Shambhala Publications makes every effort to print on recycled paper.
For more information please visit www.shambhala.com.

Distributed in the United States by Penguin Random House LLC
and in Canada by Random House of Canada Ltd

Designed by Deborah Hodgdon

Library of Congress Cataloging-in-Publication Data
Fincher, Susanne F., 1941–
The mandala workbook: a creative guide for self-exploration, balance,
and well-being/Susanne F. Fincher.
p.   cm.
Includes bibliographical references and index.
ISBN 978-1-59030-518-8 (pbk.: alk. paper)
1. Mandala. I. Title.
BL604.M36F564 2009
203'.7—dc22
2009010584

May the words, images, and activities of

The Mandala Workbook bring positive experiences

into the lives of those who find it

Contents

Acknowledgments   xiii

Introduction: What Are Mandalas?   1

Before You Get Started   33

Stage One: Resting in the Darkness   41

Mandala of Resting in the Darkness   44

Through the Circle   45

Qualities of the Circle   45

Qualities of the Circle, Variation I   46

Qualities of the Circle, Variation II   46

Circle of Self   47

Spider Web Mandala   47

Earth Mandala   48

New Moon Mandala   49

Womandala Bag   50

Mandala Card One   51

Stage Two: Floating into the Light   55

Mandala of Bliss   58

Million Star Mandala   58

Water Mandala   59

Rebirthing Mandala   59

Child's Play Mandala   61

Mandala of Possibilities   61

Soothing Mandala   62

Mandala of Abundant Potential   63

Mandala Card Two   64

Stage Three: Turning Toward the Journey   67

Mandala of Turning Toward the Journey   71

Loopy Thread Mandala   71

Umbilical Mandala   72

Mandala of Turning Points   73

Dream Mandala   74

Mandala of the Breath of God   75

Dream Catcher Mandala   75

Finger Painting Mandala   76

Labyrinth Mandala   77

Spinning Inward Mandala   79

Celtic Spiral Mandala   80

Mandala Card Three   81

Stage Four: Embracing the New   83

Mandala of Beginning   86

Madonna and Child Mandala   86

Mandala of Baby Me   87

Discovering the New Mandala   88

Nesting Mandala   89

Nurturing Flower Mandala   89

Mandala of Welcoming What's Up   90

Ancestors Holding Mandala   90

Pregnancy Mandala   92

Mandala Card Four   93

Stage Five: Claiming Selfhood   95

Hildegard's Mandala   97

Little Me Mandala   98

Bindu Mandala   99

Target Mandala   100

Family Circle Mandala   100

Defensive Shields Mandala   102

Standpoint Mandala   104

Nesting Boxes Mandala   105

Sphere of Influences   106

Sacred Flower Mandala   108

Blessing Words Mandala   108

God's Eye Mandala   109

Mandala Card Five   111

Stage Six: Igniting the Inner Fire   113

Mandala of Igniting the Inner Fire   117

Archetypal Parents Mandala   117

Mandala of Taming the Dragon   119

Adolescent Me Mandala   120

Mandala for Exploring a Dilemma   120

Summer Solstice Mandala   121

Mandala of Choosing Your Name   122

Mandala Card Six   123

Stage Seven: Squaring the Circle   127

Mandala of Firm Foundation   130

Squaring the Circle Mandala   130

Solar/Lunar Metallic Mandala   132

Mandala of the Sacred Marriage   133

Your Personal Shield Mandala   134

Medicine Wheel Mandala   135

Tree Mandala   136

Mandala of the Four Quadrants   137

Mandala Card Seven   138

Stage Eight: Functioning in the World   141

Mandala of the Functioning Ego   144

Mandala of the Shining Star   145

Star Me Mandala   147

Problem-Solving Swastika Mandala   148

Mandala Series for Healing   149

Mandala Invoking Your Creative Energy   150

Whirled Peace Mandala   151

Mandala Card Eight   152

Stage Nine: Reaping Rewards   155

Yantra Mandala   159

Basic Mandala Grid   159

Basic Mandala Grid for Impatient People   162

Mandorla Mandala   163

Eight-Pointed Star Mandala   164

Eight-Pointed Star Mandala, Variation   168

Solomon's Seal Mandala   169

Sublime Flower Mandala   170

Mandala of Your Higher Power   171

Mandala of Crystallization Moments   173

Mandala Card Nine   174

Stage Ten: Letting Go   177

Mandala of Sacrifice   180

Mandala of Letting Go   181

Burning Wheel Mandala   182

Ghost Catcher Mandala   183

Treasured Body Part Mandala   183

Mandala Gateway to the Worst Thing That Can Happen   184

Mandala for the Lost and Gone   185

Mandala for Facing It   186

Mandala Mask for Letting Go   187

Kali Yantra   188

Mandala Mask   189

Kinesthetic Mandala of Letting Go   190

Mandala Card Ten   191

Stage Eleven: Falling Apart   193

Mandala of Fragmentation   197

Mandala of Tearing Apart   197

Mandala of Your Least Favorite Color   198

Memory Mandala   200

Mandala of People I Dislike   202

Crazy Quilt Mandala   203

Mandala of Broken Mirrors   204

Falling Apart Mandala   205

Scratch Art Mandala   206

Mandala of Abiding Order   206

Pizza Mandala—with Everything   207

Mandala Card Eleven   208

Stage Twelve: Opening to Grace   211

Mandala of Receiving Grace   214

Mandala of Offering Up   214

Ecstatic Mandala   215

Mandala of Light at the Center of Darkness   216

Mandala of the Sacred Chalice   217

Mandala of Transient Beauty   217

Dancing Your Body Mandala   218

Mandala of the Winter Solstice   219

Mind's Eye Mandala   220

Mandala Card Twelve   222

Completing the Circle: Stepping to the Center   223

Mandala of Looking Back   224

Mandala of the Great Round Mandalas   224

Exploring Your Opposites   225

Mandala of the Great Round of the Year   226

Liturgical Year Mandala   227

Mandala of the Twelve Astrological Signs   227

Medicine Wheel Mandala   228

Mandala of Cards   229

Womandala Bag Reprise   230

Group Clay Mandala   230

Enso   232

Appendix A: Mandala Templates and Coloring Mandalas   235

Appendix B: Yoga for the Great Round   252

Appendix C: Songs for the Great Round   277

Appendix D: Using *The Mandala Workbook* with a Group   286

References   289

Index   293

About the Author   301

Acknowledgments

Many thanks to the women who joined me for a yearlong mandala group and allowed me to include their mandalas in the book: Diana Gregory, PhD, Edna Bacon, Kaaren Nowicki, Patty O'Keefe Hutton, Maureen Shelton, Era Sue Kahn, Annie Kelahan, and Annette Reynolds. Thanks to the numerous friends who inspired my creativity.

Thanks to the artists who allowed me to include their work: Donald Cooper (Sandler Hudson Gallery, Atlanta) and Joshua Rose (ZaneBennett Gallery). Thanks to Jonathan Lerner for permission to publish King Thackston's mandala. Thanks to the Oglethorpe University Museum of Art for permission to include the Francisco Roa painting.

Thanks to Brandylane Publishers, Inc. (www.brandylanepublishers .com) for permission to include an illustration by Rachel G. Norment from *Guided by Dreams: Breast Cancer, Dreams, and Transformation* (2006).

Thanks to Elizabeth Rucker for sharing her mandala and Medicine Wheel knowledge with me.

Thanks to Marilyn F. Clark (www.invitedbymusic.com) for her support and consultation related to music for the mandala group.

Many thanks to Maureen Shelton for her inspiring original music. Thanks also to Matthew Shelton (www.mandalaCD.com) for his technical expertise and assistance.

Very special thanks to Patty O'Keefe Hutton (www.contemporary icons.com) for her generous contributions of word mandalas, yoga illustrations, and written yoga instructions.

The
MANDALA
WORKBOOK

What Are Mandalas?

Mandala is Sanskrit for "magic circle" and, in the most basic sense, a mandala is simply a circle. Since ancient times in many cultures the mandala has had a powerful role in depicting, containing, and expressing the sacred. Mandalas can come in many forms, from stone carvings to domed cathedrals, ritual dances, and calendar cycles. No matter their form, mandalas offer us a profound way to examine our inner reality, to integrate that understanding with our physical selves, and to feel connected to the greater universe.

In this book, mandalas are used as an instrument for communicating messages in a nonverbal language, from unconscious parts of our psyche to our ego. Because the circle organizes and safely contains symbolic imagery, creating mandalas supports the conscious, discerning, and thoughtful part of us (our ego) in our dialogue with the unconscious. Mandalas offer a protected space where we can establish or regain our sense of balance.

Creating the mandalas in this book, whether danced, drawn, or visualized, is beneficial to our health and well-being. Our mandalas activate pathways between mind and body. Mandalas strengthen the roots of our ego—body image, preverbal aspects of self-image, and bodily sensations outside our awareness. Because they are symbolic, and symbols can contain many layers of meaning, mandalas can simultaneously express our earliest sense of identity, help us integrate present-day experiences, and open up future directions for growth.

When mandalas are witnessed with respect, their messages can become conscious. Then the information can more easily be integrated by our egos in the gradual process C. G. Jung called individuation. When we decipher the messages in our mandalas, we can also learn more about the deep inner guidance of the Self, the true center of our psyche. This allows us to be more fully informed about our wants and needs when making decisions.

> The Circle has been universally accepted as a religious image of perfection, a shape of total symmetry, hermetically closed off from its surroundings. It is the most general shape, possessing the fewest individual features but serving at the same time as the matrix of all possible shapes. —Rudolf Arnheim

Creating mandalas offers us a creative way to know ourselves better. Self-discovery was the goal of the women who joined me in a yearlong mandala group that was the source of many of the exercises in this book. Mandalas from this group are shown in plates 9–33. Before moving on to the exercises presented in this book, let's take a closer look at the historical and psychological meanings of mandalas.

Mandalas and the Sacred

The oldest mandalas known are carved or painted on rocks dating back to the Stone Age. They are scattered from South Africa to Scandinavia, from the southwestern United States to Australia.

Often these ancient mandalas are used to set apart a particular space, time, or action as non-ordinary or sacred. For example, a mandala shrine that was built an estimated ten to twelve thousand years ago survives in India and consists of a circular platform of beige sandstone supporting fragments of a red stone triangle. This shrine is thought to be associated with veneration of the Great Mother (Jayakar 1990), and the circular platform likely served as the focus of ritual celebrations in her honor.

This sense of mandalas indicating a sacred space is not just present in the physical spaces themselves, but also in how a physical structure is used. In the ancient religions of the East, mandalas are embedded in the beliefs and ritual practices. For example, Japanese pilgrims begin in the deep darkness of early morning to trudge up the volcanic cone of Mount Fuji, striving to reach the top for the auspicious rising of the sun. Fuji and the countryside around it were declared a mandala by the Shingon Buddhist sect centuries ago. Thus, pilgrims making the climb traverse a mandala to its core, the top of the peak, a place thought to be saturated with sacred energy.

Similarly, Bodh Gaya, the place of Buddha's enlightenment, provides another example of a mandala site. Pilgrims circumambulate a temple reputed to hold a relic of the Buddha. A similar arrangement exists in Borobudur, Indonesia, where a huge shallow dome representing the sacred

Corresponding to the spatial order of the world mountain, the four quarters, and the ever-cycling spheres, there is everywhere an associated temporal order of precisely measured days, months, years, and eons.
—Joseph Campbell

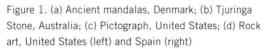

Figure 1. (a) Ancient mandalas, Denmark; (b) Tjuringa Stone, Australia; (c) Pictograph, United States; (d) Rock art, United States (left) and Spain (right)

mountain is surrounded by pathways, steps, railings, and statues creating a sacred mandala space for pilgrimages.

The dome as sacred mountain is transposed to an interior experience of space in buildings dedicated to religious practices in the Middle East and Europe. To sense what it is like in these spaces, first imagine that you are standing on an open, grassy plain beneath a clear blue sky. Taking in your surroundings, you will notice that the sky overhead is like a vast blue bowl. The edges of the bowl touch Earth at the horizon line, which forms a perfect circle around you, with you as its center. This expansive feeling is evoked by domes that naturally lift your attention upward and allude to an infinite space beyond their surfaces. Early Christian churches and the mosques of Islam use this quality of domed architecture to create inspiring sacred spaces. A renowned example of domed Islamic architecture is the Blue Mosque (see plate 1) in Istanbul, dating from around 1616. The blue, white, and ochre tiles that cover the interior walls are decorated in graceful designs that resemble fanciful blossoms. Golden calligraphy and subtle arabesques in blue, ochre, and ivory highlight the domes overhead. The lively patterns tend to make surfaces ambiguous, and one has the impression that the structure is but a gauzy veil separating the interior from infinite space beyond.

Some of the structures described above are examples of sacred spaces based on the cosmic mandala of traditional Eastern thought, where the Cosmos is represented as a mandala, which is conceived as a vast circle with a heavenly abode in the center. Others are buildings that utilize both the engineering strengths of the circle and the ability of circular space to create the feeling of safe enclosure, which fosters a spiritual sensibility. Still others utilize the circle as a device to lift the gaze upward, toward the heavenly realm, and even suggest sacred reality beyond the physical structure.

Just as mandalas are used to create a sacred space, they are also utilized to express, contain, and regulate sacred energy. Like an electrical transformer, circular images translate the power of the sacred into a form that can be safely taken in by human beings. Ceremonial mandalas are

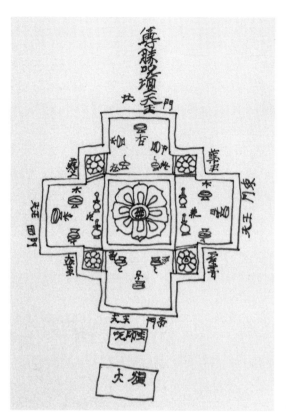

Figure 2. Oldest known ink drawing of a mandala,
ninth- to tenth-century China (Brauen 1997)
Figure 3. Body and mandala symbolism in Buddhism
(drawing inspired by Brauen 1997)

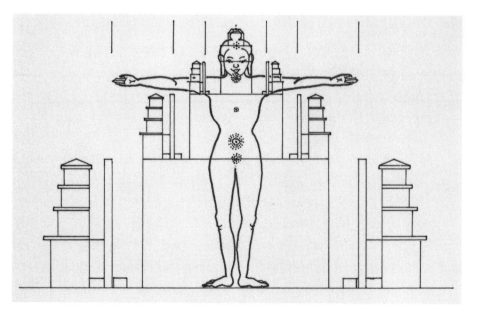

believed to attract and hold the attention of gods, goddesses, and ancestors during rituals. Mystics who have direct experience of the sacred often find circular images the best way to describe what they have encountered.

Hildegard of Bingen, a Christian mystic living in Germany during the fifteenth century, had visions of God as "a circle, a wheel, a whole" (Fox 1985, 24). Looking into the heart of reality, she experienced a mandala.

Hildegard of Bingen was not the only mystic who experienced sacred reality best expressed by a mandala. As a result of their study and reflection on the mystery of human existence, Jewish mystics developed the Kabbalah, a complex system of spiritual thought and practice that continues to enrich the lives of many today. A traditional circular diagram illustrates one of the Kabbalistic explanations for God's creation of the Cosmos. It is thought that there have been ten separate emanations of God, each resulting in creation. The diagram is comprised of ten concentric circles intersected by a line to the center. This line represents God's penetration into all ten emanations.

Christian iconography utilizes circles, as halos, to designate those who are divine beings (see plate 2). Also, great European cathedrals, such as the Notre Dame in Paris, have as their focus grand circular stained glass mandalas, or rose windows. The rose is a symbol for the Virgin Mary, and so the windows allude to her as the vessel, while the center of the rose window is usually occupied by Christ, her son. He is enfolded in swirling patterns of jewel-like color that highlight his prominence and organize the visual experience. The viewer's attention flows between center and periphery in a rhythmic, repeating pattern that is meditative, calming, and exhilarating.

Tibetan Buddhist ceremonies often begin with the construction of a sand mandala. These ritual mandalas invite and contain sacred energies in the form of deities. It is thought that their presence is of great assistance while meditations, teachings, and rituals are taking place. When the activity concludes, the mandala is ritually destroyed. The colorful sand is swept into a nearby stream, or dispersed among participants. By these actions any benefits generated by the practice are released for the good of all.

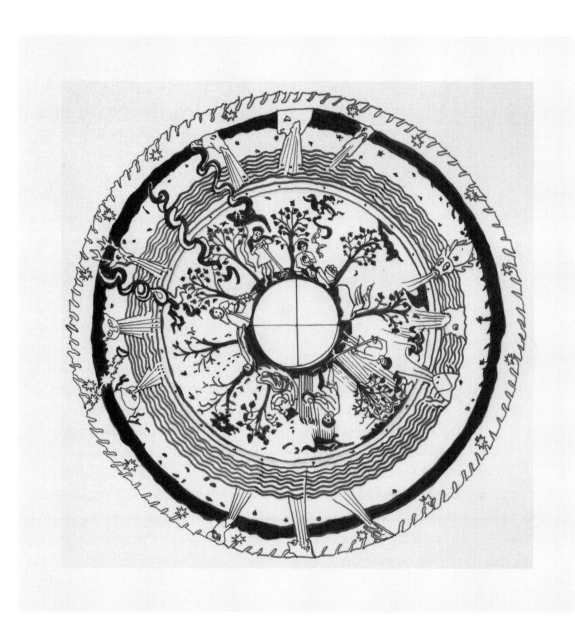

Figure 4. Medieval worldview from a manuscript of Hildegard of Bingen

Figure 5. Diagram inspired by Kabbalah

In a strikingly similar practice, Navaho wisdom keepers of the southwestern United States create circular dry paintings as part of ritual observances on many occasions. For the Blessing Way ceremony, dry paintings are constructed of cornmeal, pollen, and pulverized flowers sprinkled on a smooth background of sand or animal hide. The paintings serve as a central element in Blessing Way rituals that "place the Navaho in tune with the Holy People, and so ensure health, prosperity, and general well-being" (Kluckhohn and Leighton 1962, 212). These Navaho dry paintings are mandalas that, like the Tibetan sand mandalas, are respectfully dismantled when the ritual is completed.

These are just a few of the many and varied examples of mandalas being used to create, attract, focus, and contain sacred energy.

Mandalas and Movement

Mandalas are not limited to physical depictions, but can also be created through movement. Mandalas can be walked, danced, and visualized as well as drawn, sculpted, and built. The experience of movement teaches us about our body's physical center and helps us establish our balance.

Figure 6. *Bird People and Four Seasons* imagery associated with the Navajo Blessing Way ceremony

Once balanced we are able to move and maintain our alignment with our physical center. The simple movements we make when we stand balanced, extend our arms, and turn in place define a circular space that can be thought of as a movement mandala.

In the dancing of ancient people, circling movement was a symbolic joining with the paths of the moon, sun, and stars. As Maria-Gabriele Wosien explains: "Celestial motion being circular, man, by imitating it, partakes of the cosmic dance-round and begins to experience reality as order round a center" (1974, 20).

Once the proper centered balance was achieved, ancient peoples believed that one's physical being became a conduit of sacred energies as well as the medium for establishing a sacred, centered space: a mandala. These beliefs seem to live on in the movement mandalas created by the whirling of a dervish, the postures of a yogi, or the concentrated stillness of a monk spinning mandala visualizations.

Dervishes are members of a mystical sect of Islam established by the followers of the poet Rumi. Dressed in long skirted white robes and tall brown felt caps, they gracefully circle in prayerful devotion (see plate 3). Just as the moon and planets revolve on their own axes and also around the sun, dervishes spin while circling the center of the dance chamber. Through their meditative dancing they yield their bodies to sacred order so as to merge with the One.

In another example, yoga represents a Hindu approach to creating movement mandalas. Body stretches extending from a balanced position are practiced in order to achieve suppleness, comfort, and concentration. Indian practitioners cultivate steady balance by imagining the mythic thousand-hooded serpent with Earth poised on its head. The yogini's movement and imagery align her body vertically and horizontally. This makes of her body a place of balanced stillness—a mandala—where the distractions of physical discomfort have been eliminated.

Mandalas created by movement have a venerable history in Europe as well. Archaic spirals carved on megalithic stones may well represent the pathways trod by ceremonial dancers. Folk dances handed down from ancient times still use circling or spiraling lines of movement. These dances emphasize the relationship between center and circle and evoke the connection between dancer, community, and Cosmos. From these simple beginnings, more elaborate danced and moved mandalas evolved. As Wosien explains: "The primal maze, as traced outside prehistoric cave-sanctuaries, became the mandalic road of high religions" (1974, 26).

The *mandalic road* is exemplified today in American Christian churches by labyrinths, many based on the one in Chartres Cathedral. These offer worshippers a mandala comprised of a circuitous, but reliable, pathway to the center of a circle and back out. Walking into the center of the labyrinth can symbolize the spiritual journey toward God. This pathway also carries the worshipper toward contact with his or her own center and an inner experience of the sacred. According to Lauren Artress: "The labyrinth is a sacred place that can give us firsthand experiences of the Divine" (1995, xii).

The sound of footsteps, the vocal expression of traditional songs, and the rhythms of breath, beating hearts, and musical instruments create special sounds that are integral to sacred dance. Rhythmic sounds, especially, attune dancers to the creative thrust of the life force. Drums, rattles, and hand clapping often set the lively tempo of dances marking the life cycle of growing things. In a ritual practice transplanted from Africa, Black Americans of coastal Georgia and South Carolina perform a circle dance known as the ring shout.

> The ring shout combines call-and-response singing, hand clapping, percussion, and a precise shuffle and rhythmic movement complementing the song. The female shouters complement the song with small, incremental steps in a counterclockwise circle, never crossing their feet, and sometimes gesturing with their arms to pantomime the song. (Cyriaque 2003, 3)

The dance is performed in African American churches, often on New Year's Eve, or Watch Night. Dancing, singing, and rhythmic clapping of the ring shout help mark the turning of the year. Clearly, the ring shout demonstrates "the fixation of the ritual gesture and the creation of the enclosed sacred space that holds surcharged energy and power" (Jayakar 1990, 51). It is, therefore, a mandala.

It may seem strange to include perfect stillness as part of a discussion on mandala movement. However, stillness and movement go together like the center and circumference of a circle. To be perfectly still is to occupy the center point, while moving comes outward from the center point of balance. Therefore, I consider the mandala visualizations of Tibetan monks to be a form of mandala movement.

Seated in meditation pose, Tibetan monks use their imagination to visualize a huge mandala in front of them. Often the Buddha is seated at the center on a regal throne. More and more details are added to fill the mandala with symbolic images. After completing the visualization, the elements of the mandala are systematically merged into the central Buddha figure, which is then pictured flowing into the body of the meditator through the top of his head. So the Buddha mandala is taken in and becomes part of the practitioner.

These examples demonstrate that movement is much a part of mandalas. Meditative whirling dance induces a direct experience of the sacred. Labyrinth walking supports a contemplative journey inward. Circle dances are mandalas that re-invigorate a community. Even the very still, meditative generation of inner mandalas depends on the ability to be physically balanced. So we see how intimately involved the body is in creating mandalas that are danced, walked, and created in the mind's eye.

Mandalas and Cycles

The Sanskrit word *mandala* also means "a complete cycle through time." Mandalas from ancient cultures often symbolize the revolutions of time itself in an attempt to show orderly changes in nature and the affairs of human beings. One of the most widely known mandalas of cycles is the zodiac. The repeating cycle of the solar year and the apparent movements of stars and planets form the basis of the zodiac. In its simplest form the zodiac divides the year into twelve segments ruled by constellations. This mandala has been a source of information and predictions since invented by priests in Mesopotamia thousands of years ago.

The Native American Medicine Wheel, like the zodiac, is a mandala of a complete cycle. The Medicine Wheel can be created by laying stones on the ground in a circle with a center hub and four spokes oriented to the directions north, south, east, and west. The four spokes also represent the four seasons and the four times of day (dawn, noon, sunset, and midnight) as points of orientation in space and time. Symbolic animals are used to teach the varying qualities of the fourfold cycle. As Hyemeyohsts Storm explains, the Medicine Wheel represents "change, life, death, birth, and learning. It is the cycle of all things" (1972, 14).

Mandalas sometimes arise to record cycles. They can serve as a calendar, marking the passage of time and also allowing the prediction of important events. Ancient peoples in the British Isles built numerous stone circles that seem to relate to the seasonal cycles of sun, moon, and

Figure 7. Aztec Sun Stone is an elaborate calendar

stars. One of the largest and most complex is Stonehenge, constructed around 2200 B.C.E. The summer solstice is clearly identified by the alignment of the rising sun with certain stones in the circle.

Similar motives seem to have inspired the Aztec people of Mexico to create their massive-carved-stone calendar mandalas. About five hundred years ago the Aztecs were a small but powerful group living near where Mexico City is today. They crafted the Sun Stone, a disk of dark basaltic rock twelve feet in diameter. Although the concepts illustrated by the Sun Stone are of such complexity that their iconography has yet to be fully understood, it is thought that the Sun Stone tells of the beginning of the Aztec world, its evolution, and its inevitable end. It seems that the Sun Stone helped the Aztec people define their place, both in earthly affairs and in the universal passage of time over which their deities presided.

Marking the passage of time was also important in Christian monastic communities. Having a system for counting time allowed coordination of the activities of monastic life. This need gave rise to another mandala of time: the canonical hours Vigils, Lauds, Prime, Terce, Sext, None, Vespers, and Compline. These hours divide the twenty-four-hour day so as to order the activities of prayer, work, and rest. Eventually, this way of observing time evolved into our presentday concept of a day as comprised of twenty-four equal segments, or hours.

The Buddhist Wheel of Life is another example of a mandala of cycles. It is frequently seen near the entrance of meditation halls where it is placed to educate and inspire practitioners. The twelve vignettes around the outer edge of the mandala illustrate the repeating stages of human existence that inevitably cause suffering. Buddhists strive for enlightenment in order to set themselves and others free from this ongoing cycle.

A similar view of life as an ever-turning cycle is the basis of ancient stories from the Middle East. Apparently based on the vegetative life cycle so important in early agriculturally based cultures, this motif is identified by Sylvia Perera as the *great round of nature* (1981, 21). The stages in this schema are based on the activities of agriculture: planting of seeds, sprouting plants, cultivation of crops, and harvest. Then follow

Figure 8. Buddhist Wheel of Life

the thrashing, separation of seeds, and processing of raw grains into food. The cycle begins again with the next planting.

We find this Great Round in the stories of gods and goddesses who must leave an abundant, light, lively existence, and fall into periods of darkness, exile, or death. After a time, they are miraculously revived. Upon returning to life, they are beings transformed, bringing back wisdom and the renewal of life for all. The myths of Inanna, Isis and Osiris, and Demeter and Persephone fit within this paradigm of the Great Round: the mandala of nature's cycles.

Peoples separated by time, place, and custom have used circles to designate sacred space, to regulate sacred energies, and to mark the repeating cycles of nature. This widespread reliance on circles, circular movement, and mandalas when addressing deep human concerns demonstrates that the circle has remarkably universal appeal. Could it be that the circle is especially useful for organizing human experience?

Mandalas and Self-Understanding

At the root of many, if not all, mandalas is the human longing to know oneself, to experience harmony, and to grasp one's place in the Cosmos. The process of developing self-awareness and understanding one's place in the order of things begins, of course, in infancy. Even prior to birth a baby is imprinted with an experience of circular space as she is closely held in the rounded space of her mother's womb. Then she is born through the circular birth canal and feeds at her mother's round breast in mutual loving gaze with her mother, whose rounded face further imprints the circle.

Reflecting on the stages of human development, we find that the circle is an ever-present reference point that supports the emergence of a body image, that is, a sense of oneself as a physical being (Cash and Pruzinsky 2002). An infant soon becomes capable of viewing most of her own body while lying in her crib. Because her eyes are spherical, her visual field is circular. Using her visual perceptions, she has enough information to know her body as that which is always present (within her circular visual field).

The imagery of centering is archetypal. To feel the whole in every part. —M. C. Richards

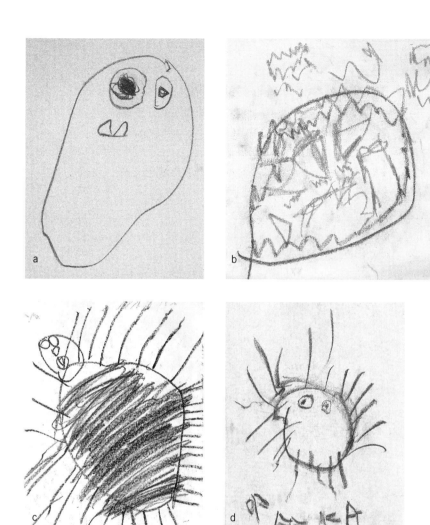

Figures 9a–e. A series of drawings made over a period of six months by a four-year-old girl shows the normal progression in children's art from mandala to human figure

Subsequent development takes place as a toddler matures and explores his physical and social environments. If all goes well he develops the capacity to be conscious of himself as a source of willed, goal-directed behaviors. He develops a self-image, or ego, which functions as the psychological center of consciousness. Nonetheless, rootedness in the early body image seems to remain the basis for his self-awareness as explained in Johnson's book *The Body in the Mind* (1987). Children's drawings suggest that this is the case.

Circles are among the earliest intentional drawings produced by children, beginning around age two (see figures 9a, 9b, 9c, 9d, and 9e). Then mandalas, such as beaming suns, begin appearing. Later drawings, from around ages three to five, depict people as circles with arms and legs attached. These designs appear to be based on early observations within the circular field of vision merged with the child's increasing social and kinesthetic awareness.

Circular structures in the human body shape our experience and perception. These structures are associated with gestation, vision, and nurturing during infancy. The body image made possible through these early experiences converges with the capacity for self-awareness to form a personal identity rooted in the physicality of the body and its potentials for feeling, moving, seeing, thinking, and self-expression. These early experiences establish an image of self that is the basis for development of a child's ego, a psychic structure that is further shaped in relationships with important others. The development of a child's self-image is reflected in the mandalas he or she creates.

As adults, creating mandalas can continue to provide us with insights into our own self-image. A survey of the work of artists reveals a widespread use of circular designs with awareness of complex personal, cultural, and historical meanings. Concerning his circle paintings (see plate 4), Joshua Rose comments:

> The circle: symbol of the Sun, the Moon, geometric perfection, Western rationalism, Eastern mysticism, the cycle of life, eternal love, the enclosure of the heart, simplicity and spontaneity, the Zen symbol

"supreme," a mirror, the universe, all and nothing, a zero, a wheel, the wheel, enlightenment itself, etc. *I use the circle as a vehicle to carry with it all of the competing notions and ideas of both clarity and confusion that populate my world* [italics added]. It allows me to do this while paying honor to all the other possible uses and users of the circle even as I try to make it mine. (Rose 2008)

During his travels in South Asia, Don Cooper noticed that a central dot often appeared in the painting and sculpture there. The dot, known by the Sanskrit term *bindu*, represents the "sacred point of origin and return." Inspired by this concept, Cooper now begins a painting by making a central dot—a bindu (see plate 5). He then lets

concentric circles radiate from this point and represent eternal cycles of cosmic evolution and involution and a link to the Whole. *The process of creating these works is both ritualistic and meditative. Hopefully they inspire similar experiences for the viewer* [italics added]. (2008)

Don Cooper's radiant mandalas generate a feeling of calm elation and lead the viewer toward an experience of being centered.

King Thackston created some eighty mandalas during his lifetime. They began as simple forms and became more and more complex through time. Jonathan Lerner comments that Thackston "referred to the later mandalas as journals, and *they are full of imagery having to do with what he was doing or going through*" [italics added] (Lerner 2008).

The time and attention to detail that King Thackston gave his mandala journals indicate that they were deeply meaningful to him (see plate 6). He has left a legacy of dazzling images that reflect the unfolding of his life journey.

Francisco Roa's *Sands Flowers* might not be recognized as a mandala at first (see plate 7). His painting depicts an arrangement of decaying flowers in a fragile glass vase set on a mantle in front of a weathered metal

BINDU

dot

drop

point of origin and return

nucleus of condensed energy

consciousness

expanding

receding

endless form

inner space

being

—Don Cooper

circle. There is here a celebration of the beauty of entropy, a necessary stage along the way in nature's cycle of the Great Round, but one rarely honored in modern times. The metal circle frames this bouquet and sets it apart from its surroundings. It is held up as *the* bouquet, a symbol for life itself. We are invited to appreciate the beauty of every fragile moment we live. This painting is a mandala that celebrates the delicate point of balance established by conscious being.

In examining the work of women artists, Judy Chicago noticed that much of their work was constructed around a center and that "there seemed to be an implied relationship between their own bodies and that centered image" (1982, 143). Her Great Lady series exemplifies this centered circular imagery. The use of circles in the self-expression of women is affirmed, sadly, in the art of mothers who have experienced pregnancy loss. Predominant images in their artwork include "circles, ovals, and soft organic shapes that speak to us of being held, contained, and centered" (Seftel, 77).

Contemporary artists explore circular art forms—mandalas—as a reflection of their personal encounter with the mysteries of human existence. Circles with centers appear to be aligned with body sense, especially in the self-expression of women. Artists frequently describe the creation of circles as a relaxing, meditative, or soothing activity. Moreover, viewing their mandalas can be a positive experience for the artist and others as well because, as pointed out by Robert Henri:

> The object which is back of every true work of art is the attainment of a state of being. [The work of art] is but a by-product of the state, a trace, the footprint of the state. These results become dear to the artist who made them because they are records of states of being which he has enjoyed and which he would regain. They are likewise interesting to others because they are to some extent readable and reveal the possibilities of greater existence. (Goldwater and Treves 1945, 401)

[The spiritual background of mandalas is] the yearning to find out a way from time to eternity, to help the primeval consciousness, which is fundamentally one, to recover its integrity. —Tucci

Through the work of these artists we can see that the circle holds us, creates a place for us to know ourselves, and helps us grasp our place in all that is. Why is it so that adults as well as children are moved to create circles and mandalas? The ideas of C. G. Jung can be useful for exploring this question further.

Mandalas and Jung

Swiss psychoanalyst C. G. Jung pointed out that circular designs are significant in the process of becoming an authentic individual. Jung discovered through his own creative self-expression, as well as that of his patients, a spontaneous desire to construct circles filled with shapes and colors. He began calling these mandalas because they were reminiscent of the mandalas he knew from the sacred art of Asia. He surmised that mandalas are a manifestation of the self-regulating system of the psyche, which maintains our orderly functioning and, when necessary, restores stability. Jung wrote:

> The severe pattern imposed by a circular image compensates the disorder and confusion of the psychic state. This is evidently an attempt at self-healing on the part of Nature, which does not spring from conscious reflection but from an instinctive impulse. (1973, 3–4)

Jung's experience led him to believe that mandalas are associated with an inborn urge to grow toward wholeness, defined as the full expression of one's potentials. This growth process is governed by a psychic center in each of us that Jung called the self [hereafter "Self" except in direct quotes from Jung's writings]. Just as an acorn knows how to grow into an oak tree, the Self holds the pattern for our wholeness. It also generates the urge to fulfill our potential in a process of growth Jung referred to as *individuation.* The mandalas we spontaneously create have their source in the dynamism of the Self. They reflect our grow-

Every mandala I drew became a discovery about who I am. —Laurie Downs

ing toward wholeness and our acceptance of the Self as our psyche's generative center point.

Mandalas come to us in many forms. They can be created with art media, they can be danced, and they can be dreamed. Jung was aware of the full range of mandala expression:

> Among my patients I have come across cases of women who did not draw mandalas but danced them instead. The dance figures express the same meanings as the drawing. My patients find that they somehow express and have an effect on their subjective psychic state. (1978, 25)

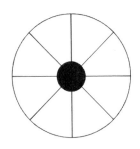

Figure 10. Mandala dream image of a hat smashed against the wall (Jung 1974)

Jung often encountered mandalas in the dreams of his patients. He describes one series of dreams where mandalas appeared as a snake circling the dreamer; a hat smashed against the wall; yellow balls rolling around in a circle; yellow light like the sun with eight rays going out from the center, but obscured by fog; and a starry circle rotating, with pictures representing the seasons at the cardinal points (1974).

Artist Meinrad Craighead writes of a recurring childhood dream she experienced during family transitions. It is rich in mandala imagery. Here is a portion of her dream:

> Gradually earth and sky separate and on the horizon a dark speck appears. [My white puppy and I] walk toward the object and it grows as we come to it. . . . The tree and the sea announce their identity simultaneously. The earth ends in the sea; the tree grows at its edge. We continue walking toward the great pine and enter the substance of the tree. In the darkness my dog disappears but this does not grieve me. I circle through the multiple concentric rings of the tree, shrinking and aging within each ring. At last the spiraling ends. I arrive at the small dark spot of origination. When I touch this innermost center I realize I am already there. I have been journeying to where I am. (2003, 36)

As suggested by Ms. Craighead's story, dream mandalas and the urge to create mandalas are pronounced during stressful times. Jung maintains that mandalas are a natural healing response. This is born out by the mandalas of Laurie, a cancer survivor. While undergoing treatment she spontaneously began drawing mandalas and continued drawing them for several years. Creating mandalas provided a positive way to affirm her existence as more than just a cancer patient. She said her mandalas helped her *"find out more of who I was and where I came from"* [italics added] (Fincher 1991, 181).

In a similar example, Rachel Norment got the idea for her mandala while she was receiving radiation treatment for breast cancer. Several months later she developed her idea into a painting that uses symbolic composition and colors to depict what had happened during her successful treatment (see plate 8).

> While each treatment was taking place *I visualized healing energies coming into my body through the crown chakra* [italics added] and by means of the actual radiation. I visualized the radiation beams vaporizing any remaining cancer cells to eliminate them from my body. (Norment 2006, 99)

From these examples we can see how mandalas express healing energies. While times of crisis, especially, lead to mandala making, it is natural to create mandalas during all of the many stages of our life's journey. Just as a wheel must have a hub in order to turn, the journey of a lifetime requires a centering point as well. Mandalas can connect us to our center even when the turning of the wheel pulls us into a busy lifestyle. Through time we can come to trust the centering force that is the Self, as Jung did.

> I began to understand that the goal of psychic development is the self. There is no linear evolution; there is only a circumambulation of the self. Uniform development exists only at the

The mandala is the center. It is the exponent of all paths. It is the path to the center, to individuation. —C. G. Jung

beginning; later, everything points toward the center. (Jung 1965, 196–97)

In this way of looking at life, no experience is lost or wasted. All events are viewed as meaningfully placed on a spiraling cycle that unfolds according to the mysterious pattern of our wholeness. As a *circumambulation of the Self,* our life may be viewed as a mandala comprised of countless moments—of ebbs and flows of energy and varied states of consciousness anchored by our psyche's center point. Life is a process of becoming. As Verena Kast explains: "All boundaries that are currently valid, and that define us at the moment, must be repeatedly questioned, sacrificed, and traversed" (1992, 114).

Figure 11. Contemporary European mandala drawn by a patient of C. G. Jung

Jung found a variety of mandala forms associated with personal growth. Though he identified no particular order in their appearance, these are mandalas that Jung observed in the artwork of his patients:

1. Circular, spherical, or egg-shaped formation.
2. The circle is elaborated into a flower (rose, lotus) or wheel.
3. A center expressed by a sun, star, or cross, usually with four, eight, or twelve rays.
4. The circles, spheres, and cruciform figures are often represented in rotation (swastika).
5. The circle is represented by a snake coiled about a center, either ring-shaped (uroboros) or spiral (Orphic egg).
6. Squaring of the circle, taking the form of a circle in a square or vice versa.
7. Castle, city, and courtyard (temenos) motifs, quadratic or circular.
8. Eye (pupil and iris).
9. Besides the tetradic figures (and multiples of four), there are also triadic and pentadic ones. (Jung 1973, 77)

The notion that mandalas are associated with natural cycles of human experience was investigated further by Joan Kellogg (1983, 1984). Inspired by Jung's work, she collected and codified mandala designs into a system

Figure 12. Archetypal Stages of the Great Round of Mandala (Kellogg 1978; drawn by Susanne Fincher 2003)

she called the Archetypal Stages of the Great Round of Mandala. Let us explore these in more detail.

Archetypal Stages of the Great Round of Mandala

The Archetypal Stages of the Great Round of Mandala (Great Round hereafter) consists of twelve stages in a "spiraling path of psychological development" (Kellogg and DiLeo 1982, 38). The stages one through twelve are designated: Void, Bliss, Labyrinth, Beginning, Target, Dragon Fight, Squaring the Circle, Functioning Ego, Crystallization, Gates of Death, Fragmentation, and Transcendent Ecstasy. Kellogg identified prototypical mandalas associated with each stage.

Kellogg's Great Round reflects the dynamic relationship between ego, the center of consciousness, and Self, the center of the whole psyche residing in the unconscious. Stages of the Great Round reveal the ego's experience of the flow of energy from the Self. Energy is high in stages when ego is closely aligned with the Self. Energy is low during stages when it is withdrawn from ego into unconscious processes.

The Twelve Stages of the Great Round are a schema for describing a continuous, cyclical pattern of personal growth. Through time you naturally experience all of the stages of growth described as the Great Round. As the spiraling stages are experienced again and again, you can better integrate an awareness of the Self, the center point guiding your process. The mandalas you create both mirror and support your growth process.

Unlike many developmental theories that posit a linear progression from simpler, less mature states to more complex mature states, the concept of the Great Round is grounded in ancient ideas of life as a spiraling journey toward greater wisdom and wholeness. In this way of looking at life, all your experiences are viewed as meaningfully placed on a cycle that revolves around the Self as you more and more fulfill your potential for wholeness. Let us explore the stages further.

> The mandala can be considered as a chalice for receiving all the contents of consciousness.
> —Joan Kellogg

Stage One

Stage One recalls the quiescence of winter, and *resting in the darkness* of a moonless night. It is aligned with the month of January, but has its true beginning at the winter solstice, the longest night of the year. The sun is low and temperatures are cool. Living things are dormant or hibernating. Seeds are buried underground and out of sight.

mandala one

Stage One is reminiscent of your earliest memories encoded at the cellular level even prior to your birth. During your initial visit to this stage early in your mother's pregnancy, you lay inert, a simple-celled creature attached to the wall of her womb. Outwardly, your mother's body showed no signs of pregnancy. The intrauterine environment was dark deep inside her body. Yet the mysterious process of becoming human had begun even as you were *resting in the darkness.*

Stage Two

Stage Two corresponds to the month of February and to the pink and gold predawn sky. In traditional cultures young herd animals are born this month. Ancient observances of the flame of life are perpetuated in candlelit vigils on the Eve of St. Agnes. St. Bridget, the Celtic midwife of Jesus, is honored in folk traditions. A straw dolly likeness of her is freshly clothed for the arrival of spring.

mandala two

Stage Two is a place of sublime peace, where we are rocked upon the waters of a gentle world. Time moves slowly. We experience ourselves as all loving and infinitely loved. In this drowsy predawn existence, we hardly notice that something important is missing: our individuality. We are content peacefully *floating into the light.*

Stage Three

Stage Three recalls the month of March. This stage is a time of new energy, when conditions, like spring weather, can change from mild to bracing before you turn around twice. The first plants have emerged, and brave flowers have begun to appear. Stage Three is first experienced when we become active in our mother's womb. Later, Stage Three is a time when

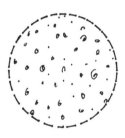

mandala three

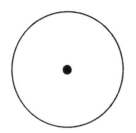

mandala four

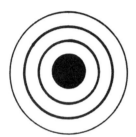

mandala five

mandala six

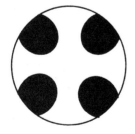

mandala seven

you find yourself at one with the unfolding cycle of nature's living things as you are actively *turning toward the journey.*

Stage Four

Stage Four aligns with the month of April, when growing things burst into bloom. It recalls the risen morning sun, full of light and promise, and the waxing moon brightening the evening sky. Stage Four is first experienced during infancy when you bond with the one who cares for you. Your back becomes strong and you sit proudly upon mother's lap. In Stage Four you will find yourself *embracing the new* in your life.

Stage Five

Stage Five is reminiscent of the heightened energy of May, the warming sun of late morning, soft evenings lighted by the moon—almost full, yet promising more. Stage Five is first experienced when you begin to assert your independence from your beloved caregiver. As a toddler you discover your dislikes and communicate these by saying "No!" Of course you still want to be cuddled and comforted, too. The conflicting needs for independence and security set the tone of Stage Five, as you are *claiming selfhood.*

Stage Six

Stage Six carries us into the brightness of June: the year's longest day, and a moon bright enough to read by. It is like a long, warm, late morning building toward noontime heat. Stage Six is first experienced during adolescence as you struggle to complete your separation from the world of your parents and experience yourself as a unique being. Your ego, as the carrier of individual consciousness, is now beginning to shine its own light instead of reflecting that of the elders. During this stage we are *igniting the inner fire.*

Stage Seven

Stage Seven presents us with the intensity of July, the clarity of midday, and the moon peering down like a wide-open eye on a velvety summer night. Stage Seven reflects a high point of self-awareness, experienced first in young adulthood. Consciousness is bright, alert, and intense as the sun at high noon. We have the ability to learn, to plan, and to love another as we are owning the light and *squaring the circle.*

Stage Eight

Stage Eight recalls August, the heart of each year's growing season. The productive activity following a pleasant noontime break typifies this stage. The moon is just less than fully rounded. Stage Eight is comparable to the active young adult phase of life. Our education is complete and we are doing our work, enjoying expanded opportunities and finding cooperation with others agreeable. We are *functioning in the world.*

mandala eight

Stage Nine

Stage Nine may be compared to the month of September: crops are completing the growth hoped for when seeds were planted. The sun's intensity recedes into the golden glow of late afternoon. The moon is like a silver disk shaved smaller with each night that passes. Stage Nine compares to the decades of adult accomplishment when we are making a home, earning our living, and raising our families. Activities settle into a harmonious and satisfying pattern. We are *reaping rewards.*

mandala nine

Stage Ten

Stage Ten reminds us of the month of October: the last of the harvest is gathered in. The sun is dipping lower in the west, burning as it goes. The moon of this stage is waning, shrunk to less than half its full size. Stage Ten corresponds to the midlife crisis, whether experienced at thirty or at eighty. Parental responsibilities are less compelling, we are no longer busy with an important project, or perhaps we are retiring from a busy career. It is a time of *letting go.*

mandala ten

Stage Eleven

Stage Eleven is like the month of November when stubble is left in the field to rot. The sun has departed leaving behind only lurid fragments of color

mandala eleven

along the horizon. The moon of Stage Eleven is a slender, waning crescent. A cold wind out of the north may be our uninvited companion. Stage Eleven is a time when leaves turn to mush on the ground, snow is on the way, and the trail is hard to see. Likely we feel as if we are *falling apart.*

Stage Twelve

mandala twelve

Stage Twelve brings us to the month of December and the longest night of the year. The sun is gone from view, but its rays sparkle in the dancing polar lights. The moon is a curving silver line at the edge of an invisible disk. Stage Twelve coincides with the wisdom and peace of mind that can be attained later in life. We begin to experience a center—our center—that holds all experiences in a pattern of wholeness. We are *opening to grace.*

Prototypical mandala forms are associated with each stage of the Great Round. Every stage has challenges and opportunities for growth and development. During each stage we tend to experience certain feelings, cognitive and motor functioning, and even ways of viewing reality. Energy levels vary from stage to stage. Moving from Stage One through Stage Twelve, we are aware of a quiet beginning, then increasing energy and accomplishment, and finally the natural end of the cycle with decreasing energy and meaningful resolution by Stage Twelve.

The stages comprise a cycle that is lived not once but many times. When we find ourselves returning to a stage again, we resonate with all our previous visits to this stage. We then have an opportunity to rework and realign past experience in light of the present, and to weave the past and present into a harmonious pattern that opens up new possibilities for the future.

Since ancient times mandalas have been drawn, danced, dreamed, and built. They have been used to designate sacred space, to provide a container for the expression of intense spiritual emotion, and to honor a connection among Cosmos, community, and individual. Today mandalas are created spontaneously by children as they develop their sense of being a person, by artists exploring the qualities of center and circle, and by adults seeking self-awareness, creative self-expression, and healing.

Mandalas both express and move us along our growth process toward wholeness. They facilitate communication between conscious and unconscious and support our ego as we discover our connection to the Self, our true center. In this process we learn that our ego is not a static entity, but that it will be frequently redefined as a natural part of our growth process.

The Archetypal Stages of the Great Round of Mandala reflect the variations in our ego's lifelong relationship with the Self. Differences among the stages in consciousness, emotions, productivity, and developmental tasks reveal a natural rhythm. Accepting that life is a flow and that all stages are equally valuable means that no experience is lost or wasted. Learning to appreciate our mandalas as an outward sign of our inner experience enhances our ability to know ourselves. We can then better align our choices with the deep wisdom of the Self.

The Mandala Workbook offers you a sequenced experience of creating mandalas. Carefully devised mandala exercises resonant with ancient and modern approaches inspire creative self-expression and support your personal growth. Guidelines for relating to your mandalas offer a valuable resource for deriving personal meaning from the mandalas you create. *The Mandala Workbook* is organized to support your exploration.

Before You Get Started

The Mandala Workbook is itself a mandala that invites you to join a complete cycle of creation, from beginning through completion. Chapters 1 through 12 describe stages inspired by Joan Kellogg's Great Round (as described in the introduction), including their qualities of consciousness, levels of energy, developmental issues, and challenges and opportunities for personal growth. A number of mandala projects for exploring each stage are included. Choose as many or as few as you like. Project goals, a materials list, and directions are given for each mandala. Although mandala projects are designed for individuals, they are also appropriate for groups (see appendix D).

Exploring the chapters in order will move you systematically through the Great Round. Completing the whole cycle helps you appreciate the natural ups and downs that are a part of life. You may find moving through the whole cycle helps you to develop skills for living in stages that are less familiar. It is also fine to start with a stage that relates to what you are feeling and experiencing in the present moment. Follow your intuition for the order in which you explore stages.

The concluding chapter, "Completing the Circle," offers activities that promote a synthesis of the experiences of the previous chapters. The projects in this chapter highlight the connections among mandala stages and offer a satisfying conclusion to the creative process delineated in *The Mandala Workbook.*

The Mandala Exercises

Creating mandalas is a simple activity that enriches your creative self-expression. There is no right or wrong way to create a mandala. Therefore, I encourage you to cultivate an attitude of respect for the mandalas you create. Mandala projects described here are not intended as a substitute for therapy, but as support for your self-awareness, personal growth, and creative self-expression.

Before you begin, assemble your art materials and your journaling supplies. The Basic Art Materials list on page 36 will provide what you need for most of the mandalas in this book. When additional materials are required for a particular mandala project, they will be listed above the directions for the mandala. Of course you are welcome to improvise with materials you have on hand or to follow your intuition about what the right materials are for your creative work.

Find a private and convenient place to create your mandalas. Set aside a special time—at least an hour—for exploring exercises. You may want to light a candle or incense to mark the space and time as set apart from your regular daily routine. I suggest that you begin your time of creating mandalas by relaxing and centering.

You will find the simple yoga postures described in appendix B helpful for this. The yoga is carefully structured to align your energy with the qualities of each mandala stage. As a way to further integrate your experience of the stages, the words and melodies of evocative original songs by Maureen Jenci Shelton can be found in appendix C. Singing these songs is a pleasant warm-up for your creative self-expression. You can listen to Maureen's recording of these songs on her CD available at www .mandalaCD.com. Her voice is pure healing sound. The tunes are easily remembered and can serve as affirmations as you live into each stage of the Great Round outside your sacred mandala space.

Once you have established your space and begun creating mandalas, you may find it helpful to use some of the following techniques for relating to your mandalas:

Be open to the inner dialogue that happens as you create your mandala. The back and forth in your thoughts as you add to your mandala, respond to it, and decide what to do next can be informative and meaningful.

Handle your mandala carefully, as something worthy of your attention. Once a mandala is completed, hold it and turn it until you locate the top. Mark the top with a small *t*. Hang up your mandala and look at it. Open yourself to seeing it without judging it. You may be surprised to find important details, unnoticed before, that will tell you something important.

Assign a title to your mandala as a way to get more information about it from your unconscious. Let your title be the first words that come to mind as you are looking at your mandala. Write the title on the front or back of your mandala. Make a note of the mandala project as well. Then add your name or initials and the day's date.

Do some journaling about your mandala. For example, write about why you chose that particular mandala project: did it seem like fun or did it touch on a current concern? Describe the process of creating your mandala: did you pick colors you like or dislike? Why? Write about what you see and feel as you look at your mandala: does it give you a jittery feeling or is it calming to look at? Write about what areas in your mandala are most strongly associated with the feelings.

To go further, list the colors and forms in your mandala and write your free associations about each one. That is, just put down on paper whatever comes to mind as you are looking at your mandala. If you find your thoughts drifting, bring them back to focus on your mandala. You can go through the same process for exploring the lines in your mandalas: are they thick, thin, wavy, zigzag? What words come to mind for each kind of line? Do you have feelings associated with them?

Take note of which mandalas are easiest or most enjoyable to create. These probably indicate stages of the Great Round most familiar to you. Likewise, mandalas that are difficult may reveal your growing edges. By working with the mandalas of each stage, you can gain insights from your experience, develop your ability to accept the gifts offered by each stage, and perhaps even resolve some difficulties encountered during past visits to the stage. After completing a shattered mirror mandala, Katherine noted that looking at her broken reflection was comforting because her outsides now matched the fragmentation she was feeling inside during a time of grief and loss.

Choose a way to keep your mandalas. They might be displayed on a bulletin board, tucked in a file folder, layered on a closet shelf, or stored in a sturdy box in your home office. Making a place for your mandalas will not only protect them, but will also increase your enjoyment of the activities in the "Completing the Circle" chapter.

If or when it becomes necessary to let go of your mandalas, do so with respectful intention. Your mandalas are intimate reflections of you, and your handling of them should be guided by the positive regard you justly have for yourself. My friend Susan says a prayer of gratitude while tearing her mandala into shreds and dropping it into her recycling bin. Others burn, bury, or use pieces of their mandalas in new works of art.

BASIC ART MATERIALS
Drawing pencil and eraser
Colored markers, colored pencils, chalks or pastels, and charcoal
Watercolor, tempera paints, acrylic paints, and colored inks
Brushes of various sizes
Liquid glue (a glue gun is also useful)
**Compass (one that can open to a spread of at least 5" so you can
    create a circle with a 10" diameter)**
Ruler
Protractor (the 360 degree round variety)
Scissors
12" x 18" (approximately) drawing paper in white, black, gray, and manila
12" x 18" (approximately) construction paper in various colors
Collage materials (paper, magazine pictures, fabrics, found objects, etc.)
Journaling materials

Interpreting Your Mandalas

I do not think it is helpful, appropriate, or even possible to interpret some-one else's mandalas unless you are in a therapeutic relationship together bound by trust, confidentiality, and professional ethics. Even then, what we see says as much about us as it does about the person who created the mandala. Therefore, when discussing the mandalas of another person, I encourage you to preface your remarks with this phrase: "If this were my mandala it would be telling me that . . . "

Delving into the meaning of your own mandalas, however, can in-crease your self-awareness. For example, Judy's mandala was filled with lines and had a random, confused quality. When she propped it up and looked at it, the jumble of lines she saw made her realize that she was more stressed than she had known. Understanding this message, Judy changed her plans for the afternoon. She went for a relaxing walk and met a friend for a cup of tea and conversation. Afterward, Judy's stress level was much lower. Her mandala had helped her take care of herself.

You may notice images in your mandala that you did not intention-ally place there. Consider these images as valid information from your unconscious, just as any others that appear in your mandala. Recognizing, accepting, and taking ownership of the imagery shifts the meaning from unconscious to conscious. This enriches your self-knowledge and sup-ports your becoming a more complex, integrated, and flexible person.

For example, Bob was surprised to see the image of a pheasant in his mandala. He was immediately reminded of his father, a good-hearted man who had died two years earlier. The phrase, "just give it your best shot," came into Bob's awareness. Although he was not a hunter like his father, Bob found the words encouraging. He realized that in his job as a teacher he, like his father, valued making his best effort and letting results take care of themselves. This new awareness from his mandala increased his acceptance of his father's positive influence in his life and at the same time enhanced his own self-confidence.

Consider each mandala you create a special message to you, from you. Witness your mandala without judgment. Open yourself to receive what it is communicating. The process of creating your mandala may give you a feeling, shift your energy level, or stir a memory. Notice what you become aware of as you focus on the colors and shapes in your mandala. Do some journaling about your creative experience and further explore feelings, sensations, or memories stirred by your mandala.

Over time, you will become acquainted with your own personal vocabulary of lines, symbols, and colors. For example, the color pink is traditionally associated with baby girls. However, for you it may signify illness, celebration, or a favorite room. Possible associations are limitless.

Your mandalas are yours alone—and yet they are also the creation of something beyond your awareness. You can never know all there is to know about your mandalas. It is my belief that the mandalas you create contribute something to the evolution of consciousness in this epoch. Robert Johnson wrote:

> Never before has mankind been in such need of the healing power of the mandala as at present. Our fractured, disintegrating world cries for that cohesive force which is the great power of mandala. (Fincher 1991, Foreword)

Therefore, creating mandalas benefits others as well as you. May you find *The Mandala Workbook* a useful guide for self-expression, balance, and well-being.

SPIDERWEB • RE-CREATION • TIMELESS AND ETERNAL • PRIMARY STATE BEFORE VOID • SEPARATION • DARK • WOMB • BEFORE FORM • BEFORE FORM • SLEEP • RESEMBLES • HIBERNATION • OPEN TO NEW POSSIBILITIES • WHITE VOID • QUIET • RECEPTIVE • HEALING • PATIENT • SLOW • FORGETFUL • WEIGHTED • NON-DUALITY • TRANSCENDENT STATE OF

Resting in the Darkness

Jenny was recovering from pneumonia. Weak as a wobbly stick, she sat in bed staring out the window. Still, she felt better than the day before. She reached for her journal. Writing was too hard, so she drew a little circle instead. Then, using her ballpoint pen because she was too tired to go looking for her markers, she darkened the circle with spidery crisscrossing lines. It certainly was not much to look at, but it gave Jenny a sense of hope. Then she set aside her journal, settled down under the covers, and took a nap.

In this example, Jenny was living through Stage One of the Great Round. This stage is a time of rest, renewal, and healing. Your first visit to this stage was as a tiny creature in your mother's womb. Snuggled inside her body, you grew like a seed planted in nourishing soil. During this, the first of twelve stages of growth, you are called again to be like a seed pressed into the dark earth, passively receiving nourishment from the soil and water around it. This is a time when you sink into your innermost being, gathering energy from the darkness within and without. You return to this womb-like matrix again and again to hibernate and to await—sometimes not so patiently—what is to come.

Stage One in some ways resembles sleep because motor functioning, mental processes, and emotions tend to be depressed. You can have the feeling of being weighted down. You tend to be forgetful. Life is experienced as a waking dream and you are a sleepwalker. Later in your life journey, re-entry to Stage One may sometimes be experienced as a fall into darkness. Metaphorically speaking, this is the point at which consciousness enters matter. Kellogg names this stage the *Void* (1984). The mandala of Diana Gregory, a member of the mandala group, conveys the quality of this stage (see plate 9).

With faith in an ultimate order you may take comfort here. Stage One is the place of the Great Mother, the sacred feminine that generously creates life and lovingly receives the dead back into her womb. In Native American tradition she is known as Spider Woman. According to folklore, she welcomes the twin heroes into her dark, smoky abode, and with her guidance they gain knowledge about their father, learn a proper outlook on life, and discover their true purpose. Her final advice to them is, "Be still."

Such mythic stories give reassurance that the peace you first experienced in your mother's womb is not lost, but ever-present. As Joseph Campbell explains,

> Protective power is always and ever-present within the sanctuary of the heart. One has only to know and trust, and the ageless guardians will appear. Mother Nature herself supports the mighty task. (Campbell 1971, 71–72)

The "mighty task" is to submit to the unknown within and without and to allow yourself to be transformed by the experience. In the past, traditional cultures induced the state of consciousness associated with Stage One as part of their initiation ceremonies. Fasting, going without sleep, and separation from the community were often part of these rituals of transition.

For example, in the 1930s, an anthropologist reported that in some northern Australian tribes, when a girl began to menstruate, she was isolated in a hut for three days. Afterward, the women bathed her and led her in procession to the main camp. There she was greeted by all who met her with a new name—she was now a woman, no longer a girl (Eliade 1994). The culturally prescribed withdrawal supported the girl's psychological transformation.

Our lives sometimes plunge us into an experience of the unknown— and it shapes us. A beginning is also an ending. Such is the paradoxical nature of this stage. Larvae literally dissolve in their cocoons prior to becoming butterflies. So it is that you are required to surrender and trust nature's process working through you during this stage. With faith, trust, and the memories of having survived past experiences of this place you can find this a time of *resting in the darkness.* However, it is not always easy.

Intentions for Stage One

If you expect yourself to function at high levels of energy and efficiency, you will be frustrated when experiencing this stage. The natural rhythm of this stage is slow, and if you can come to appreciate this and accept the gifts of deep rest, then this experience can even be welcomed. The tasks for Stage One are waiting, keeping faith, trusting the process, and being patient with your poor performance. The stage of *resting in the darkness* is a natural part of life, but if you find yourself lingering here longer than a few weeks, it is important to seek the support of helping professionals.

It is a paradox that you begin your journey of the Great Round in a place of being still. The challenge is to accept this paradox and not to force yourself into activity for the sake of feeling some *progress.* This stage is about microscopic changes, like the swelling and softening of a seed just before germination begins. You can see none of this growing activity on ground level above, yet scientists who measure such things tell us it is happening. And it is the same for you. Subterranean energies in the unconscious are stirring, even though you cannot discern what is happening.

Darkness holds everything, embraces everything, including you and me." —David Steindl-Rast

Stage One Mandalas

Mandalas created while experiencing this stage may be dark or completely black. Sometimes they are simply circles left uncolored. Mandalas here have little or no form other than the circle. This is partly because the activity of drawing is difficult when experiencing Stage One. The circle gives you a safe place for *resting in the darkness.* It is the beginning point for your exploration of mandalas of the Great Round.

Mandalas associated with Stage One emphasize the circle as boundary, container, womb, and web of life. It is the *process*, not the *product*, that matters in art making here. Stay in the present moment with creative self-expression and let go of expectations for beautiful results, *right* symbolism, or meaningful color choices. A simple approach can open a vast appreciation of the circle itself, the matrix of all mandalas.

Exercises

Before beginning your mandalas, take some deep relaxing breaths. Performing the yoga position suggested for Stage One can help you become grounded and centered for your creative self-expression. When creating the mandalas suggested below, pay attention to what it is like for you. Is it calming to repeat circles and lines or does the drawing provoke anxiety or frustration? Do you become aware of associations, memories, inner dialogue, and snippets of songs during your work? How is it for you having your color choices limited? Following each mandala, do some writing in your journal as you witness and reflect on your art-making experiences.

MANDALA OF RESTING IN THE DARKNESS
Materials You'll Need:
Basic Art Materials (see page 36)
Coloring Mandala 1 (see appendix A, page 240)

During Stage One you experience a moment beyond ordinary time, a dreamtime when your inner world is profoundly reordered. In the metaphorical language of spirituality, it is a time when spirit enters matter and takes the form you know as your body. The Mandala of Resting in the Darkness is offered as a way for you to transition into your experience of Stage One. See what it is like for you to color this mandala using shades of flesh, dark blue, black, and gray. Describe the experience of coloring the mandala in your journal, if you like.

THROUGH THE CIRCLE
Materials You'll Need:
Basic Art Materials (see page 36)
Cardboard, tagboard, or other stiff material, approximately 10" x 10" or larger

Through the Circle outlines simple steps to create a circular viewfinder. By observing your surroundings through the circle you can become attuned to the organizing capacity of the circle. This is an effective starting point for your mandala making.

Trace a circle on stiff paper or cardboard and cut it out. Set it aside. Holding up the cardboard frame as a sort of viewfinder, look at your surroundings through the circular opening. See how the circle organizes and brings definition to your field of vision. Notice what it is like to have your environment structured by the form of the circle. How is this different from or the same as your ordinary way of viewing the world? Share your insights with a friend or write in your journal.

VARIATION

Use an empty cardboard paper towel roll, a wedding ring, or a Hula-hoop as your circular viewfinder.

QUALITIES OF THE CIRCLE
Materials You'll Need:
Basic Art Materials (see page 36)

The purpose of Qualities of the Circle is to experience the physical motion of circle making and then to transpose the movement into making marks on paper. This activity reiterates some of your earliest drawing experiences as you discovered your ability to control your arm and hand movement to create circles with a crayon. This is a simple, repetitive activity that introduces the creation of circles as a self-soothing meditation.

In a quiet setting with a relaxed frame of mind, reflect on the qualities of the circle as a boundary for safe space. After a few minutes of reflection, take a drawing implement in your hand and make circular motions in the air as if drawing. Now transfer this same free movement onto paper, drawing a freehand circle. Go over and over the circle, keeping breath and movements relaxed (see plate 10). Continue for fifteen minutes or so. Then stop your drawing and sit quietly, integrating the memory of your circular movements.

QUALITIES OF THE CIRCLE, VARIATION I
Materials You'll Need:
Basic Art Materials (see page 36)

With your dominant hand you put into action much of your willed behavior. The discovery of hand dominance occurs early in life and is facilitated through drawing and other activities relying on manual dexterity. Touching the paper with your hand increases the kinesthetic feedback of the circling motion. By performing this simple drawing exercise with your non-dominant hand, you may invite some forgotten experience of your early life.

For Qualities of the Circle, Variation I, draw a circle using your non-dominant hand. You may enjoy using soft chalk so that you can set the chalk aside once your circle is established and smooth the lines with your fingers (see plate 10). When using your fingers, keep the same relaxed circular motion as when drawing and attend to thoughts, feeling, and memories that come up. After your drawing experience, share with a friend or write about it in your journal.

QUALITIES OF THE CIRCLE, VARIATION II
Materials You'll Need:
Basic Art Materials (see page 36)

By introducing more color choice and simultaneous right- and left-hand movements into the circle making, Qualities of the Circle, Variation II is designed to promote the integration of dominant and non-dominant aspects of the psyche.

Choose a different colored chalk or marker for each hand. Draw a circle with your dominant hand. Then draw over this circle using the color in your non-dominant hand. Now continue drawing your circle, using both hands at the same time. Notice what your experience is like, and when your circle drawing is complete, share with a trusted other or describe it in your journal.

CIRCLE OF SELF
Materials You'll Need:
Basic Art Materials (see page 36)
Paper, approximately 36" x 36"

Circles have been used since ancient times to demarcate a special, often sacred, space. Circles have defined ceremonial dance floors, mandalas for meditation, and grand domed sanctuaries. Circles are reminiscent of nurturing womb space, and they are also among the earliest drawings produced by children, where they appear to be linked with the development of a sense of self. This project offers a soothing visit to the circle as safe and sacred space constructed especially for you, by you. The Circle of Self also affirms personal boundaries by contrasting experiences of *inside* and *outside* the circle.

Explore the circle as safe and sacred space by placing a large, sturdy piece of paper on the floor. Sit in the center of the paper and breathe deeply into a relaxed state of mind. You might enjoy singing "In the Darkness Deep" (see appendix C, page 278).

Then draw a circle around yourself where you sit. You will probably find it easier to draw half the circle with your left hand and the other half with your right hand. Adjust the circle to suit you: make the line thicker, add colors, or create openings. When your circle is complete, take time to experience the feeling of being *inside*. Then move outside the circle and notice what it is like to experience the circle from that vantage point. Add or subtract from the circle as you wish until it feels complete.

SPIDER WEB MANDALA
Materials You'll Need:
Basic Art Materials (see page 36)

The spider is prominent in mythologies of Native American tribes. She is also found in the creation stories of India, where it is said that the spider brings the world into being through her delicate, rhythmic weaving. Robert Johnson has pointed out that the spider and her web represent the energy source from which the evolved mandala springs (Fincher 1991).

Stage One activates memories of your intrauterine experience. According to Kellogg (1983), the spider's web symbolizes the connection of the fetus to the lining of the womb. If your early life in the womb was uncertain, either because you could not thrive or the uterine environment was unwelcoming, you may find yourself spontaneously creating spider's web mandalas in black and white or dark blue and yellow.

When you create the Spider Web Mandala, you may find you are reaching back to heal some of your earliest experiences by producing a safe holding environment for yourself. If your gestation was a healthy, welcoming time, creating a Spider Web Mandala might refresh pleasant memories of life in the womb. Experiencing either possibility during your mandala making offers the potential to reshape your assumptions about reality as you begin your passage through the Great Round.

Using black paper and white pencil or white paper and charcoal, draw a circle freehand. Place your pencil or chalk on the circle and draw a line freehand through the center and across the circle, connecting to the opposite side of the circle. Continue until you have drawn at least six lines in this manner. You will then have at least twelve lines radiating outward from the center. Now, like a spider weaving her web, begin near the center. Place your pencil on any one of the lines at a point slightly off the center. Without picking up your pencil, draw from line to line, spiraling outward to the edge of the circle. Move very slowly. Let your breathing be deep and relaxed as you draw.

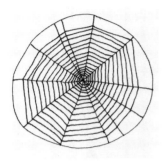

Spider Web Mandala

EARTH MANDALA
Materials You'll Need:
Stones, sticks, moss, feathers
Compost or potting soil
Seeds (optional)

The gravity of Earth offers an ultimate safe holding environment. Ancient peoples revered Earth as the Great Mother, source of nourishment and new life. Growing appreciation of the delicately balanced cycles of Earth has inspired ecological awareness and a feeling of emotional connection with the natural environment. Produce your Earth Mandala as a tribute to Mother Nature, ever patient, accepting, and amazingly resilient—up to a point. She deserves our respect.

In a sheltered place out-of-doors, arrange the natural materials you have gathered so that they form a circle. Fill the circle with compost or potting soil. Reflect on your circle as an empty place with nourishing potential for life. Perhaps you will plant some seeds in your circle. Even without seeds, you may want to step into your circle and pack the soil in place with rhythmic steps accompanied by song, drum, or rattle. In closing, sprinkle water on the packed earth in your circle as a gesture of appreciation that will also benefit any seeds you have planted there.

NEW MOON MANDALA
Materials You'll Need:
Black paper
White chalk or pastel

Some years ago when I was visiting England a friend invited me to accompany her on a visit to the stone circle at Castle Rigg. Set in the countryside away from farms and villages, Castle Rigg is located at the center of a wide valley. The earth slopes gently up into rolling hills on all sides. The stone circle is about 30 feet across, formed of irregular standing stones from 4 to 6 feet tall.

It was dark when we arrived, but my friend insisted that we not use flashlights so our eyes could adjust. I groped my way to the circle with her help and settled safely at the base of the first stone I touched. Sure enough, in about half an hour I began to see details of the magnificent boulders. Stars shone brightly overhead, where before I had seen none.

My friend stood nearby, leaning against a monolith. I was amazed when I realized that she was drawing. Using white chalk on black paper, she was sketching away as if it were daylight, capturing the weathered features of the venerable stones. You may not have a stone circle nearby, but you can explore the possibilities of drawing in the dark just as my friend did.

Find a safe, dark place—perhaps a natural setting on a moonless night—and settle in with your art materials. Take several deep breaths to relax. Be patient while your eyes adjust to the dark. After a few minutes, you should be able to see well enough to draw. When you are ready, draw your circle and let your New Moon Mandala unfold in the darkness.

WOMANDALA BAG
Materials You'll Need:
Basic Art Materials (see page 36)
Leather or fabric square, at least 5" x 5" (this makes a small bag;
    adjust dimensions according to your preference)
Awl or other sharp hole puncher
Leather cord, ribbon, yarn, string, or embroidery floss
Craft paint, beads, stones

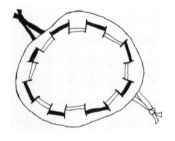

Womandala Bag

The edges of a circle can be gathered together to create an enclosed space. Any object that contains an inner space resonates with *the* enclosure: the safe holding environment of the womb. So, in the construction of the Womandala Bag, you use a circle to create a container where tender wishes, longings, and inspirations can be safely held and protected. Your Womandala Bag can hold precious objects that need to be set apart to honor a memory, mourn a loss, or nurture an aspiration.

Choose a piece of leather or fabric in a color and texture that speaks to you of the dark, nurturing power of Mystery. Measure and cut out a square or a circle from the material you have chosen. You may leave the edges ragged if you like.

Now with a compass or other circular template, trace a circle on your material on one or both sides. Leave at least 1/2" between the circle you draw and the outside edge of your material. The space inside the circle(s) on one or both sides of your material can be decorated with craft paint, beads, and embroidery to incorporate symbols of the light at the heart of darkness. Of course you may leave your material plain if you prefer.

Make an even number of slits or holes along the circle with scissors, an awl, or another hole puncher. Weave a leather cord, ribbon, or yarn through the holes. End with your material flat on your work surface with what will be the outside of your bag facing up and the ends of the cord trailing loosely from the first and last holes you threaded. Securely knot the ends of your cord together.

Weave a second cord through the holes beginning in the hole opposite the one in which you began the first cord. End at the hole opposite the ending hole of the first cord. Knot the ends securely. Now pull the knotted ends of both cords to gather and shape your bag.

Let this Womandala Bag be a special place for you to put things that need to be nurtured, invoked, or held in safety. This might be prayers, intentions, or affirmations on small pieces of paper. Other possibilities include pictures or objects symbolic of something you want to welcome into your life on this turning of the Great Round.

Reflecting on Stage One

Stage One is a time of deep rest, an interval of quietly knitting together new structures as yet unseen, and a moment of joining with the primordial waters of creation. Look back at the mandalas you have created here and remember what it was like for you as you made them. What have you experienced? What have you come to appreciate, understand, and know through your time focusing on Stage One? Let your reflections on the essence of this stage be a starting point for creating Mandala Card One.

MANDALA CARD ONE
Materials You'll Need:
Basic Art Materials (see page 36)
Pieces of cardboard, tagboard, or other stiff material (in a size and shape you find comfortable to work with; 3" x 4" or larger is suggested)
Images of empty circles (drawn or cut out of magazines)
Slips of paper with words and images that evoke *resting in the darkness*

Mandala cards can be large enough to stand alone or small enough to tuck in to your pocket. They can be any size or shape that you like, but they should be large enough to hold the designs and images called for in each exercise. This card project invites the distillation of your experience of Stage One into a form that can serve as a reminder or reference point in the future. Your card for Stage One may be the beginning of your personal deck of the Great Round.

Create a design evoking the qualities of Stage One. Use drawing, painting, or collage, and incorporate an empty circle, a spider web, or a dark solid-colored disk into your work. Add textures, colors, images, and words on one or both sides of your card illustrating Stage One, *resting in the darkness.* Allow your card to dry flat. You may want to press it under a heavy book. Store your Mandala Card One in a safe place.

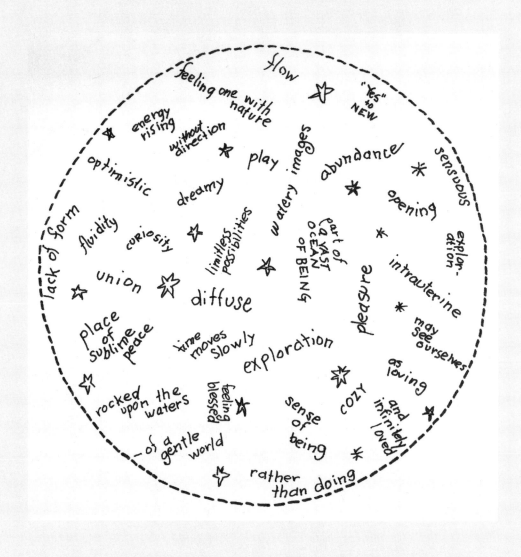

Floating into the Light

Marian was past the early queasiness of her pregnancy and eager to make the most of the weeks remaining before the birth of her daughter. On a sunny morning in late February, she pulled on her jogging pants, laced up her walking shoes, and layered sweaters under her fleece windbreaker. Marian picked up the old glass-bottomed bucket, latched the back door, and set off for the wetlands at the end of the road.

Soon she was on the boardwalk heading for a pond where she could see springtime in action. Once at the edge of the pond she kneeled down and lowered the wooden bucket halfway into the water. She peered in and saw the life of the pond revealed beneath the glass bottom. Tiny nymphs, baby dragonflies, larval mosquitoes, tadpoles, and fish too small to identify swirled in the tannic waters of the marsh in the circular bucket viewfinder. "It's just like a mandala," she said to herself. She felt a *whoosh* in her womb, as if her voice had startled awake a little fish. She patted her belly and smiled as she looked across the water glistening in the sunlight.

Marian and her daughter were experiencing Stage Two of the Great Round. This is the stage that corresponds to the blissful intrauterine experience of midterm pregnancy. During your first experience here as a tiny creature in your mother's womb, you did not know or care what was *me* and what was *mother*. Consciousness here is thought to be diffuse, dreamy, and lacking any sense of ego boundaries. Infinite possibilities exist in this stage. It is a time of suspended action and passivity, of *floating into the light*.

When we experience Stage Two later in life, we find our perspective is somewhat disengaged, perhaps a bit impersonal, yet marked by a relaxed enjoyment of the world and its pleasures. You may find that you identify with the nourishing, cosmic rhythms of the universe in a kind of *participation mystique*. If your intrauterine experience was not positive, returning to this stage may be unpleasant. However, you can heal this harm through sensitive inner work. The story of Sandra shows how mandalas can help with this healing process.

Sandra's mother was disowned by her parents because her boyfriend—Sandra's father—was black. When Sandra's mother became pregnant she was a malnourished adolescent, and Sandra was born underweight. With the care of her father's mother, Sandra soon became healthy; however, given her difficult start, Sandra was haunted by a feeling of insecurity as an adult.

After years of courageous inner work, Sandra discovered a mandala coloring book, and something important, but indescribable, came together for her. She went on to create her own mandalas, "messing with the paint," as she said. The soothing colors she chose seemed to nourish a starving place in her soul. After a few months of painting mandalas, Sandra realized that she was less anxious. It was a good feeling.

Intentions for Stage Two

In this place on the Great Round, energy is rising, though it does not have a clear direction or goal. When experiencing Stage Two you are swimming in the joy of feeling yourself a part of nature. There are limitless possibilities for when, where, and how to express your new energy. The richness of these options gives you a feeling of abundance and buoys up your optimism that amazing things are possible.

During Stage Two you are far from doing anything *productive*. It is more of a time for play, for exploration of what you are curious about, for following your intuition and joining with the flow of life around you. Just as a toddler forms paradigms for how the world works when she plays with blocks, sand, and mud, during this stage you have the opportunity to open yourself to new ways of looking at things, to practice new behaviors, and to say yes to things when you might previously have said, "No way." This stage is a nice time to relax, turn your face to the sun, and enjoy the bliss of being.

Since this is a uterine space, its connection is to images of water, water that fertilizes, purifies and dissolves. —Joan Kellogg

Stage Two Mandalas

Stage Two mandalas are a window on a watery world. Mandalas created during this stage are characterized by fluidity in the designs. Numerous tiny forms scattered like stars float within the mandala. Sometimes the mandala looks like an aquarium filled with fish eggs, miniscule creatures, or strange plants. There is the suggestion of fertility, but no clear sense of what is developing. The mandala of Sue Kahn, a member of our mandala group, illustrates the quality of Stage Two (see plate 11), which Kellogg calls *Bliss.*

Reflecting a lack of boundaries characteristic of Stage Two, artwork may spill over to the space outside the mandala circle. Colors tend to be light blues and yellows, pale orchids, and pastel pinks. A touch of red in these mandalas may emphasize generativity, as in the yolk of a fertilized bird's egg. Dark shades of blue can possibly reflect an early negative experience in this stage.

Exercises

When you begin your creative time with mandalas, take a few moments to settle first. Let your body relax and just breathe for a minute or more. Explore the yoga movements suggested in appendix B (see page 253). Consider singing "We Are One" (appendix C, page 279). This will allow you to transition into the present moment and prepare to focus on your creative experience.

Several of the mandalas for this stage give opportunities for playful exploration with water and paint. What is it like for you to let yourself experiment with no particular goal in mind? What thoughts are going through your mind as you drip paint on paper or make a mess? How is it to intentionally create something that is soothing to you? Are you comfortable exploring what your birth was like? Writing about your mandalas after creating them helps you reflect more deeply on your experience.

MANDALA OF BLISS
Materials You'll Need:
Basic Art Materials (see page 36)
Coloring Mandala 2 (see appendix A, page 241)

Stage Two is reminiscent of our time in utero. To consider this stage later in life brings us to an awareness that life is pregnant with possibilities. The tiny babies in this mandala symbolize the possibilities of who we can become, what we can produce, and what we can discover on our sojourn through the Great Round. Color this mandala with baby colors of pale blue, yellow, pink, and lavender. Let this exercise be your introduction to the qualities of Stage Two, Floating into the Light.

MILLION STAR MANDALA
Materials You'll Need:
Basic Art Materials (see page 36)

There is a gnarled old redbud tree near the entrance to my neighborhood. Its thick twisted trunk, blackened bark, and broken branches attest to its age. Its stark silhouette is beautiful during the winter and, in my opinion, fully justifies its being there. Yet, amazingly, each spring this old thing puts out new growth—fresh, bright purple blossoms and greenery—just as if it were a youngster. The lesson for me is that the life force innocently blossoms wherever conditions allow. This blissful fecundity is celebrated in the Million Star Mandala.

Before beginning to work with your materials, sit quietly, taking a few deep relaxing breaths. Ponder the marvels of nature: the multiplicity of forms in plants, animals, rocks, and bodies of water. Notice the endless fertility revealed in all we experience around us in the natural world: early buds appearing on leafless trees, teeming life in springtime ponds, countless stars in the nighttime sky of late winter. As you meditate on these images, draw a circle and fill it with small, simple star shapes. Let your mandala take form as an expression of the vast ocean of being that is nature.

WATER MANDALA
Materials You'll Need:
Basic Art Materials (see page 36)
Newspaper
Watercolor paper
Sponge or paper towel

Stage Two evokes the experience of blissfully floating in our mother's womb. We were water creatures then. No wonder we are attracted to water. The Water Mandala gives you an opportunity to have fun with water, to experiment with its fluid possibilities, and, perhaps, to resonate with your own nonverbal memories of prenatal existence in a fluid environment.

Lay down several layers of newspaper to absorb extra moisture. Place a sheet of watercolor paper on top of the newspaper. Draw a circle with pencil on the watercolor paper. Wet a sponge or paper towel in clean water and moisten the watercolor paper. Pick up paint or ink with a brush and allow drops of it to fall randomly on the wet paper. Your painting will be inside and outside the circle. Just let it happen. Observe the movement of color on the surface of the paper: natural process in action. Add more water and colors as you wish, either dropping paint onto the paper or developing the blots of color on the surface with your brush (see plate 11).

REBIRTHING MANDALA
Materials You'll Need:
Basic Art Materials (see page 36)

Stage Two highlights the experiences around pregnancy and birth. The Rebirthing Mandala allows you to look back on your birth with the eyes of an adult. You may wish to consult your family members and others before beginning. Gathering information in this way can spark insights, deepen your understanding of your origins, and fill in missing pieces of your personal history. You may find that you are revising the story of your birth, and that this is a bit like a corrective birthing experience, or a *rebirthing*.

Reflect on your own early life, holding in gentle loving acceptance your mother and the tiny being you were then. What was the month, season, and place in which you were born? What time of day or night were you born? What was it like for you and your mother during her pregnancy with you? What was your birth process like? You might expand your focus to include the milieu of your family and other important people around you as you were welcomed into the world.

Circles symbolize the womb, so it is appropriate to create a mandala to represent your mother's womb space. Draw a circle and with color and form create an abstract or realistic image of yourself (and siblings if you were a multiple) inside the circle. Add forms and colors that convey what your prenatal environment was like. You may add details outside the circle to flesh out your mother's body or to include people who supported you and your mother as you came into the world.

Some of us come easily into the world. Some of us find beginning life harder. With your work on this mandala, emotions may surface. Feel the feelings, whatever they are, and just continue breathing. Stay with your breathing and your painting and let the creative process carry you through your rebirthing experience. There is no right or wrong way to birth a mandala—or yourself. Once your mandala is completed, share your rebirthing experience with a trusted witness or respond to your mandala by writing in your journal.

When your mandala stirs intense emotions, you may wish to establish a special place for your Rebirthing Mandala. Perhaps you will take a few moments over the next days or weeks to pause, look at your mandala, and honor your birth experience by placing some flowers or lighting a candle there. Maureen's song for Stage Two, "We Are One" (see appendix C, page 279), might help you voice your feelings as you witness your mandala. Or you might like to draw a circle and create a second mandala in response to your Rebirthing Mandala. Your aim in these activities is to arrive at a sense of completion—for the moment—with your birthing experience.

CHILD'S PLAY MANDALA
Materials You'll Need:
Basic Art Materials (see page 36)
Foam plates

While babysitting my three-year-old grandson one day, I began drawing. I put a foam plate face down on the paper and drew a circle around it. Seeing what I had done, he also put a plate face down, but he did not reach for a pencil.

He dipped his fingers into nearby acrylic paint and dabbed a design on the bottom of the plate. Then he carefully turned the plate over and pressed it onto the paper, then lifted and pressed it again, several times, creating a colorful mandala print. This Nana was most impressed by her brilliant grandson!

I offer you this simple, enjoyable mandala making project, so appropriate for Stage Two, Floating into the Light. Spread a sheet of paper on the table. Dip fingers or brush into acrylic paint (include some soft colors such as pink, blue, soft yellow, lavender) and dab on the bottom of a foam plate. Turn the plate over and press onto the paper. Lift the plate and enjoy the unpredictable mandala design that appears. This project demonstrates the importance of what is easy, unexpected, and playful in your growth process.

MANDALA OF POSSIBILITIES
Materials You'll Need:
Basic Art Materials (see page 36)
Collage images

When visiting Stage Two, the boundless potentials of life open before us. This is not a time of making choices, but of reveling in possibilities. It is a time to *brainstorm* without the limits of what is reasonable, appropriate, or affordable. Let your imagination play and simply take notice of what comes, as you did when you were a curious toddler. This is the first step toward dreaming up something new.

Draw a circle on pastel-colored paper. Cut out a dozen or so small circles containing pictures that represent something interesting, even exciting, to you at the moment. It might be an image of a person, a picture of something from nature, a famous place, or a special object. Do not think about what your choices represent just yet. Arrange the cutout circles in your drawn mandala circle and glue them in place. Overlap pictures if necessary to completely cover the space inside the circle.

Look at your Mandala of Possibilities and identify the theme(s) you see expressed in your choice of images. Is the out-of-doors prominent? Are certain activities emphasized? Do your images depict cozy home interiors? Let the theme be a title for your mandala. Write it on the paper near your mandala or in your journal. Study your title and the images in your mandala to answer this question: What new possibilities am I inviting into my life now? Your answer to this question may give you clues to the preferences that will guide you toward being who you really are.

SOOTHING MANDALA
Materials You'll Need:
Basic Art Materials (see page 36)

It is very important that we have ways to soothe ourselves when we feel the need. With skills that allow you to take care of yourself, you can better withstand the natural stresses of life. It is empowering to know that even when a loved one is unavailable to cheer you up, you can still help yourself feel better. This Soothing Mandala is intended for use when you feel the need for nurturing.

Choose chalks or pastels in colors that you like and find comforting. With one of your colors draw a circle on paper of a soft color. Without any planning, begin filling the space inside and around the circle, using the side of your chalk or pastel.

From time to time put down your chalk. Inhale deeply and exhale slowly as you move your fingertips along the lines in your mandala, blending and softening. Work slowly and rhythmically with relaxed concentration on the task of softening any sharp edges.

When your mandala is completed, set it a few feet away and enjoy the results of your process with your favorite soothing colors. Notice how you feel now, as compared with your state of mind when you began the mandala. Remember the Soothing Mandala next time you need to slow down and relax.

MANDALA OF ABUNDANT POTENTIAL
Materials You'll Need:
Basic Art Materials (see page 36)
Cardboard, tagboard, or other stiff material, approximately 12" x 12"
Beans, peas, grains, or seeds of varied colors

The potential for new life is stored in beans, peas, and seeds. Each one is encoded with the pattern of the plant it can become, and it contains a bit of nourishment to give it a good start. We, too, have a unique inner pattern of wholeness. An inborn, often unconscious urge activates our responses to life's challenges as we naturally grow toward wholeness. Create this mandala as a metaphorical reminder of your own potentials and the countless possibilities for personal growth that life offers.

On the cardboard draw a circle, then spread on an even layer of glue inside it. Begin your mandala design with a random scattering of beans of a single color. Fill in around these with beans, peas, seeds, or other materials in colors of your choosing. You may want to add glue and colored materials to the space outside your mandala as well.

When completed, look carefully at your mandala. Notice the rich possibilities for growth represented by each tiny bean, pea, seed, or grain. Seeing there is such potential in a handful of beans, consider how much you, in all your complexity, are capable of.

As a next step, you might enjoy laying your mandala on a plate or in a garden space, covering it with potting soil, and watering it generously. Over time you can see the design literally sprout and come alive. Let this abundance inspire reflection on your own unexplored potentials and the myriad opportunities each moment brings.

Reflecting on Stage Two

Stage Two is a dreamy, contented time in the cycling of the Great Round. We are often blissfully unaware of life's difficulties when experiencing this stage. It is reminiscent of our very earliest memories of a time when we were cared for by others. We return to this stage for rest, renewal, and healing.

Stage Two invites us to remember the boundless potentials that life offers. Through the mandalas of this stage we have explored soothing atmospheres, dreamy optimism, and creativity as play. Now, reviewing your experiences and your mandalas of Stage Two, become aware of the essential qualities of this stage for you. What have you learned here? Take your realizations into the creation of Mandala Card Two.

MANDALA CARD TWO
Materials You'll Need:
Basic Art Materials (see page 36)
Cardboard, tagboard, or other stiff material, 3" x 4" or larger
Collage images

Cut out a card from your choice of card stock in the size you prefer. Reflecting on your recent and past experiences in Stage Two, create a mandala design on your card with collage, paint, or drawing. Consider including a circle teeming with little things. Add other images, words, textures, and colors to express the quality of *floating into the light.* Allow your card to dry flat, then store in a safe place.

THE JOURNEY BEGINS

GROWING

ENTRY INTO THE TEMPLE ◎ INTUITIVE ◎ FOCUSED ◎ DIFFUSE ◎ INTUITIVE ◎ DIFFUSE ◎ VAGUE SENSE OF DIRECTION ◎

BEGIN PROCESS OF SEPARATION ◎ FEELING A DESIRE TO MOVE, CREATE ◎

BRINGING OURSELVES INTO BEING ◎ BOTH FREEING AND FRIGHTENING ◎

ABLE TO TRANSLATE KNOWLEDGE INTO ◎ MYTHIC CONNECTION ◎ ACTION ◎

INSEMINATION ◎ NO CLEAR SHAPE ◎ BECOME ◎ CONSCIOUSNESS ◎

UMBILICAL CORD: BOTH CONNECTING AND SEVERING ◎

EPHEMERAL ◎ ACTIVATION OR REACTIVATION OF LIFE FORCE ◎ LEGS? LEGS ◎

DISCOVERY ◎ HEIGHTENED CONSCIOUSNESS ◎ DOUBLE HELIX OF DNA, RNA ◎

MIND ◎ THE ID RATHER THAN EGO ◎ BRINGING LIFE AND MOTION FORTH ◎

AKIN TO: ◎ BRINGING LIFE AND MOTION FORTH ◎

SEEKING WITHOUT KNOWING WHAT IS SOUGHT ◎ INTUITIVE ◎

MOVEMENT FROM UNIVERSAL TO INDIVIDUAL CONSCIOUSNESS ◎

SEPARATION: BOTH FREEING AND FRIGHTENING ◎

DIFFERENT WORLDS CONNECTED BY MYSTERIOUS PASSAGES ◎

MOVING FROM ONE STATE TO ANOTHER ◎

ALERT ◎ MYSTERIOUS PASSAGE ◎ FEELING A DESIRE TO MOVE, CREATE ◎

INTUITIVE ◎ BREATH OF GOD UPON THE WATERS ◎

TREE OF LIFE ◎ A SENSE THAT SOMETHING IMPORTANT HAS BEGUN ◎ EGO DIFFUSE ◎

STAIRWAY TO HEAVEN ◎ WAKING UP ◎ LIKE A BABY: BREATHING, STRETCHING, MOVING ARMS, SWIM ◎

ROAD TO THE GRAIL ◎ NO FIRMLY DEFINED SENSE OF SELF ◎ ENERGY QUICKENS ◎ BEING SWEPT ALONG ◎

Turning Toward the Journey

Karla went into labor around midnight, and by 8:30 A.M. her son Elijah was born headfirst, which was not unusual, except that he had been facing the opposite direction when labor began. Of his energetic turnaround, the midwives chuckled, "It's as if he was ready to get this show on the road!" Karla's husband Dan had taken pictures of his son's birth.

"Look here, Honey. This is when his head first appeared. It looks like one of those things you like—what are they called?" Karla looked at the pictures of her son crowning, his head a bright pink as it pushed through the circular muscle of her cervix. "A mandala," said Karla, gently brushing her son's head with her lips.

Your first visit to this stage was probably late in your mother's pregnancy with you. The looping umbilical cord would have been your close companion as you developed your senses, pushed, kicked, slept, and hiccupped in the womb that held you tight and tighter as you grew. During gestation you were a true shape shifter, beginning life as a tiny fertilized egg, then developing a tail and hands like fins, losing your tail and developing gills, and finally taking on the shape of a human being. At last, the time to commence your life journey *outside* arrived. With your mother's help, you navigated the birth canal and experienced your first breath of air.

Turning, spirals, and labyrinths are associated with Stage Three. Kellogg has named this stage *Labyrinth.* Some say that the labyrinth was originally inspired by the umbilical cord. You are a creature of the earth, and labyrinths, spirals, and other circling movements recall your connection to Mother Earth: the sweep of her weather and the currents of her oceans. And here is another link: ocean water is virtually the same substance as the amniotic fluid in which you swim before birth.

Stage Three is the beginning of something new. You may not know how it will come out, only that it is coming. What it is at first may not be at all clear. This is a time your will to thrive manifests. Think of the red-faced baby demanding its meal of breast milk. You, too, may feel such determination. Because the urge to grow is so strong in this stage, you persevere until you find what is truly nourishing for you.

Yolanda had persevered with her education and by the age of thirty-one, she had become an accountant in a large firm in the Midwest. One Saturday morning she went to her neighborhood coffee place, as usual, to read the paper. On her way to sit down, she glanced at the bulletin board posting local events, and a new one grabbed her eye. The spring green flyer read: "Contemplative Group Circle Dancing," along with the date, time, and location information. Yolanda caught her breath as her heart skipped a beat. She had not realized that she was looking for something new. An inner yes confirmed her intuition. She did not know where it would lead, but she was going to the dance group that night.

Stage Three is reminiscent of the month of March and the early stirrings of spring. You may find your energy increasing. Often you will feel excitement about beginning, yet have no detailed plans of what to do. It is a time to enjoy letting your intuition guide you to the next right thing. Renewed enthusiasm can draw you into new classes, new relationships, and ambitious plans for your garden. Stage Three of the Great Round finds you *turning toward the journey*.

Consciousness in Stage Three is alert, intuitive, and focused. This stage marks the beginning of a process that culminates in an individualized consciousness. Here you begin a journey, whose final goal is yet a mystery. Stage Three is a seeking without a clear idea of what is sought after. As Kellogg and DiLeo explain:

> Out of numerous stars and out of the many potential consciousnesses, one star, one individual consciousness, will finally emerge at stage eight. That point marks the completion of the first half of the journey. From Universal Consciousness we come to a single individualized consciousness. (1982, 41)

If you have ever seen fish eggs released, you can imagine this space as threads of milky substance. There is no nucleus here; it is as though the stars from the Milky Way have sent down a lifeline. It is reminiscent of the umbilical cord, laid out in a map-like fashion. —Joan Kellogg

The Cosmos, which was all of a piece in Stage Two, is now differentiated into a top and bottom in Stage Three. This layering of consciousness is symbolized in mythology as different worlds connected by mysterious passages, such as the road to the Grail Castle, the bowels of the behemoth, the stairway to heaven, or the ladder down to the underworld. When you are living in Stage Three, you become aware that consciousness occurs in varied levels because they are easily accessible to you.

Stage Three brings with it a time of heightened awareness. Along with increasing energy, you may feel the desire to move, stretch, and become. Perhaps you will sense that you are growing. The rapid rate at which you are changing here may actually cause you to feel dizzy from time to time. Your mood may shift quickly as a reflection of your ephemeral sense of identity. A project can be a helpful focus during Stage Three, as Winda discovered.

Winda fell in love with labyrinths at a church retreat. She came home with the determination to create one in her own back yard. Clearing and leveling the space, marking out the pathways, and moving rocks to mark the lines became her big spring project. The physical labor helped her stay grounded during the excitement of building the labyrinth. Being outside more than usual deepened her awareness of nature in her part of the world. She slept well after working and had lovely dreams of a white-haired crone walking the land where she was building.

You may find that you are remembering your dreams. You may have a keen sense of the presence of absent loved ones or a renewed awareness of the divine patterning of persons, relationships, and events in your life. While you are capable of important insights into the nature of reality, you are limited in your ability to act effectively because you lack a firmly defined identity to direct complex ventures. Ego boundaries are diffuse.

Intentions for Stage Three

Our task for Stage Three is akin to that of the shaman who is challenged to visit extraordinary levels of consciousness and to bring useful knowledge acquired there back to share with the tribe. Like Winda and her labyrinth, you are to take the information you receive from various states of mind, your dreams and inspirations, and shape them into a form that can be understood, appreciated, and used by others. With this arduous work you bring yourself into being as well.

Stage Three is exciting and a bit dizzying, pulling you in several directions toward exciting possibilities. During this stage you touch into the indomitable life force of new growth. Your challenge is to settle on a special *something* by the end of this stage that will give you focus for the stages to come. However, sometimes you only discover what this is in retrospect. What is most important is that you embrace life by *turning toward the journey.*

Stage Three Mandalas

The mandalas of Stage Three often suggest depth and the twists and turns of plant tendrils along a mysterious path through the jungle. The possibility of moving from one level—of experience, consciousness, emotion—to another is often suggested by mandalas of this stage. The mandala of Annette Reynolds, a member of our mandala group, is a good example (see plate 12). Colors are usually springtime pastels, especially light blue, lavender, and pink, although bright colors are not unusual. Curving lines are typical of Stage Three mandalas. They have no pronounced center.

Exercises

Before beginning your mandalas, do some stretching and breathing. The yoga movements for Stage Three (appendix B, page 225) are helpful for this. As you explore Stage Three, notice your energy. How does it compare with your level of energy during Stages One and Two? Several mandalas for this stage require you to become actively involved. How is it for you to *move* your mandala? Dreams are a source of personal insights for some. How are your dreams related to the challenge of this stage, *turning toward the journey*? Respond to your mandalas and your experiences exploring Stage Three by journaling.

MANDALA OF TURNING TOWARD THE JOURNEY
Materials You'll Need:
Basic Art Materials (see page 36)
Coloring Mandala 3 (see appendix A, page 242)

Stage Three ushers in rising energy. You may feel that you have begun an important journey, though where your journey is leading you remains unknown. There is excitement, a sense of expectancy, and anticipation as the path opens before you. As you color this mandala, consider using lighter shades of blue, green, yellow, pink, or lavender in the center and darker shades toward the edge of the circle. This will give your mandala the feeling of depth that is typical of Stage Three. Notice thoughts, feelings, or memories that come to mind as you color. Recording these in your journal can help you remember what it was like as you turned toward your journey for this circling of the Great Round.

LOOPY THREAD MANDALA
Materials You'll Need:
White glue
Colored yarn, thread, or ribbon
Cardboard, tagboard, or other stiff material, approximately 8" x 8"

During Stage Three, we are called to experience process without a clear goal. We first encountered this approach to life as infants. With our blocks we performed experiments about texture, gravity, and balance. Our findings helped us develop a model of our environment.

Each time we return to Stage Three later in life, an attitude of serious play serves us well. Inspirations bubble to consciousness during this stage. Creative elements of the unconscious are like fish who only surface when they like the bait and feel safe. Creating the Loopy Thread Mandala is like casting your line with a juicy worm attached. Stay alert for the inspirations that, like fish, may suddenly surface. Most will have to be tossed back, but one of them might be worth keeping and nurturing into your next big project.

On a piece of cardboard draw a circle in pencil. Coat the surface of the circle with white glue or decoupage liquid. Take thread, yarn, or ribbon in a color you like and let it fall from your hand in loose coils onto the glue-covered surface (see plate 13). Press to secure. Add a contrasting color as background to highlight the loops. You may want to apply the background first and dip your looping material in the liquid glue before dropping it onto the surface. You may prefer to use no glue and let your mandala be a transitory object whose materials are released at the end of your creative self-expression.

UMBILICAL MANDALA
Materials You'll Need:
Basic Art Materials (see page 36)

Sometimes you may have the sense that your life is in a period of rapid change, but you cannot see where you are heading. This is a time when it is important to trust in the unfolding process of life, and *turn toward the journey,* even though you do not know what the future will bring. When you were in your mother's womb, you were an amazing shape shifter. For awhile you had a tail, gills, and fin-like hands. Throughout all these changes, you were firmly attached to your mother with the umbilical cord. This attachment even continued after birth until the umbilical cord was cut.

Native peoples often assign another umbilical connection to initiates as a source of stability through their life's journey. The constancy of the North Star, the steadiness of the force of gravity, or the predictable rising and setting of the sun are sometimes designated as a point of attachment. Before creating the Umbilical Mandala, choose one of these, or another if you prefer, to be a point of constancy for you. Let this point suggest to you a safe connection that is always present for you, even as you experience unpredictable changes. The Umbilical Mandala is a kinesthetic demonstration of this principle.

Draw a circle. At the point where ends meet to close the circle, make a dot. Let this represent your point of constancy. Beginning from this point, without lifting your pencil, chalk, or marker, create gentle loops that fill your circle. As you are making your looping lines, keep in mind the still point of attachment where you began. Let your Umbilical Mandala be a reminder that you can feel safe during changes brought on by the unknown possibilities of life.

MANDALA OF TURNING POINTS
Materials You'll Need:
Basic Art Materials (see page 36)
Leather cord, ribbon, yarn, string, or embroidery floss
Beads, feathers

During Stage Three, you become engaged with your life's journey, and the pace of living seems to speed up. There is much to see, learn, and discover. This stage encompasses important turning points when life suddenly expands, contracts, or moves in a different direction. This Mandala of Turning Points allows you to reflect on some of your past visits to this stage of the Great Round.

Begin by focusing on the turning points in your life: those times when your life could have gone a different direction, but turned instead along the path that brought you to where you are today. You might want to write these in your journal or ask a trusted person to listen as you describe them. Cut a piece of yarn, or other material, at least 3' long. Make a sturdy knot at one end to symbolize the beginning of your life journey. Then, for each turning point you recall, tie a knot in your string.

That move from grandma's house to your parents' own home: tie a knot. The birth of a baby brother: tie a knot. The first day of school: tie a knot. Enhance your knots with beads, cloth, feathers, and so on, to better portray your turning points. Once completed, lay down your knotted cord, letting your first knot be the center and spiraling the cord out into a circular form.

Ask for time with a trusted person or group to tell the story of each knot as you unwind your cord. Take note of the many changes you have negotiated during your lifetime. Congratulate yourself on your flexibility, adaptability, and endurance. Then decide what you want to do with your cord once you have told your story. Will you wear it as a necklace? Store it in your Womandala Bag (see page 50)? Bury it as some people do their baby's umbilical cord? The choice is up to you.

DREAM MANDALA
Materials You'll Need:
Basic Art Materials (see page 36)

Dreams are an important communication from your unconscious. Remembering them, journaling about them, drawing them, and sharing them in a dream group are ways to integrate the healing messages they convey. Dreams of mandalas are especially significant as symbols of the natural ordering principle of the Self. Mandala dreams most often appear during personal stress and have the potential to soothe, balance, and reorder your existence during a time of chaos.

No doubt you have experienced a dream in which a mandala appeared, although you might not have recognized the mandala. Here are some examples of dream mandalas that could go unrecognized: the dreamer is part of a group seated around a table; the dreamer circles around an object, place, person, or animal; or a person, animal, or object circles the dreamer.

Sometimes mandalas appear in dreams as circular objects. They can be as simple as a clock face or as complex as a stained glass rose window. They can be cooking pots, buckets, orbs, stones, wheels, moons, or suns. One of Jung's patients reported a dream in which he noticed a hat hanging on the wall. Jung identified the hat as a dream mandala (see figure 10 on page 22).

Stage Three on the Great Round is a time of remembering and bringing dreams to consciousness. For this project, I invite you to draw a mandala that has appeared in your dreams. It can be a recent dream or one from the past. You may draw the dream context where the mandala appears or simply draw the mandala without surrounding dream details.

When your Dream Mandala is complete, set it up and look at it. (It can be difficult to fully capture the quality of a dream, but even your attempt to do so allows the energies of the archetype of the Self to be present for you.) Study your drawing for additional information about the content and message of your dream. In your journal, complete sentences that describe your mandala: "You are ___." When you have several of these sentences completed, go back and substitute "I am" for "you are." This is a way to help you integrate information from your unconscious, and this technique can balance your conscious outlook.

MANDALA OF THE BREATH OF GOD
Materials You'll Need:
Basic Art Materials (see page 36)

Wind blowing across a body of water sets spiraling currents in motion. The writers of the Bible used this image as a symbol for the presence of God. They personified the wind as the breath of God, a force that enlivens all of creation. In preparation for creating the Mandala of the Breath of God, you may wish to attune with the Biblical imagery and place yourself at one with the Cosmos by singing the lovely song "Breath of God" (see appendix C, page 279).

When you are ready, draw a circle. Then, if you like, continue singing as you let yourself move gently into creating a mandala that reflects the presence of divinity in the spiraling movements of nature. This is your Mandala of the Breath of God.

DREAM CATCHER MANDALA
Materials You'll Need:
Twig, vine, or flexible bamboo
Wire
Ribbon, yarn, or string
Beads, feathers

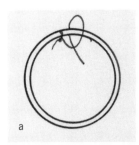

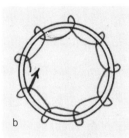

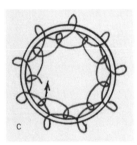

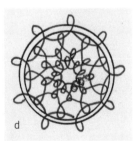

Diagram for making a dream catcher

Dreams are elusive and often dissolve as we are waking up. Dreams bring us pleasant messages from hidden parts of ourselves. Sometimes even helpful dreams are disturbing, however. Dream catchers, inspired by Native American customs, were devised as talismans to *catch* dreams and to allow only pleasant dreams to come through to the dreamer.

Part of our challenge during Stage Three is managing information that comes to us from dreams and other levels of consciousness. Creating a Dream Catcher Mandala is a seriously playful way of affirming an intention to be receptive to new information, while at the same time exercising our ability to screen and organize the information as needed.

Twist a pliable piece of twig, vine, or bamboo into a circular hoop and secure with wire or string. The circle should be about 5" across (see figure a). Choose a color of yarn, string, or ribbon that you like and knot the end securely to your hoop. Now loosely wrap the yarn around your hoop at nine places, about 2" apart (see figure b).

Create a new row of loops inside by continuing your looping pattern in the nine loops already secured to your hoop (see figure c). Continue on in the same way, creating two more rows and leaving an opening in the center to allow your dreams to come through (see figure d) Tie the end of your yarn in a sturdy knot and cut off any you do not need. Decorate with beads, feathers, or tiny written invitations to your dreams (see plate 14).

Native American peoples appreciate dreams as sacred messengers. Hang your Dream Catcher Mandala near the head of your bed. Perhaps it will help you find in your dreams the special *something* you are meant to develop during the rest of your journey of the Great Round.

FINGER PAINTING MANDALA
Materials You'll Need:
Finger painting paper
Finger paint
Newspaper

The motif of the spiral is often seen in mandalas of Stage Three. Also, the active exploration of possibilities is typical of this stage. The Finger Painting Mandala brings both these together into a hands-on exploration of media. Allow yourself to have fun with this and afterward reflect on your creative experience.

Place a piece of finger painting paper on a layer of newspaper. Drop several dollops of finger paint onto the paper in colors of your choice. Spread the paint with your hands and play with the possibilities of paint on paper for awhile. Try making circling movements with your fingers, hands, and palms. Finally, develop the form of a circle that fills most of the paper. Set aside to dry.

Lay down a clean piece of paper, add more paint, and create another Finger Painting Mandala. Continue creating Finger Painting Mandalas until you have a series of at least three or four. Lay them out and respond to your mandalas by writing in your journal about what you see, feel, and appreciate in your paintings. Complete your journaling by answering these questions: What did this experience show me about color, play, and the energy of spiraling movement? How can I apply this information to my life?

LABYRINTH MANDALA
Materials You'll Need:
Basic Art Materials (see page 36)
Stones, sticks, or moss
Ribbon, yarn, or string

A labyrinth is a meandering pathway to the center of an enclosed space. There are no dead ends or traps to one walking the path of the labyrinth even though it may appear that there are. Most labyrinths are constructed inside circles, so they are mandalas. It is appropriate to create a labyrinth during Stage Three because Kellogg named this stage of her Great Round the *Labyrinth.*

Walking a labyrinth teaches that the path to the center is trustworthy. You need only keep putting one foot in front of the other, and you will

Diagram for drawing a labyrinth

arrive at your destination. This is a powerful metaphor for the journey of life: there are no wrong turns. The labyrinth is also embraced as a symbol of the spiritual path to God. Walking a labyrinth, then, can be a form of meditation. When you create the Labyrinth Mandala, you, too, can experience this walking meditation. Annette Reynolds of our mandala group is pictured walking a labyrinth she created in plate 12.

Practice drawing a seven-circuit labyrinth following the steps illustrated above. Once you have mastered the technique, create a labyrinth large enough to walk by drawing lines on a sandy beach, mowing the design into a grass lawn, or laying down yarn, sticks, stones, or moss. Use whatever materials are available. (I have even used biodegradable toilet paper and empty soda cans to create a labyrinth!)

When your Labyrinth Mandala is completed, stand for a moment at the entrance and state an intention, question, or concern to be the focus of your walk. Then enter the Labyrinth Mandala and walk mindfully, noticing what you experience as you turn left and right, moving toward and away from the center, until finally arriving and stepping into the center. Spend a few moments there reflecting on your walk and any information you have received about your intention.

Before leaving the center, invite inspiration about how to put into action the wisdom you are receiving on your labyrinth walk. Take a deep breath and slowly retrace the pathway to the entrance. After stepping out of the Labyrinth Mandala, take a few moments to discuss or journal about your experience.

VARIATION

Draw a Labyrinth Mandala on a piece of paper. Form an intention as described above. Then trace the pathway with your finger. Respond to your experience by journaling.

SPINNING INWARD MANDALA
Materials You'll Need:
Basic Art Supplies (see page 36)
Scarf or lightweight cloth (optional)

Turning in place, or spinning, is a movement that comes naturally. As children we discover the intoxicating sensations produced by whirling, and it becomes a part of our play. It is also an exploration of our body in space, of balance, and of gravity. Just as mandalas seem a natural part of children's identity development, their spinning mandalas may serve a similar purpose. The Spinning Inward Mandala allows you to revisit this childhood activity by creating your own movement mandala.

Choose soft, rhythmic, instrumental music to support your movement. Traditional music selections from Africa, Latin America, and the Middle East, as well as contemporary acoustic works, seem to create a good atmosphere for moving mandalas. Begin the music and stand quietly in place for a few moments, holding a scarf or a piece of flowing cloth. Straighten your spine, relax your shoulders, and notice the feeling of being upright and tall, with feet firmly planted. When you feel ready, begin slowly turning counterclockwise, gradually extending your arms up and out, then down. Allow yourself to fully inhabit the space that your body touches while turning and staying securely balanced.

If it feels safe to do so, speed up your spinning and let your movements become free and fluid as you are guided by the music. Continue until you feel your experience is complete. Then turn to spin in a clockwise direction, gradually slowing your turning until you are once more standing still with your arms folded across your chest. Remain standing just a moment as you breathe and integrate your experience of turning. Then sit and respond to your Spinning Inward Mandala by drawing or writing in your journal.

CELTIC SPIRAL MANDALA
Materials You'll Need:
Earthenware clay, polymer clay, or silver metal art clay
Rolling pin
Clay tools
Circle template (anything that makes a circle the size you want)
Beads, feathers, leather pieces
Leather cord, ribbon, yarn, or string
Wire jewelry loops
Small needle-nose pliers

Spirals are prominent in the ancient stone carvings of Celtic Britain. Folk dances originating in the Celtic areas of Scotland, Ireland, Wales, and Brittany often incorporate spiraling movements to the center of the circle and back out. The Celtic spiral seems to represent the idea of death and rebirth, with the spiral path being like an umbilical cord attached to the womb of the Great Mother, or Earth Goddess. Creating the Celtic Spiral Mandala is a way to symbolize your own connection to the earth, to the sacred feminine, or to the ancestors many of us claim from Celtic lands.

Shape a handful of clay into a ball. On a flat surface covered with cloth, press the clay to flatten it. Use the rolling pin if needed to shape the clay into a slab about 1/4" thick. With a template, mark and cut a circular piece of clay from 1" to 6" across. Push a pointed stick through the clay to make a hole near the top of your Celtic Spiral Mandala.

With a clay tool or stick draw one or more spirals into the round piece of clay. Create additional holes if you would like places to attach beads, feathers, and other symbolic items. Let clay dry and harden, then fire if appropriate.

Decorate with paints, glazes, or stains, and fire clay mandala again as needed. After the firing attach beads, feathers, and leather pieces as you wish. Once complete, attach a wire jewelry loop and string onto a cord if it is to be worn as a pendant. Otherwise, attach a cord for hanging your mandala in a special place. If very small, your Celtic Spiral Mandala might even find a place in your Womandala Bag (see page 50).

Reflecting on Stage Three

Stage Three is a time of quickening energy. Alertness increases. You may become aware of new possibilities and meanings during your visit to this stage. Or you may be inspired by dreams that point toward something new, but do not give specific guidance. This stage of the Great Round can be a bit confusing because you are growing in many ways, yet no clear direction has yet manifested. This is a stage of exciting possibilities. Let Mandala Card Three be a place to express the essence of your experience of Stage Three, Turning Toward the Journey.

MANDALA CARD THREE
Materials You'll Need:
Basic Art Materials (see page 36)
Cardboard, tagboard, or other stiff material, 3" x 4" or larger

Creating Mandala Card Three is a way to summarize your exploration of Stage Three. Draw, paint, or collage a spiraling mandala image on your card. You might create a labyrinth or a meandering line with no visible beginning or end. Add other images, textures, colors, or words that suggest to you the experience of Stage Three, when we are *turning toward the journey.* Let your card dry flat and then store in a safe place.

IN WE TAKE PLEASURE IN NURTURING SOMETHING NEW, YOUNG AND TENDER IN OURSELVES ◉ LIKE A DEPENDENT INFANT SEPERATE BUT CONTAINED WITHIN THE MOTHER'S WORLD ◉ SEEING THINGS ◉ ACTIVE ENGAGEMENT ◉ LOVE, WARM FEELINGS ◉ WITH FRESH EYES ◉ AN OPPORTUNITY FOR DEEPENING COMPASSION ◉ WE FEEL A CONVICTION THAT WE ARE UNIQUE ◉ THIS IS WHERE WE LAY THE FOUNDATION OF EGO ◉

REFINING OUR SKILLS FOR ◉ LOVE AND CARING FOR OTHERS WITH RESPECT ◉ GRATITUDE ◉ ◉ ONE CORRESPONDS TO ORAL STAGE OF DEVELOPMENT ◉ CAN RETURN HERE FOR RENEWAL ◉ OPTIMISM ◉ NORMAL TO FEEL NARCISSISTIC OR SELF-ABSORBED ◉ HERE ◉ A CALL TO FOCUS ◉ MOTHER- INFANT BOND ◉ WARM FEELINGS ◉ ACTIVE ENGAGEMENT ◉ COMFORT ◉ AN INVITATION TO GROW ◉ A DAWNING SENSE OF SELF ◉

◉ GATHERING INFORMATION FROM ELDER(S) ◉ ◉ COMFORT OF THE CLOSE BOND BETWEEN MOTHER & INFANT ◉ ◉ INNOCENT DELIGHT ◉ LOVING EMBRACE ◉ EASY TO TRUST ◉ CHOOSING FROM THE MYRIAD POSSIBILITIES ◉ EMBRACING THE NEW ◉ WE TAKE RESPONS- IBILITY FOR ENFOLDING, AFFIRMING AND NURTURING OUR INNER CHILD AND OURSELVES ◉ BECOMING ◉ ABSORBING LOVE ◉ NOURISHMENT

Embracing the New

Stage Four on the Great Round is a time of active engagement, optimism, and warm feelings. This stage calls you to focus (or re-focus) on one relationship, project, or goal selected from myriad possibilities that invite you to invest your energy. Stage Four is a time of open-minded curiosity. We are learning a lot from our mother, or motherly friends.

Stage Four is the domain of the *good mother.* It is reminiscent of your first relationships as an infant. Babies are curious about their surroundings, often putting anything they can hold into their mouths. As they become more independent and learn to walk, they make brief forays away from mother's lap to explore. From time to time the little one returns to mother for reassurance. Through these early interactions with loved ones babies learn about being human and develop a sense of what the world is like.

The early pairing of mother and baby is the inspiration for some of the world's favorite art. From statues of Isis and the child Osiris to Renaissance tondos of Mary and the baby Jesus, these works convey a sense of the robust innocence of new life and the nurturing support that sustains it. We encounter these qualities each time we experience Stage Four.

Kellogg named Stage Four *Beginning.* During your first visit to Stage Four, you developed a sense of yourself joined with another: your caregiver. Returning to this stage gives you an opportunity to again look at your world with fresh eyes, to try new behaviors, and to refine your skills of caring for yourself and others. Psychologically, Stage Four supports the development or re-working of your ego, your conscious sense of self.

Stage Four is a natural time for *inner child* work. Revisiting this space allows you to gently enfold your little inner child of the past, to affirm what was real for you then, and to take adult responsibility now to provide safety and nurturing for yourself. Wholeness means, among other things, being a good parent to yourself. And who better to know what your little

This space speaks to the beginning of the world, of a person within the world or within the universe of the womb. It is related to the fertilized egg or the completed fetus, which is still part of the Great Mother, separate, but still contained. This also refers to the oral stage of development. —Joan Kellogg

inner child needs than you yourself? Trisha learned this when she moved in with her partner of two years.

Trisha and her partner had a stormy relationship. They thought things would be better between them once they moved in together, but they were not. The same suspicions and insecurities kept their interactions volatile. Trisha often got her feelings hurt because her partner responded with irritation when Trisha sighed and let her face sag into a discouraged frown. Trisha wanted nurturing, but her partner got up and left the room.

A wise friend encouraged Trisha to take care of herself by finding some activities she could do alone that would cheer her up when she was down, rather than always relying on someone else to bring her spirits up. At first this advice made Trisha feel even more lonely. However, one day Trisha saw some crayons in the grocery store. They were just like the ones she had loved as a girl. As a splurge, Trisha bought the largest box, and a pad of paper, too, and brought them home.

She sat down at the coffee table and started coloring. Trisha began with the same house, tree, and flower drawings she had made as a six-year-old when her parents had divorced. Back then, she had carried her pictures to her mother, hoping to make her smile. Now, the simple activity calmed Trisha's nerves. Very soon she was making more complex drawings. She noticed how soothing it was to draw anything in a circle. And so Trisha learned a new way to take care of herself. Funny, she mused, that her partner now seemed so mellow.

Intentions for Stage Four

During Stage Four you may find yourself filled with the innocent delight of seeing things as if for the first time. Or perhaps you will be sheltering your creative process, making time for careful listening to your muse or resisting premature production of your inspiration. The *something new* you are welcoming may be familiar, but overlooked until now. Or the new may come as a complete surprise, as it did to Trisha.

The new might even arise from your unconscious as a powerful symbol leading to a new realization. Like a parent who gets twins when one baby was predicted, this new arrival may take some getting used to. *Embracing the new* is an act of trust, faith, and love. No doubt you will find something worthy of gratitude and loving embrace as you experience Stage Four.

Stage Four Mandalas

The mandalas of Stage Four convey the sweetness of mother and child together and often incorporate a comma shape that can easily be seen as a fetus. Other typical forms include an upward-pointing triangle, a circle with a center point, or a welcoming nest. A flower or womb-like forms that can shelter something new are also seen here. As a general rule, mandalas with a pronounced center and little detailing in the surrounding circle can be associated with Stage Four.

Trisha learned about mandalas at an art therapy workshop. It was there that she drew her first mandala. Its colors were light pink, blue, and yellow, with a touch of orange. It looked like the inside of a cloud at sunrise. Trisha liked her mandala, although she was puzzled by the small golden shape in the center: something like a fish. Reflecting on what was new in her life, as the art therapist had suggested, she could only think of the upset stomach she had experienced the last few weeks. It was not until she gave birth to her son eight months later that she could understand what her mandala had been showing her.

Exercises

Before beginning your mandalas, pause to get a body sense of Stage Four by performing the yoga movements suggested in appendix B (see page 257). The song "Grace Notes" (appendix C, page 279) might also help you center. When you feel relaxed and ready, begin your creative work by choosing one of the mandalas below that feels comforting and safe.

Notice what colors you like for these. You might follow this mandala with one that challenges you to become acquainted with your inner child of the past. What surprises do you get from looking at pictures from your past? How is it for you placing the pictures inside a circle? Is it sheltering or does it feel constricting? Did you include any of the colors you used in your comforting mandala? Why or why not? Journaling will help you clarify your insights.

MANDALA OF BEGINNING
Materials You'll Need:
Basic Art Materials (see page 36)
Coloring Mandala 4 (see appendix A, page 243)

During Stage Four you are producing something new, even though its final form cannot yet be seen. The dot at the center of this simple mandala design can be used as a beginning point for your own design. Building upon the center dot, let your mandala design evolve without much thought. Use bright springtime colors. When your mandala is complete, look at it carefully. Perhaps it will give you information about something you are "birthing."

MADONNA AND CHILD MANDALA
Materials You'll Need:
Basic Art Materials (see page 36)
Image of a mother and child

Stage Four evokes the archetypal imagery of mother and infant. This iconic image appeared in sculptures of ancient Egypt and in even older statuettes of Eastern Europe and the Middle East. The images from these times depict the mother as goddess, and the worshipper probably identified with the child on her lap, as one protected by her. The iconography of Christianity adapted the imagery to show the mortal Mary nurturing the divine Christ child. These images convey the idealized qualities of the *good mother,* who loves, protects, and cares for her child.

The qualities of the good mother are imprinted on your unconscious as an archetypal potential. Life experiences with your own mother contribute to the actualization of the archetype. However, when there have been deficits in the relationship with a real-life mother, images of the archetypal realm can be invoked as a soothing corrective. In reality, you are mothering yourself: who better than you to know just what you need? By creating the Madonna and Child Mandala you give expression to your own potential to give and receive good mothering.

Draw a circle and fill it in with a soft, nurturing color. Glue the image of Madonna and Child in the center. Add more details of decoration and embellishment to highlight personal meanings in the ancient imagery of mother and child. Perhaps you will add a frame to your Madonna and Child Mandala and create a special place to display it.

VARIATION

Create the Madonna and Child Mandala with an image of yourself seated on the lap of God, Goddess, or your Higher Power. Write a letter to the nurturing Higher Power symbolized in your mandala. Write a letter from your Higher Power to you and your inner child.

MANDALA OF BABY ME
Materials You'll Need:
Basic Art Materials (see page 36)
Photo or photocopy of you as an infant

The nurturing qualities that are activated during Stage Four can be useful for celebrating our inner child of the past. Our inner child is a part of our identity formed early in life based on the outlook and capabilities of a very young person to gather, process, and interpret information about the world. Our inner child sometimes perpetuates a narrative of our lives and who we are that influences our view of the world. Sometimes this can cause us pain and misunderstandings even as adults.

Creating the Mandala of Baby Me can be an empowering step toward focusing an adult's viewpoint and mental capacities on what your early life was like. This may add subtleties and nuances to the story of your early childhood and make it possible to forgo old debts, and forgive past failings. Creating the Mandala of Baby Me can also be a testament to your resiliency and the good will of those who cared for you. Doing this expressive work is a way of taking responsibility for the love, care, and nurturing your inner child of the past needs in order to feel loved and worthy in the present.

Draw a circle and glue a photo of you as an infant in the center. Add color, form, and texture to create a mandala that holds and supports the image of you as a baby (see plate 15). When your mandala is completed, light a candle and sing "Happy Birthday" to baby you.

Respond further to your mandala by journaling. You might answer the questions: What do I notice about me in this mandala? Am I safely held? If not, what is needed to create a feeling of safety? Taking another direction to learn more about yourself as a baby, you might write down family stories you have heard about you and your early life.

DISCOVERING THE NEW MANDALA
Materials You'll Need:
Basic Art Materials (see page 36)

One of the best ways to receive information from your unconscious is through an expressive process that you allow to happen with as little control as possible. Cultivating an attitude of expectant nonattachment allows hidden, or tenderly emerging, aspects of oneself to appear in our imagery. Discovering the New Mandala guides you through a process of visual, kinesthetic, and written dialogue with hidden parts of yourself.

Draw a circle and fill it in with soft, blended colors that help it seem like a safe, nurturing, holding space. Next take a pencil and place the point near the center of the circle. Make a dot. Then, without lifting your pencil, and with eyes closed, let your pencil move, expressing the emerging of something new and unknown.

After letting your pencil move randomly for a few moments, open your eyes. Study the pencil marks in your mandala and find an object, design, or simply a shape to develop. You may add more lines and colors, if you wish. When your mandala feels complete, set it up where you can see it clearly.

In your journal, write an imaginary conversation between you and the new that has appeared in your mandala. Ask the new questions such as: "Who (what) are you? What do you need (want) from me? What do you have for me? What are you bringing into my life?" Pause between questions to let the new respond, and then record the dialogue.

NESTING MANDALA
Materials You'll Need:
Basic Art Materials (see page 36)
Twigs, grass, raffia, yarn (optional)
Plastic egg(s) (optional)

Draw circles with a soft color to build a nest. If you like, add texture to your nest with twigs, grass, yarn, and anything else you'd like. Now draw or cut out a picture, in the shape of an egg, of something you want to nurture in yourself and your life. You may prefer to use a plastic egg and put inside words or symbols that refer to something tender and new that you are *hatching*. Add symbols or words to the nest that spell out specific actions you can take to nurture the egg you have placed in the center of your mandala.

NURTURING FLOWER MANDALA
Materials You'll Need:
Basic Art Materials (see page 36)

The process of creating the Nurturing Flower Mandala is designed to be relaxing and affirming. When your mandala is completed, you will also have a reminder of self-nurturing activities, affirmations, and settings whenever you need inspiration. Begin by consciously relaxing. Then you might enjoy singing "Grace Notes" (see appendix C, page 279).

Draw a circle. Inscribe a smaller circle inside. The smaller circle will be the center point of a flower. Place a symbol of yourself in the center circle. Add petals to fill the space between the inner and outer circles. You can use drawing materials, paint, or pieces of colored paper to create petals. On each petal write or draw activities, settings, affirmations, tastes, or scents that give you a feeling of being nurtured and cared for. Refer to this mandala when you need a reminder of nice things to do for yourself.

MANDALA OF WELCOMING WHAT'S UP
Materials You'll Need:
Basic Art Materials (see page 36)

Stage Four calls for *embracing the new.* Kellogg identifies upward-pointing triangles as a common indicator of something coming into awareness. This Mandala of Welcoming What's Up allows you to identify something new in your life, explore how you are feeling about it, and develop ways you can support yourself and the new coming into your life. New enthusiasms can sometimes pull us into overdoing, so this mandala also helps you clarify some self-care activities that go along with the new.

Draw a circle on paper. Place an upward-pointing triangle in the center. Reflect for a few moments on something new you would like to welcome: a friendship, a skill, field of study, or perhaps a challenging situation. Write this above your circle. Inside the triangle, jot down any thoughts or feelings that arise now about your new project or situation. In the space between the triangle and the outside circle, write the self-nurturing behaviors and other forms of support you can utilize to help you fully develop the potentials of this new project or situation. When complete, highlight items that show what you want, need, and hope for from the new situation.

ANCESTORS HOLDING MANDALA
Materials You'll Need:
Basic Art Materials (see page 36)
Seeds, grains, beads, or small objects

Grounding in tradition can be a powerful container for new discoveries about yourself. The purpose of Ancestors Holding Mandala is to bring to your awareness some of your family inheritance in terms of the lives of those who have gone before. Creating the mandala can provide a bridge between you, the roots of your being represented by the ancestors, and the new that you embrace as you become more and more yourself.

You may know the history of your family: ancestors who gifted you with your life and handed down memories, skills, and traditions as well as your DNA. Weave stories about your grandparents and great-grandparents into the creation of the Ancestors Holding Mandala. For example, have you been told that grandmother was a gifted seamstress? Include a needle and thimble to represent her in this mandala. Was great-grandfather a sailor? Include the image of a boat.

When you have little or no information about older generations of your family, invoke your ancestors by including symbols to represent your ethnicity, the country or region where you grew up, the language(s) you speak. You might wish to include qualities of your older friends, teachers, or mentors and the religious, moral, or spiritual beliefs that you embrace.

Begin by drawing a circle about 10" across. Inside this circle draw another circle 8" or 9" across. Leave the inner circle empty. In the space between the inner and outer circles create a border filled with symbols representing your grand- and great-grandmothers and fathers.

Take some deep, relaxing breaths as you sit quietly reflecting on your mandala and the matrix of support generated for you by those who have gone before. Then scatter a few seeds, grains, beads, or other small objects in the empty center space of your mandala.

Be open to discovering a helpful message among the random objects. This might be a new way of looking at your life from the perspective of those who have lived a long time. It might be an inspiration for a new venture that continues an important family tradition. It might even be permission to move on and let the past be in the past.

When you are ready to end this time reflecting on your ancestors and the part they continue to play in your life, clear away the items from the middle of your circle. Put your Ancestor's Holding Mandala someplace for safekeeping. You may want to bring it out again in the future.

PREGNANCY MANDALA
Materials You'll Need:
Basic Art Materials (see page 36)
Mementoes of pregnancy (optional)

Stage Four is about new life. This stage evokes the archetype of pregnancy and birth. The Pregnancy Mandala gives you a place to explore feelings and memories about these important events in the lives of you and your loved ones. The Pregnancy Mandala offers a place to remember and celebrate the gifts of your experience. Creating the mandala is a way of honoring baby and parents.

Every pregnancy is different. Even before birth, babies have distinct personalities. Was your baby relaxed and easygoing or were you awakened in the night by elbows in your ribs? Did you have pet names for your baby before birth? There are bound to be unexpected events during pregnancy that can be humorous, endearing, frightening, infuriating, and sad. Reflect on the pregnancy you or your loved one experienced and complete the Pregnancy Mandala.

Draw a circle and place a picture or symbol of your baby in the center. Fill in the space around the center with written memories, words, images, and other mementoes of the pregnancy and birth. Add words that you would like to communicate to your baby: gratitude, prayers, parental advice. Place your Pregnancy Mandala on a home altar and light a candle in front of it.

Reflecting on Stage Four

Stage Four is about the appearance of the new and our challenge to accept it. Something new may be a cause for joyful celebration after long anticipation. The new can also surprise us because it is not what we expected, or we feel unprepared. This stage requires that we open our hearts to the new, regardless of what it is, and commit to it our best care. Bring forward the essence of your experience of Stage Four, *Embracing the New,* into creating Mandala Card Four.

MANDALA CARD FOUR
Materials You'll Need:
Basic Art Materials (see page 36)
Cardboard, tagboard, posterboard, or other stiff material, 3" x 4" or larger
Collage pictures

Cut a piece of card stock in the shape and size you want for your Mandala Card Four. For your card, select images to collage or create illustrations of something young or new to express the theme *embracing the new*. On your card create a mandala design that incorporates the images you have selected as well as an upward-pointing triangle, a dot, or the comma form of a fetus typical of Stage Four. Use additional images, words, textures, or colors to complete your card design. Lay flat to dry and then store in a safe place.

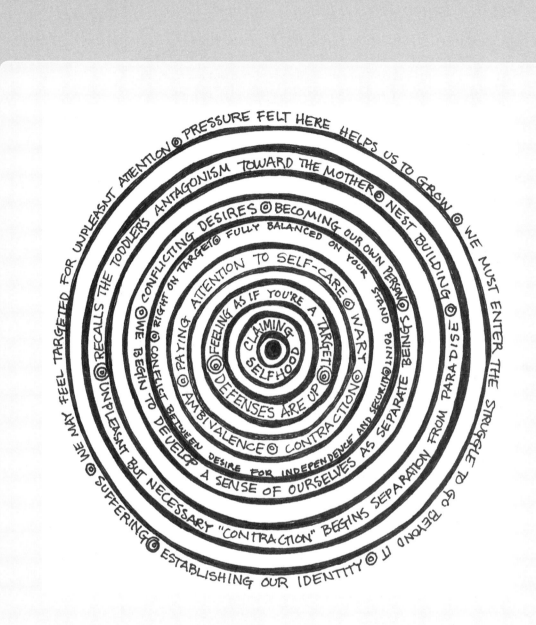

STAGE FIVE
Claiming Selfhood

Energy and emotions intensify as we are *claiming selfhood* during Stage Five. It is not unusual to feel anger, frustration, fear, and even courage during this stage that Kellogg calls *Target.* From the perspective of Stage Five, the world can appear to be a dangerous place. Paranoia may arise when you suspect you are being singled out for negative attention. You can also feel excited and *on target* here as you discover your standpoint and gain a sense of individuality.

Stage Five is first experienced when you are around two or three years old. At this time your abilities to stand and walk independently for short periods allowed you to develop a sense of yourself. When your desires clashed with those of your caregiver, you said no and risked disapproval from the most important people in your life. This helped you to surrender your claim to the blissfully dependent state of infancy, even though it may have seemed you had nothing to put in its place. No wonder it is called the *terrible twos.*

When we return to Stage Five as adults, it remains a significant point for changing our ego, the self we know. During this stage we experience conflicting desires for independence and security. You may encounter protest when you say no to requests from others or when you disagree with others on the best course of action to take. You may unconsciously project your anger and fearfully expect others to vindictively retaliate. It may seem important to marshal your best defenses. It is also a time to pay special attention to your self-care.

For Sandy, high school algebra tests were the worst. He got so nervous the night before that he could not sleep. Once he threw up during an algebra class. Somehow what happened got around at school, and Sandy felt humiliated. The next day his algebra teacher consoled him: "I used to feel the same way about algebra! Why don't you get some tutoring?" Sandy did just that and also got some advice from his tutor on how to manage his nervousness. Now, whenever Sandy has a business presentation to make, he has a sort of ritual that helps him stay calm. He prepares thoroughly well ahead of the deadline, gets lots of exercise the day before his presentation, and plays soothing music to help him go to sleep. This routine enables him to wake up with energy and feel confident about making a good presentation.

It is not unusual to feel stuck during Stage Five as conflict plays out between different parts of yourself in ambivalence, procrastination, or self-criticism. Irritation can boil into anger as you stew in the seemingly insoluble dilemma of choosing to do *this* or *that.* The conflict is not usually enjoyable, but like a boiling pot with a tight lid, it generates energy, the psychic energy that fuels your personal growth. Through the push and pull, both within yourself and in relationships with others, you are coming to know yourself more clearly.

Interestingly, some mystics find the pattern of concentric circles an apt expression of their spiritual experiences. Hildegard of Bingen conceptualized ranks of angels in this arrangement (see Coloring Mandala 5 on page 244). Hindu tantric art also makes use of concentric circles to symbolize the eternal cycles of cosmic evolution and involution. It is possible that your Stage Five mandalas will be similarly inspired.

> Ritualistic behavior can be initiated when one is in this space. . . . The compulsive nature of this space can be seen in the instinctual habits of nest building, repetitive rounds of behavior of a stereotyped nature. —Joan Kellogg

Intentions for Stage Five

The tasks for Stage Five are to take responsibility for yourself and confront your fears as you push against your inner parent for autonomy. Stage Five might be compared to cooking a pot of gumbo: lots of ingredients are put together, but they must be patiently simmered in order to become the smoky yet subtle dish many crave. Enduring the conflicts typical of Stage Five is required for *claiming selfhood.*

Stage Five Mandalas

Mandalas of Stage Five usually resemble a target: concentric circles around a defined center point. Sometimes a mandala of this stage has a striped design, like a beach ball being viewed from one side. Bright colors are most often seen in Stage Five mandalas. Complementary colors such as red/green, purple/orange, and blue/yellow are frequently used together. They visually express the upsurge of energy in this stage. The mandala of Maureen Shelton, a member of our mandala group, is a good example (see plate 16).

Exercises

Before you begin creating your mandalas, take a few minutes to stretch and breathe into Stage Five. A good way to accomplish this is to perform the yoga movements for this stage (see appendix B, page 259). As you do the yoga, reflect on how it feels to extend your arms wide and fill space with a movement mandala centered on your heart. Then, as you work on your mandalas, keep in mind these questions: Do you feel like a target, or are you *on* target? What sort of defenses help you feel safe? Is it more important to you to feel safe or strong? Journaling about your mandalas and your responses to these questions can provide useful information about yourself.

HILDEGARD'S MANDALA
Materials You'll Need:
Basic Art Materials (see page 36)
Coloring Mandala 5 (see appendix A, page 244)

This mandala depicts Hildegard of Bingen's vision of all beings together, dancing, singing, and celebrating God's creation. Nine circles of angels and human beings surround an empty circle representing "the mystery of the center where beauty is born" (Fox 1985, 77). Use your brightest colors to fill in these concentric circles of angels and human beings. This will help you grasp the intense energy typical of Stage Five.

LITTLE ME MANDALA
Materials You'll Need:
Basic Art Materials (see page 36)
Cardboard, 3" x 4" or larger (optional)
Photograph (or photocopy) of you as a toddler

Stage Five was first experienced when you were a young child around three years old. This was a time in your life when you were making important discoveries about relationships, boundaries, right and wrong, and your sense of being an individual with a will of your own. Creating the Little Me Mandala honors the curious little person you were. It also highlights your family and other important people in your life.

Exploring your early life identity and relationships will raise to awareness some of the conclusions you came to during that time in your life. Most will still be useful, such as: *falling down can hurt.* Others may need revising when compared to your present-day perspective. An example of one of my own toddler opinions in need of an update: naps are a boring waste of time.

Make a dot in the center of a piece of drawing paper or cardboard, and draw five circles of various sizes around the same center point. In the center circle place an image of you as a toddler. (You might want to create a cardboard support so the image can stand vertically upon the paper.) Into the next circle, place names, symbols, or images of your immediate family—those people with whom you lived when you were the age you are in your center image.

In the next circle place members of your extended family who were important to you when you were a preschooler, but who did not live in your home. Grandparents, aunts and uncles, cousins will probably fit here. A caregiver that you were attached to but did not live in your family home would belong in this circle, as would family members whose absence or death touched you during this time.

In the next circle, place names, images, or symbols to represent your neighbors, family friends, preschool friends, church and kindergarten teachers, priests, or ministers who were important influences in your life during this time. Finally, in the outer circle place elements of the larger culture that you liked at the time: playthings, cartoons, songs, games, TV programs, movies, superheroes, and so on.

When your mandala is complete, take a look at it. Note the many relationships you had as a toddler. Reflect on how your circles of influence supported and shaped you—or hindered you—as you established your own identity. How has the person you are now been shaped by this period in your life? How has your sense of trust been touched by your experiences as a toddler? Do you still hold ideas about the world from that time that you would like to affirm or revise now? Add words or images to your mandala to claim the ideas you now hold or would like to make more a part of who you are in the present.

BINDU MANDALA
Materials You'll Need:
Basic Art Materials (see page 36)

Bindu is Sanskrit for "point of beginning" and "point of return." Bindus mark the center of *yantras*, circular designs from the culture of India. Like other mandalas of Eastern origin, yantras summon, focus, and contain sacred energy. In yantras the bindu conveys the message that life is a constant flow of creation and destruction.

Visually, adding the bindu to a circle enlivens the design by providing a focus point that organizes all the other design elements. In the creation of this mandala, you will experience the shift that occurs when you add the center point, the bindu. Open yourself to awareness of what this occurrence means to you.

On a piece of paper lightly pencil in a dot for the center of your mandala. Place the point of your compass on this point and create a circle. Using the same center point, make four or five more circles each larger than the last such that you create a design of concentric circles. Add color to your circles, staying neatly within the lines as much as possible. Once your mandala is filled with color, take note of the interplay of lines and colors. Next, make a dot at the center of your mandala in red or black. You may find that your mandala becomes enlivened by the presence of the bindu, as complexities, potential forms, and myriad visual relationships snap into alignment.

TARGET MANDALA
Materials You'll Need:
Basic Art Materials (see page 36)

Our lives are comprised of moments when we feel competent, capable, and focused. We also experience times of feeling incompetent, vulnerable, and confused. Usually reality is somewhere between these two extremes. The purpose of this mandala is to give you an opportunity to explore these dynamics in your own life and possibly come to a point of balance.

On a piece of paper mark a dot for the center of your mandala. Place the point of your compass on this dot and draw a circle. Using the same center point, create three or four more circles equally distant from each other. Use bright complementary colors such as red/green, purple/orange, and yellow/blue to fill your circles. As you color, reflect on situations in your life where you feel as if you are *the* target for positive or negative attention from others. Also, consider the situations where you feel you are *on* target, at the right place at the right time. In the centermost circle of your target—the bull's-eye—use a color that symbolizes your own strong center point.

FAMILY CIRCLE MANDALA
Materials You'll Need:
Basic Art Materials (see page 36)
Earthenware clay, polymer clay, or modeling clay
Cardboard or wood, approximately 16" x 16"

The family that raises us shapes our attitudes and behavior. This intimate group teaches us how to be a human being and gives us our start in life.

As adults we have a choice to accept or not to accept the stories we were given about relationships, values, and our own identity. Making choices is made more difficult, however, by the fact that these stories are deeply embedded in our memories and may even be outside our awareness in the unconscious. The Family Circle Mandala creates a container for discovering, exploring, and even changing these stories about you and your family.

Sculpt clay figures to represent you and your family: the people with whom you lived from ages two to four. On a flat piece of cardboard or wood, arrange the figures to reflect your family group. Staying with the memory of your family as it was when you were a toddler, put the most important person(s) in the center and place other clay figures in relationship to this one. Indicate close relationships by placing figures near to each other. Make the distance greater between figures to show less of a connection. Draw a freehand circle around the figures of your family.

Notice what it is like to reflect on this portrait of you and your family. What does it tell you about your world during these formative years? Which family member's figure did you place closest to the figure representing you? You probably felt emotionally closest to this person. Identify the figure farthest from you. Any surprises about whom you are closest or farthest from in your Family Circle Mandala? How does this information align with your memories and the stories you have been told about you and your family members? Try moving figures around and noticing your feelings as distances change between your figure and those of various family members.

Now shifting into the present family situation: are there family members you would like to be closer to or farther away from? Make a new family configuration that expresses the way you would like your family relationships to be. How does this family mandala compare to your relationships with family at the present time? Are there any actions you would be willing and/or able to take now, based on what you have observed in your Family Circle Mandala?

DEFENSIVE SHIELDS MANDALA
Materials You'll Need:
Basic Art Materials (see page 36)
Posterboard or heavy paper, approximately 12" x 12"
Yarn or string

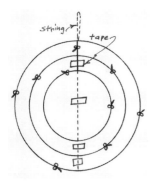

Defensive Shields Mandala

Knowing that you can protect yourself helps you feel safe, secure, and empowered. Levels of threat and protection vary, according to the situation. The Defensive Shields Mandala allows you to explore several levels of threat, from mild to challenging, to think through appropriate protective actions, to create affirmations that soothe mild threats, and to develop symbols that rehearse the activation of your most effective defenses when needed.

On a piece of poster board or heavy paper, mark a center point and draw at least three circles around it, equal distance from each other. Cut out the largest circle. Now draw a line from the edge of the largest circle *toward* the center point, but stop at the line for the inner circle. Cut along the line you just made from outer edge to the boundary of the center circle and then cut along all the circle lines. Next, tape each outer circle where you cut along the line to the center. When you are finished you will have one inner circle and several outer rings.

Let the inner circle represent you. Each ring demonstrates a level of protection that is available to you when you need it. Fill the inner circle with words and symbols that represent you. These could be photographs, "I am" statements, poetry, or your personal qualities such as patience, energy, humor, courage, and so on.

The smallest inner ring is for least threatening situations, such as being caught in an unexpected rain shower, receiving by mistake a piece of mail addressed to your grouchy neighbor, or passing a speed-monitoring camera going 50 mph in a 35 mph zone. List examples or illustrate such threats on one side of the inner ring. On the opposite side of the ring write, draw, or collage affirmations and options for responding appropriately in a way that makes you feel safe. Examples might be: remember that a little water does not hurt you; choose a time when my neighbor is away to put

Buddha feet in Eastern mandala

her mail in the mailbox; take foot off the accelerator; breathe deeply and relax shoulders while breathing out.

Use the next largest ring to list or illustrate situations that you experience as anxiety producing. Some examples might be bumping into a stranger on a train, misplacing your car keys, or being late for work. On the opposite side show some of the affirmations and appropriate actions that can help you feel secure or at the very least more comfortable. For example: count to ten before responding, focus on the next right thing to do, think of the last time and place you saw the keys, call the boss to let her know you are on the way.

The outermost ring is reserved for listing and illustrating the situations you find very challenging. Examples could include being confronted by a belligerent co-worker, walking on a dangerous hiking trail, or your spouse asking for a separation. The opposite side is for illustrations of the strategies and positive statements you can use to manage the challenges. Action strategies might include staying calm, getting as much information as possible, careful preparation, doing what can be done and letting go of the rest, asking for help or intervention. Affirmative statements might include: feelings come and go; just keep breathing; I use my creativity to manage whatever life sends me; I ask for help when I need it; feelings give me useful information; keep an open mind; check the facts. Use your creativity to arrange these images and phrases around the outer ring.

Now lay the inner circle on a flat surface with the rings arranged around it so they reconnect the line you originally drew. Lay a piece of string along this line, leaving enough string outside the outer ring to make a loop for hanging your piece. Secure the string with glue or tape so that the inner circle and surrounding rings can twist and turn freely. Hang up your Defensive Shields Mandala and let it be a reminder of the many options you have for self-care and protection.

STANDPOINT MANDALA
Materials You'll Need:
Basic Art Materials (see page 36)
Paper or cardboard, approximately 36" x 36"
A piece of string 12" long

In Eastern religious art we find examples of mandalas with footprints in the center. These symbolize the presence of the Buddha, just as do his written name and images of him in other mandalas. In another part of the world, we see rock carvings from the era of the Vikings that are clearly intended to represent tracings of human feet. These are placed near images of boats. Could it be that the footprints are a sort of signature attesting to one's presence at an important event, such as a boat launching?

We assert our beliefs when we *take a stand* on an issue. We also may *stand and be counted* when we cast a vote in support of an issue in a democratic process. In these instances we demonstrate verbally or physically that we are present and that we have a personal point of view. We may stand to be seen, so that others will know that we are present. In taking these actions we assert the importance of our existence and proclaim our presence as a unique individual with our own identity.

The Standpoint Mandala allows you to literally *stand your ground* in order to appreciate your existence as a physical being and as a person with your own boundaries, capabilities, and preferences. This mandala gives you an opportunity to *stand on your own feet* and celebrate yourself as a sturdy individual.

Stand in the center of a large piece of paper or cardboard and trace around your feet (with or without shoes). Then tie the piece of string to your pencil. This will be your compass. Hold the free end of the string on the paper at the midpoint between your outlined feet (this marks your center point) and, keeping the string taut, draw a circle around your traced feet. Now work around your feet or step outside the circle and use bright colors to create concentric circular shapes working outward from your foot tracings to the edge of the circle. When your mandala is complete, step once again onto the traced outlines of your feet. Stand tall and notice what it is like to define your standpoint in this way. Do some journaling about the colors you used and what they tell you about yourself and your standpoint (see plate 17).

NESTING BOXES MANDALA
Materials You'll Need:
Basic Art Materials (see page 36)
Set of three nesting circular wooden boxes from craft store

Itinerant holy people of the East sometimes carry sacred shrines in miniature, folded into a series of cleverly interlocking boxes. When the person stops to take a break on his travels, the tiny objects can be opened out to reveal a mandala of compartments sheltering images of protective deities, wisdom teachers, and symbols of good luck. In the West we are familiar with keepsake boxes where baby teeth, a lock of a loved one's hair, small pieces of jewelry, and all sorts of personal mementoes are sequestered for safekeeping.

The Nesting Boxes Mandala is a special set of boxes you create to illustrate your sources of support, inspiration, and protection. Once completed, the Nesting Boxes Mandala will shelter a special object that symbolizes you. The mandala can then be a reminder that you have many sources of help to call on when you feel the need. Boxes can be opened or closed, nested inside each other or stand separate. Objects can be added or removed. These options symbolically demonstrate that you have personal choice and flexibility in the deployment of your protective resources.

Let each box represent a layer of protection for you. Decorate the boxes with images and symbols that represent loving support, protection, and inspiration. When complete, place a symbol of you, such as a stone, a piece of jewelry, or a flower, in the smallest box. Enclose this small box in the next larger box. Then place the next larger box in the largest box. Reflect on how it feels to have these layers of protection around you, as represented by the object in the smallest box. Experiment with removing layers of protection by removing lids or setting aside one or more boxes. What is it like? Do some layers seem more necessary than others? If so, why? Why not?

SPHERE OF INFLUENCES
Materials You'll Need:
Basic Art Materials (see page 36)
2 Round balloons (inflated) or a smooth, rounded bowl (alternative: purchase wooden or foam ball from craft store)
Papier mâché (strips of newspaper 1" x 2" and glue)

Mandalas are not always flat circles. They are domes and three-dimensional spheres as well. Spheres have the same capacity as circles to impose order on disparate colors and visual images. The Sphere of Influences Mandala gives you a place to represent seemingly contradictory aspects of your personality in a way that visually unites them into the wholeness of the sphere. This can be a showing that supports your acceptance of personal contradictions, and the conflicts they sometimes generate, as a natural part of life.

Create a papier mâché sphere using a balloon or a rounded bowl. If using a balloon, blow it up and knot the end. Cover the entire balloon, with the exception of the knot, with papier mâché, using glue and strips of newspaper about 1" × 2" thick. Once it is dry, pop and remove the balloon and cover the hole with more papier mâché. If using a bowl, apply nonstick spray to the round bottom, then apply the papier mâché layers of newspaper. Allow to dry. Remove papier mâché hemisphere from the bowl. Repeat to make a second hemisphere. Spread newspaper strips and glue over the seams to attach the hemispheres together to create a sphere; masking tape or a hot glue gun can also be used. (You might like to decorate the inside before you attach the two halves.)

Trace a circle with a diameter of 3" or less on the sphere. Then set a compass to the smallest adjustment possible, about an inch between points. Next, run the point along the circle, letting the pencil in the compass draw your new line and create a new circle outside the first circle. Then run the point of your compass along this new line to mark the next line. Continue in this way, creating lines approximately 1" apart all around the sphere. End your drawing of lines when you have completed an odd number of lines and the only unmarked empty space left on the sphere is a circle about the same size of the circle where you began. These two circles will be on opposite sides of the sphere.

Let the two opposite circles represent parts of you that are so different they seem to be in opposition. For instance, these may be different yet equally important interests, such as competitive bicycling versus painting as meditation. The divide between introvert and extravert might pull you in a split between being a homebody and a social butterfly. Another important conflict to explore could be the pull to leave versus the desire to stay in a relationship.

Color the two circles on your sphere in hues that represent the two qualities you are exploring. Make your color choices vivid to emphasize the differences. Alternate your two colors for the rings around your circles. When completed, attach string so you can hang up your Sphere of Influences Mandala. Turn it and see how it shifts from circle to stripes, and back to (opposite) circle. Notice how elements in seeming contradiction co-exist on the sphere. What else do you see as you turn your three-dimensional mandala? Finally, enjoy seeing this Sphere of Influences Mandala as a representation of your wholeness.

SACRED FLOWER MANDALA
Materials You'll Need:
Basic Art Materials (see page 36)
Earthenware clay, polymer clay, or modeling clay
Fabric (optional)

The structure of flowers is that of concentric circles. The Sacred Flower Mandala allows you to construct your own flower as a visual paean to nature's beauty, symmetry, and life force. You are invited to include names of important teachers on the petals. The Sacred Flower Mandala could even be a gift or offering to honor your teachers and to affirm your commitment to their teachings.

Near the center point of a piece of drawing paper, trace a small inner circle. This will be the center of the flower. Let this circle represent you. Fill it in with one of your favorite bright colors. Now lightly draw three or more larger circles using the center point of the inner circle. Let these lines be your guide for adding petals radiating out from the center of the flower. The petals can be drawn, or cut out of paper or fabric and glued in place. On the petals write names of spiritual guides or beings whose presence you find encouraging.

VARIATION

Create angels instead of petals. This will allow you to use imagery specific to your faith tradition. Include your guardian angels, favorite angels, or loved ones who are angels. For Christian imagery refer to the coloring mandala based on a vision of Hildegard of Bingen (see Coloring Mandala 5, appendix A, page 244).

BLESSING WORDS MANDALA
Materials You'll Need:
Basic Art Materials (see page 36)
Gel pens (optional)

Words are powerful. By developing the habit of saying positive things to yourself about yourself, you can improve your self-esteem, increase your self-confidence, and lower your anxiety level. Creating the Blessing Words Mandala is an opportunity to immerse yourself in positive words. When you put the mandala on display where you will see it often, it can serve as a gentle reminder of the positive thoughts you are cultivating.

On a piece of white or colored paper draw seven circles from the same center point so that you have a target design. Begin in the center and, writing clockwise, fill the space with words that express positive emotion, encouragement, and affirmation. When the center is filled, go to the next circle and continue your writing. You may repeat words, use wise sayings of friends and family, and quote favorite lines from poems, scripture, or self-help programs. You may change colors as you move from circle to circle, or not, as you choose.

When your mandala is complete, place it somewhere so that you can refer to its encouraging messages often. Some believe that a mandala like this has energy that keeps *praying* the affirmative messages you place in it, even when you are not consciously doing so yourself. May it be so for you.

GOD'S EYE MANDALA
Materials You'll Need:
Two or more sturdy sticks 6" to 8" long
Brightly colored pieces of yarn

God's eyes originated among the Huichol peoples of northwestern Mexico. The Huichol use God's eyes as talismans to protect newborns and young children. God's eyes symbolize the power of seeing and understanding that which is a mystery. They consider some God's eyes portals through which human beings can see God, and God can view the world of human beings.

You might create the God's Eye Mandala as you pray for your own good health or the health of a friend or a family member. When completed, the God's Eye Mandala can become a physical reminder of your prayer. Your God's Eye Mandala can also serve as a symbol of an intention to deepen your self-understanding through inner work, journaling, and creative self-expression.

Arrange the sticks so that they cross at their center points and form a radiating star shape. Use bright colored yarn to secure the center point where sticks intersect. Continue wrapping the center, weaving the yarn over and under the "arms" of the star, until the sticks are completely covered where they intersect. End by knotting the yarn firmly to an arm of the star.

Now, beginning where the center wrapping ends, tie on a different color yarn. Turn the knot to the back of your God's Eye Mandala. Wrap yarn once around the stick, then carry it to the next stick, wrapping yarn close to the center wrapping. Continue in this way wrapping from stick to stick. After a few rows of this color, secure the end of the yarn with a knot.

Tie on a new piece of yarn in a different color, and continue as before. Keep tying on and wrapping with new colors until the space between the sticks is filled with bands of color. Leave raw stick ends exposed. Tie on a piece of yarn to be a hanger for your mandala. Hang up your God's Eye Mandala and reflect on how the colors you chose, the number of sticks you used, and the way you wrapped the sticks also say something about the "I" that you are.

Reflecting on Stage Five

Stage Five is a time of *claiming selfhood,* of developing your boundaries and stepping into awareness of yourself as part of a family circle. You are learning who you are, what makes you feel safe, and how to put in place necessary protections. Reflect on your experience of Stage Five and the issues of establishing boundaries, creating safety, and taking a stand. Singing "Make My Way" (see appendix C, page 280) will help bring your exploration of this stage to a conclusion and inspire your creation of Mandala Card Five.

MANDALA CARD FIVE
Materials You'll Need:
Basic Art Materials (see page 36)
Cardboard, tagboard, posterboard, or other stiff material cut to desired size
Collage pictures

Using collage pictures, drawings, or painting, develop a mandala of concentric circles on your card. Complete your design with additional color, texture, images, or words that express your sense of Stage Five, *claiming selfhood*. Let your card dry flat, and store in a safe place.

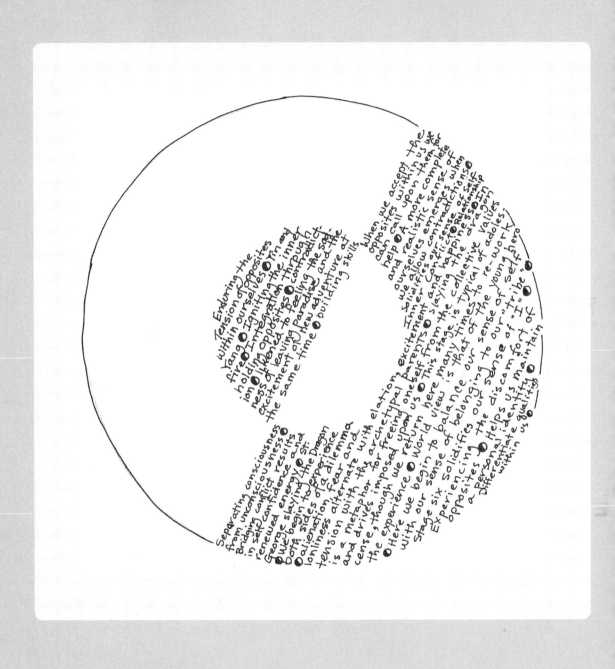

Plate 1. The domed architecture of the Blue Mosque in Istanbul leads the eye upward and inspires a feeling of awe.

Plate 2. Circles appear in Christian art as halos that encircle the heads of divine and saintly beings. Here we see Jesus Christ depicted in a mosaic on view in Hagia Sophia, Istanbul.

Plate 3. Sufis, members of a mystical sect of Islam, perform turning in circles, or whirling, as a form of contemplation.

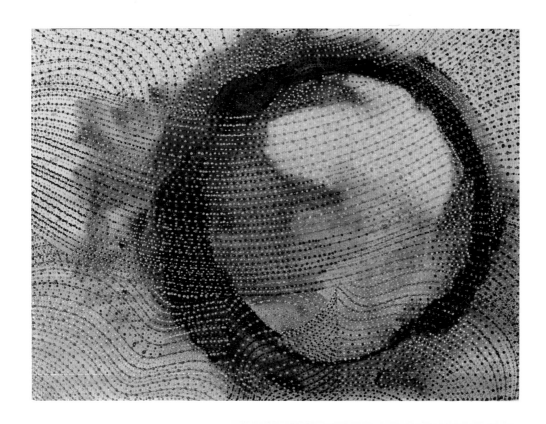

Plate 4. Joshua Rose explores the simple yet complex imagery of circles in his paintings. *ENSO: Eclipse*, 2007. (Courtesy of Zane Bennett Gallery, Santa Fe, New Mexico.)

Plate 5. Donald Cooper finds the center—or *bindu*—a focus for his engaging circle imagery. *Bindu 4.15.0622*. (Courtesy of Sandler Hudson Gallery, Atlanta, Georgia.)

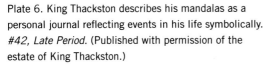

Plate 6. King Thackston describes his mandalas as a personal journal reflecting events in his life symbolically. *#42, Late Period*. (Published with permission of the estate of King Thackston.)

Plate 7. Even arrangements of natural and cast-off objects can be organized by a circle and become a mandala. Francisco Roa, *Sands Flowers*, 1994. (Published with permission of Oglethorpe University Museum of Art, Atlanta, Georgia.)

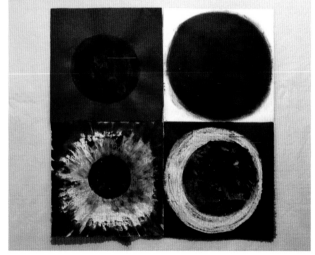

Plate 8. Rachel Norment conveys her experience of cancer treatment in her painting *Radiation Therapy,* 2006. (Courtesy of Brandylane Publishers, Inc.)

Plate 9. Diana Gregory expresses her experiences of Stage One, Resting in the Darkness.

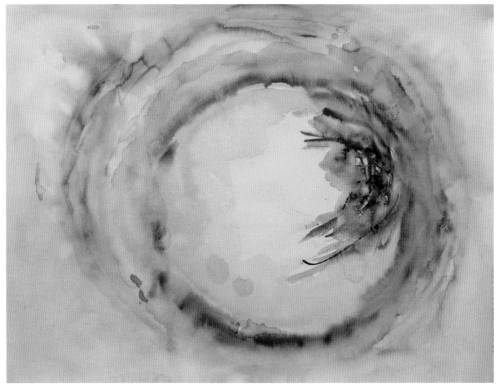

Plate 10. Susanne Fincher explores the qualities of Stage One in *Circling*.

Plate 11. Sue Kahn enjoys a watery exploration of Stage Two in her painting *Bliss*.

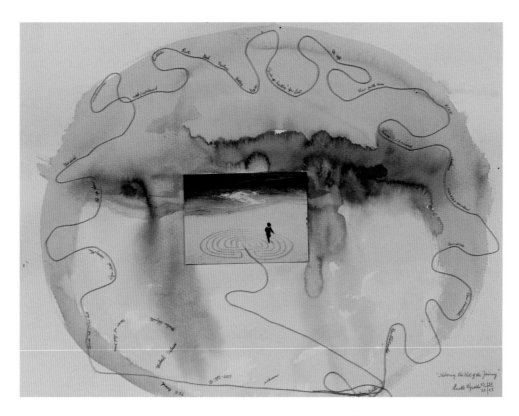

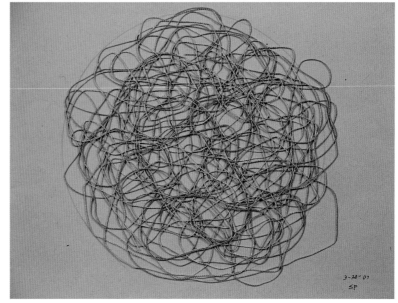

Plate 12. Annette Reynolds notes important moments in her life journey along the meandering loop that leads to the center in *Welcoming the Rest of the Journey*. That is Annette walking a labyrinth she created by the Gulf of Mexico.

Plate 13. Susanne Fincher revisits Stage Three, Turning Toward the Journey, through the creation of this thread mandala entitled *Loopy*.

Plate 14. Annette Reynolds crafts a dream catcher for Stage Three.

Plate 15. Susanne Fincher places a baby picture at the center of this Mandala of Baby Me. Creating this artwork allows her to remember and appreciate her first experience of Stage Four.

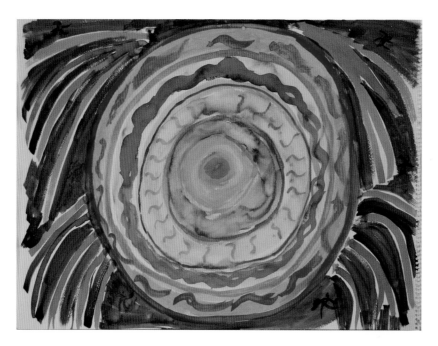

Plate 16. Maureen Shelton finds
the concentric circles typical of
Stage Five mandalas a comfortable
starting point for her colorful painted
mandala.

Plate 17. Susanne Fincher traces
around her feet to establish the
center of this Standpoint Mandala.
Creating this mandala helps her
touch into an experience of Stage
Five, Claiming Selfhood.

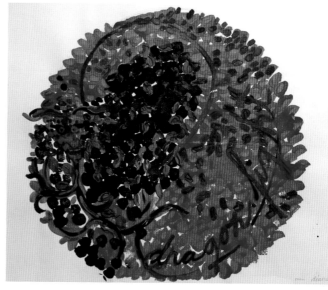

Plate 18. Patty Hutton constructs a flame-like form to bridge the opposites in her mandala. Going more deeply into the personal meanings of her *bridge* gives helpful information about how to move beyond some of her inner conflicts.

Plate 19. *Dragon Fight*, by Diana Gregory, expresses the intense energy typical of Stage Six.

Plate 20. *You Are Here . . . Now What?*
This is Patty Hutton's question to herself
as she lives into Stage Seven, a time for
discovering your life goals.

Plate 21. In response to the Stage Sev-
en suggestion to produce a mandala that
expresses your core values, Susanne
Fincher creates *Love Is the Center*.

Plate 22. The mandala *Thinking, Feeling, Sensing, and Intuition* allows Patty Hutton to explore all her capabilities for Functioning in the World, Stage Eight.

Plate 23. Sue Kahn creates *Reaching Out to Each Other* as an expression of cooperation, her experience of Stage Eight.

Plate 24. Annie Kelahan uses collage in her mandala on a theme of service to others. Hands are often seen in mandalas of Stage Eight.

Plate 25. For Patty Hutton *The Compass Rose* reflects a crystallization of spiritual insights during Stage Nine.

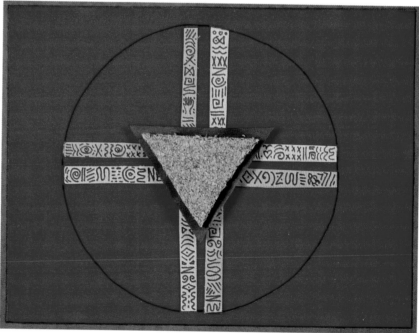

Plate 26. A kaleidoscope of colors makes a pleasing mandala design in Sue Kahn's exploration of Stage Nine, Reaping Rewards.

Plate 27. Annie Kelahan's richly colored mandala is an expression of Stage Ten, Letting Go.

Plate 28. A powerful shield mandala is Edna Bacon's response to the challenges of Stage Ten.

Plate 29. A mandala mask of *Facing My Fear* helps Susanne Fincher stay with her experience of Stage Ten.

Polyhymnia in November: Fragmentation

This time, Polyhymnia found me underneath my desk
Looking for words that had escaped,
Searching for thoughts that had declined my invitation.

Unnamed humors from someplace
Near my soul
Mingle with the mess that I had made.

I watched in dazed disorientation
As hues of groundedness, creativity, and will.
Gratitude, integrity, wisdom and wonderment were
Polyhymnia, thinking I might need some space,
Left me there underneath my desk.
With a whispered invitation to call her when I could.

She exited more quickly than she ever had before.
Still, I thought there was a woodsy scent that lingered
Long after she had wrapped up in her leafy shawl and

She watched me study paper cracks.
She saw me try to read a message?
Imagined to be written in the weaving of the rug

Fingers on her lips in thought,
She considered my distraction, undecided
Should she stay in and rescue me again?

She eyed the rainbow on my altar space.
The seven tiny crystal bowls containing all I needed to survive.
She put them on a tray and slid them to my side.

My reach was quick and urgent,
But my grip was insufficient.
And the tinctures spilled onto the fabric of the floor.

Kaaren, November 9, 2007

Plate 30. Kaaren Nowicki lets herself deepen into an experience of Stage Eleven, Falling Apart, through her collage mandala.

Plate 31. A shattered self-image is a natural part of coming to terms with the fragmentation of Stage Eleven. Susanne Fincher expresses this experience in her broken mirror mandala.

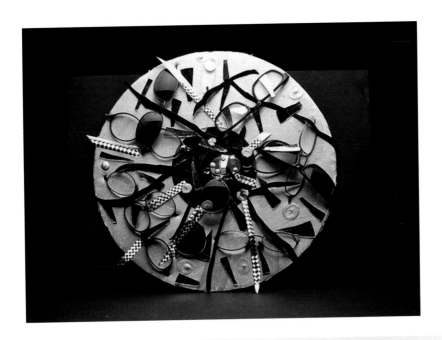

Plate 32. For this collage mandala, Diana Gregory gathers all her old pairs of eyeglasses that symbolize the many assumptions she has had to *see through* and discard during previous visits to Stage Eleven, Falling Apart.

Plate 33. Stage Twelve, Opening to Grace, is conveyed by Patty Hutton's mandala expressing an experience of joyful resolution.

Igniting the Inner Fire

Stage Six of the Great Round aligns with the month of June, with early summer, and with late morning. The psychological growth associated with this stage is reminiscent of that done during adolescence. Relinquishment of childhood attachments to parents is highlighted. Differentiation of your ego from its unconscious matrix, which began in Stage Five, solidifies your sense of being an individual. With this inner work you are *igniting the inner fire.*

This shift requires some sort of trying and testing in order to clarify personal boundaries, negotiate understandings in relationships, and create your place in the adult world. You have here the experience of leaving paradise, with sadness, nostalgia, and not a little concern for your survival. Yet you also feel the allure of high adventure, and the excitement of new possibilities pulls you forward into life. You may be industriously preparing for a career of your own choosing.

So it is that Stage Six is often a place of conflict, of experiencing both sides of a dilemma: the desire to stay and the pull to move on. Your conflicts may play out internally, in relationships with others, or in both inner and outer domains. Your first visit to this stage might have been accompanied by fights with your parents and other authority figures, inner conflicts about right and wrong, and challenges to the existing order at home, at work, and at school.

Stage Six is a time of knowing and accepting yourself as the one you are meant to be. You feel ambivalence as you are forced to confront paradoxes in your existence and endure the tension of conflicting opposites within yourself. During Stage Six it is not unusual to feel alienation, fear, loneliness, and depression alternating with elation, excitement, and delight as you are *igniting the inner fire.*

Enduring the conflicts here has the potential to increase self-awareness and develop a more complex, integrated, and resilient ego structure. Along with this change comes a surge of self-confidence, energy, and optimism. The need to bolster your sense of identity by contrary or oppositional behavior falls away, and it becomes easier to speak your truth.

European myths of heroes who battle dangerous dragons provide a metaphor for this stage. Consider that the dragon embodies the tug of the unconscious, the lure to relinquish consciousness and give oneself over to primal, unfocused states of mind where you are lacking a sense of individual identity. This lack of focus can be restful from time to time, and these states are a natural part of the early stages of the Great Round. However, it is limiting as a permanent way of being.

The slaying of the dragon symbolizes freeing the young hero from his mother as a carrier of collective drives and instincts and from his father as the transmitter of the values and traditions of his time. A feminine counterpart to the mythic dragon slayer is found in the Greek myth of Psyche, the heroine who persevered to accomplish daunting tasks imposed on her by Aphrodite, her lover's jealous mother. One of Psyche's tedious chores was to sort a huge pile of mixed seeds.

Once these challenges are accomplished, the archetypal parents wear a different aspect. As Erich Neumann says, "they are no longer hostile, confining powers, but companions, bestowing their blessings on the life and work of the victorious hero-son [and heroine-daughter]" (1974, 22). The completion of this inner work eases the relationship with the real-life parents as well.

> Establishing ego boundaries seems important [here] . . . the self plays with opposites, ambivalences, polarities, and inconceivable inequities. This makes this space a place of paradoxes. —Joan Kellogg

Intentions for Stage Six

You will return many times to Stage Six and re-work your past experiences in light of present situations each time. The worldview here is that of a young hero or heroine facing a daunting challenge. Some of your tasks in Stage Six are not unlike Psyche's: you will find it necessary to discern, sift through, and take back projections. Here is an example from Tanya's experience.

When Tanya encounters a person who is, in her opinion, too loud, overbearing, or demanding, she can see the unpleasantness in the other person, but none in herself. She pushes her own unpleasant behavior out of her awareness. Once Tanya accepts that she sometimes displays the very behaviors she disapproves of, she experiences a conflict between this realization and the person she prefers to think she is all the time: soft-spoken, tolerant, and patient. Only when she can own the unlikable qualities as also belonging to her has she taken back her projection.

When in Stage Six, it is your task to integrate such negative truths about yourself—not by willing yourself to do so, but by holding contradictory possibilities until they resolve into a more complete and realistic sense of who you are. When you are able to hold your dilemma in consciousness rather than letting one half slip into unconsciousness (and be projected onto another person), the stage is set for the emergence of a new, more complex ego configuration.

This resolution is achieved by what Jung called the *transcendent function* (1970, 200), which generates a third position that subsumes both the conflicting elements into a new synthesis. He emphasized the importance of symbolic, nonverbal modes for accomplishing the integration. Jung valued dreams and creative self-expression in general—and mandalas in particular—for this inner work.

The tasks for us in Stage Six are to cease our childlike claims on our parents (or their stand-ins later in life), to risk disobedience, and to take responsibility for our own life. It takes energy to separate ego consciousness from the unconscious matrix of infancy. More energy is necessary to develop and maintain a sense of personal identity. The conflict between opposites that sets the tone of Stage Six generates the psychic energy needed for the important inner work of (re)establishing your ego and *igniting the inner fire.* It is an exciting time full of energy, passion, and change.

Stage Six Mandalas

Mandalas typical of Stage Six reveal conflict by a division into two halves. The split down the middle is usually clearly defined. It is often a straight line, although sometimes the center division is curved, as in the traditional Chinese yin-yang symbol. Often a separate design appears superimposed upon the split between halves. This third design reflects the new ego structure.

Mandalas here are characterized by bright colors. The conflict of the opposites may also be expressed by complementary colors, which are opposites on the color wheel. For example, color combinations such as red/green, purple/orange, and yellow/blue can give a sense of energetic confrontation.

Mandalas with landscape motifs belong in Stage Six. The earth (or ocean) can symbolize *mother* while the sky represents *father*. A sun rising in the center suggests the (re)birth of your ego. Unlike the brightness of complementary colors, landscape mandalas are usually done with the softer color combinations of nature: brown, green, blue, and yellow.

Exercises

To prepare for the creative self-expression of Stage Six mandalas, first stretch, breathe, and center by doing the yoga movements suggested in appendix B (see page 260). Notice how the yoga requires right and left arms to extend and move in opposite directions, yet come together at the center near your heart. When creating the mandalas that follow, notice how this moving apart and coming together is an essential quality of Stage Six. The stretch between roots and sky is the theme of Maureen's song for Stage Six, "Hope of Sky" (see appendix C, page 281). Singing this can help you feel grounded as you open yourself to creative exploration. Pay attention to how it is for you to focus on conflicts past and present. Are you comfortably assertive, aggressive, or overly compliant? What and who are your dragons? What colors do they wear? What are your preferences, and what is your name?

MANDALA OF IGNITING THE INNER FIRE
Materials You'll Need:
Basic Art Materials (see page 36)
Coloring Mandala 6 (see appendix A, page 245)

Stage Six often requires that we endure the tension of the opposites. When we do, a new viewpoint eventually emerges that transcends and resolves the conflict. So we see in this mandala the opposites of Mother Earth and Father Sky, male and female energy. The sun rising between the earth and sky signifies the new element appearing. Like the child that inherits qualities from both parents but is identical to neither, the solution to conflict brings something entirely new to the situation. Using nature's colors for water, sky, and sun, let this mandala align your energy with Stage Six, Igniting the Inner Fire.

ARCHETYPAL PARENTS MANDALA
Materials You'll Need:
Basic Art Materials (see page 36)

Archetypes evolve from experiences that have been repeated for so many generations that the potential for these ways of behaving becomes part of our human inheritance, perhaps even encoded in our DNA. Parenting is an example of such a behavior. Father and mother archetypes are like templates of the ideal father and mother. Some of the archetypal possibilities are actualized through our lived experiences with parents and other important authorities.

We each have an inner father and inner mother constructed from our interactions, no matter how limited or intimate, with our parents and important others. Our parents transmit the values of the culture in which we live. Even so, the archetypal substrate remains important as a source of possibilities that can be activated through our continuing growth process.

The parental archetypes support our developing skills for parenting ourselves in ways that fill in deficits, correct limited notions, and heal wounds from our own personal experiences. The Archetypal Parents

Mandala allows you to increase your awareness of the father/masculine and mother/feminine qualities you have taken in from your parents and other authority figures. With your increased awareness you can explore your preferences and augment your inner capacity for parenting yourself—and others, when appropriate.

Trace a circle on a piece of paper and divide it into equal halves by drawing a line from top to bottom through the center. Let one side represent *father/masculine* and the other side represent *mother/feminine*. Fill in the halves with drawn images, cut or torn colored paper, or other materials to express your thoughts, feelings, sensations, and intuitions about your parents as carriers of *masculine* and *feminine* qualities (see plate 18).

When the two halves are complete, respond to each with journaling. Using your imagination, take the viewpoint of the father/masculine half. Using phrases that begin with "I" or "you," record the opinions of the father/masculine side of your mandala toward the mother/feminine side. For example, the masculine might express such opinions as "You look too soft and wispy," or "I am (should be) strong." Next, shift to the viewpoint of the mother/feminine and record feminine opinions about the masculine in your mandala. Again, use phrases that begin with "I" or "you."

Read back through the masculine and feminine dialogue in your journal. Be aware that the opinions expressed there belong to you, even though some may surprise you. With this awareness you gain the option to claim a different, third viewpoint about masculine and feminine.

Turning again to study your mandala as a whole, respond to the imagery as the person you are. Writing in your journal complete the following statements: "I see ___," "I like ___," "I don't like ___," "I prefer ___," "I choose ___," "I am ___." This exercise will help you clarify your viewpoint. It may or may not agree with the earlier opinions of father/masculine and mother/feminine.

Following your journaling construct a smaller mandala image on a different piece of paper to represent yourself and your viewpoint. It may incorporate all, some, or none of the colors and forms on the masculine and feminine halves of the first mandala. Now place your smaller mandala at the center of your first mandala, overlapping the father/masculine and mother/ feminine halves. You may wish to attach the small mandala, or you may prefer to leave it movable. This will give you the option to experiment with different placements within the mandala, representing varying distance or closeness with the *father/masculine* and *mother/feminine* halves.

MANDALA OF TAMING THE DRAGON
Materials You'll Need:
Basic Art Materials (see page 36)

Kellogg refers to Stage Six as the *Dragon Fight*. The dragon represents the unconscious, which must be defied in order for a child to develop a strong ego, separate from its mother's psychological atmosphere. From time to time later in life, the unconscious again exerts pressure on your ego to regress to earlier levels of functioning. The Mandala of Taming the Dragon allows you to explore this important inner dynamic as it plays out in your life.

What stops you from being the person you want to be? What are your drawbacks? Your obstacles? Your greatest fears? Trace a circle and draw or collage the image of a dragon inside it to represent the fears and blockages that you experience. Do some journaling about your dragon: what it looks like, what it might say, what it might want to do. Then ask yourself, "What do I need to tame my dragon?" You might find it helpful to complete the sentence, "If I ___, I can set myself free to be my best self." Be as concrete and realistic as possible. For example, instead of filling in this blank with *win the lottery*, list specifics such as: speak up for myself, get reliable transportation, count to ten before responding, be my own best friend, make a place for my books, set aside three hours a week for entertainment.

Now transcribe your phrases, adding in front of each one the words "I will." For example, "I will be my own best friend." Add your phrases to your dragon mandala any way you like. Some possibilities include making them into a tether around the dragon's neck, attaching paper butterflies carrying the phrases onto and around the dragon, writing them into the folds of the dragon's hide, and delivering the words on the tip of a dragon slayer's lance (see plate 19).

ADOLESCENT ME MANDALA
Materials You'll Need:
Basic Art Materials (see page 36)
Photos or drawings of yourself as an adolescent
Photos or drawings of parents (optional)

Our first experience of Stage Six is during adolescence. Many of us have loose ends from this important transition. We may harbor guilt, confusion, or other's opinions of us during this time. The Adolescent Me Mandala gives you a space to explore who you were as an adolescent, to acknowledge the important events of your life during this time, and to reflect on your adolescent self from your present vantage point. This mandala can be a celebration of the good times you had then, a remembrance of your burgeoning freedom, increasing self-knowledge, and maturing intellectual abilities. It may also highlight your awareness of fashionable dress and hairstyles! Perhaps this mandala will be a step toward acknowledging that you did the best you could as an adolescent.

Draw a circle and divide it in half with a line through the center, either up and down or side to side. Let one side represent your mother, as she was during your adolescence. The opposite side will symbolize your father. Attach the image of your adolescent self at the center of the dividing line. Complete your mandala by adding colors, forms, and textures that express what it was like for you during your teenage years. Reflect on your mandala when it is completed. What does it show you? Is there anything unfinished from that time that you would like to acknowledge and bring to closure? If so, is there a way to alter your mandala to reflect this? Make those changes now.

MANDALA FOR EXPLORING A DILEMMA
Basic Art Materials (see page 36)

Life is about making choices. We are confronted with difficult decisions from time to time. The bifurcated mandalas of Stage Six are especially useful for defining conflicts. Bringing to full awareness both sides of a dilemma is a helpful step toward finding our best choice. The Mandala for Exploring a Dilemma can be a useful tool for your decision making.

Trace a circle and divide it into equal halves. Let each half represent one side of a dilemma, a conflict, or a choice with which you struggle. Include cutout magazine pictures, drawings, or shaped colored-paper images to represent the two aspects of your dilemma. Fully explore the pros and cons of the situation in your mandala imagery.

Notice what you see in your mandala and what you learn about each side through this exploration. Do some journaling about this. Without forcing a solution, simply continue noticing any colors, thoughts, feelings, actions, snatches of music, and so forth that come to you as you ponder your dilemma. Let this information become part of your decision making. This process can stir up a new realization that will ease, bridge, or even resolve your dilemma.

SUMMER SOLSTICE MANDALA
Materials You'll Need:
Flowers, leaves, sticks, bird feathers, etc.
Soil or sand of various colors
Coffee grounds, dry powdered tempera paint, spices (optional)
Candle or fire-building materials
Wishes, prayers, intentions, gratitudes, or goodbyes written on slips
   of paper (optional)

On the Great Round of the year, Stage Six is June, the month of the summer solstice. The summer solstice is the longest day of the year. It is an important turning point because after the summer solstice days become shorter and shorter until the winter solstice in December. The winter solstice is the shortest day of the year and marks the opposite pole of the dance between day and night, light and dark.

The summer solstice is traditionally celebrated with fire, which is a symbol of the power of the sun itself. Of course June is a time of natural abundance worthy of celebration as well. The Summer Solstice Mandala brings these elements together in an observance of the beauty of nature. This mandala is built outdoors in a safe and secluded area by an individual or a group. Be sure the area is clear of flammable debris.

Mark a point on the ground to be the center of your mandala circle. Then standing on the center point, turn in place pressing a pointed stick to the ground to scribe a circle. You may want to add lines that run through the center and extend north and south, east and west. If you are building a fire, lay the wood and other materials to burn on top of the center point. Otherwise, place your candle in the center.

Fill in the circle with flowers, sticks, leaves, spices, pigment, and other natural materials. Dry powdered tempera and coffee grounds can be used for color and texture. When completed, light the fire or candle and spend time at your mandala reflecting on the blessings of sun, growing things, light, warmth, and the transformative power of fire. You can burn your prayer slips in the fire in the center as a sign of your willingness to accept the transformation each requires of you. Observe good safety practices with your fire.

MANDALA OF CHOOSING YOUR NAME
Materials You'll Need:
Basic Art Materials (see page 36)

Naming is an important aspect of identity. In tribal societies, people are given new names to mark their life transitions. While not a formal practice in our Western cultures, many of us have been known by different names during our lives. As children, our families assign us names that may have belonged to ancestors. We may also have had nicknames.

Moving from school to school or job to job, we may be called by different names. As adults, women who marry often adopt the name of their husband. Some of us may even have secret names that we call ourselves that are unknown to others. The Mandala of Choosing Your Name allows you to remember and note the sources of all the names you have had and to decide for yourself the name you now prefer.

Draw a circle. Divide the circle into two equal halves. Create a second circle from the same center with a radius of one half or less of the first circle. Place names given you during the first twenty years of your life on one side of the large circle. Put names given you from age twenty and older on the other side.

Begin with your baby names or nicknames. Include your names from elementary school, high school, and among your childhood and adolescent friends. On the opposite side of the large circle record names you received as an adult. List the names by which you have been known at work, among your friends, or in your professional career. Record names you received when you married or made a spiritual commitment that called for your re-naming.

Finally, what is the name you call yourself? Place this in the center circle. By what name would you like others to call you? Place this name prominently in the inner circle of your mandala and anywhere else you would like to see it written on your artwork. Sharing your mandala with others might be a way of informing them of the name by which you prefer to be known.

Reflecting on Stage Six

Stage Six has focused on the process of separating our own identity from the givens of our family of origin. Through experiencing conflict, paradox, and separation we ignite our sense of personhood during this stage. You have created mandalas that empower and help you more clearly define your identity and preferences. Take the personal awareness you have gained from this exploration into creating Mandala Card Six.

MANDALA CARD SIX
Materials You'll Need:
Basic Art Materials (see page 36)
Cardboard, tagboard, or other stiff material
Collage pictures

Cut out a card in the shape and size of your choice. Using collage, painting, or drawing, create a mandala on your card expressing a conflict of the opposites, your experience of wrestling with a dilemma, or perhaps even your struggle with another person. Add a third element at the center of your mandala to represent you and the third position you have discovered that somehow resolves the tension of the opposites. Add other images, words, colors, and textures that help you convey the passion ignited by these experiences. Let your card dry flat and then store in a safe place.

Chris 125

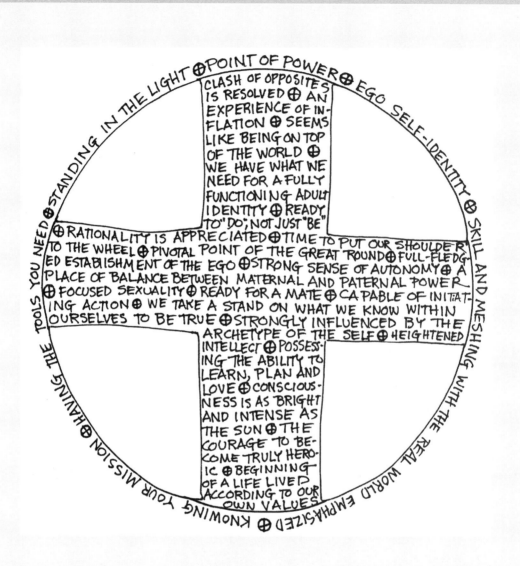

STANDING IN THE LIGHT ⊕ POINT OF POWER ⊕ EGO SELF-IDENTITY ⊕ SKILL AND MESHING WITH THE REAL WORLD EMPHASIZED ⊕ KNOWING YOUR MISSION ⊕ HAVING THE TOOLS YOU NEED ⊕

CLASH OF OPPOSITES IS RESOLVED ⊕ AN EXPERIENCE OF INFLATION ⊕ SEEMS LIKE BEING ON TOP OF THE WORLD ⊕ WE HAVE WHAT WE NEED FOR A FULLY FUNCTIONING ADULT IDENTITY ⊕ READY TO "DO", NOT JUST "BE" ⊕ RATIONALITY IS APPRECIATED ⊕ TIME TO PUT OUR SHOULDER TO THE WHEEL ⊕ PIVOTAL POINT OF THE GREAT ROUND ⊕ FULL-FLEDGED ESTABLISHMENT OF THE EGO ⊕ STRONG SENSE OF AUTONOMY ⊕ A PLACE OF BALANCE BETWEEN MATERNAL AND PATERNAL POWER ⊕ FOCUSED SEXUALITY ⊕ READY FOR A MATE ⊕ CAPABLE OF INITIATING ACTION ⊕ WE TAKE A STAND ON WHAT WE KNOW WITHIN OURSELVES TO BE TRUE ⊕ STRONGLY INFLUENCED BY THE ARCHETYPE OF THE SELF ⊕ HEIGHTENED INTELLECT ⊕ POSSESSING THE ABILITY TO LEARN, PLAN AND LOVE ⊕ CONSCIOUSNESS IS AS BRIGHT AND INTENSE AS THE SUN ⊕ THE COURAGE TO BECOME TRULY HEROIC ⊕ BEGINNING OF A LIFE LIVED ACCORDING TO OUR OWN VALUES

Squaring the Circle

Here we are at Stage Seven, halfway through our journey. In the Great Round of the year, we are in July. Light can be as intense as the sun at high noon on a summer day, or it can be softly luminous, as under the full moon on a warm summer evening. We first experience Stage Seven in early adulthood and return here again each time we are actively (re)clarifying personal identity.

Stage Seven is the place where we stand *four square* on what we know within ourselves to be right. It is the beginning of life lived according to our own values. Metaphorically speaking, we have given the parents back to each other. We no longer depend on parents as a child does because we have incorporated within ourselves the qualities of each that are necessary to be a fully functioning adult. The clash of the opposites is no longer a source of conflict.

In Stage Seven the clarity we have about our personal values can propel us toward worthy causes. So it was with Donna. Donna was an American, but her heart went out to the Mothers of the Disappeared, a group of brave women in South America. As luck would have it, Donna had an unexpected opportunity to travel to the city where the mothers were living. She knew from the moment her trip was planned that she would go and march with the women during their weekly demonstration.

On the appointed afternoon, Donna made her way through the crowd of observers in the city's main square to join the mothers. They were old, but resolute, and they carried banners, signs, and photos of their loved ones who had disappeared thirty years before during a dark period in the country. Donna felt privileged to walk with the mothers as they circled the square. Carrying one of their signs was her personal declaration of support for their cause. She knew it was the right thing to do.

During Stage Seven we are *squaring the circle.* Consciousness rules in this stage of the Great Round. Thinking is highlighted and rationality is much appreciated. It is a good time for learning, for embracing personal goals, and for enlightenment. We are ready to begin a career. Sexuality that was diffuse in earlier stages is focused on active expression in Stage Seven. We are ready to feel passionately about another person.

Behind the development of our individuality is the Self, the dynamism that compels us to become who we are meant to be. Furthermore, our ego is in close alignment with the Self in this stage, so positive energy is high. We experience a strong sense of personal power and autonomy during Stage Seven.

Stage Seven is a pivotal point on the Great Round. Stages One through Six have highlighted relatedness to the parents, especially the mother. We might describe the left side of the Great Round as the *matriarchy.* Mandalas here are characterized by curved lines. We then could think of Stages Eight through Twelve, the right side of the Great Round, as the *patriarchy.* During these stages, skills, practicality, and productivity are emphasized. The mandalas on the right side of the Great Round are notable for straight lines. Some mandalas here require planning, measuring, and numbering.

During Stage Seven, however, masculine and feminine energies are balanced. You have available both active and receptive, yang and yin, solar and lunar qualities within yourself. You are capable of initiating action rather than being the passive recipient of the actions of others. You are ready to *do,* not just to *be.*

Mandala designs typical of Stage Seven are based on the number 4. Equal-armed crosses, four-pointed stars, and flowers with four petals are often seen, as well as the classic mandala form that gives this stage its name: the square inside (or outside) a circle. The cross in a circle is an ancient symbol apparently first used to symbolize the sun. Jung recognized in this and similar fourfold symbols a reflection of the *individuation* process: "Individuation, or becoming whole, is the painful experience of the union of opposites. That is the real meaning of the cross in the circle" (1972, 98).

Intentions for Stage Seven

The task here is to put our best efforts into a quest: to find our soul mate, to identify our life work, and to make a personal commitment to living life. During Stage Seven we usually have plentiful energy, enthusiasm for life, and a sense of direction toward something worthwhile. We may even be falling in love (again). This is one of the few stages our culture encourages us to value, so enjoy your time here. Please remember, however, that Stage Seven is only one of twelve, and it is no better or worse than any of the other stages.

Stage Seven Mandalas

The mandalas typical of Stage Seven represent the integration of the masculine (straight lines) with the feminine (curving lines). They convey balance, stability, and symmetry. The mandala of Patty Hutton (plate 20), a mandala group member, is an example. The title *You Are Here . . . Now What?* conveys the readiness to move into action we often feel when experiencing Stage Seven.

Colors seen in Stage Seven mandalas include warm, bright yellows and golds. Orange, bright blue, red, shades of green, and peach are also typical colors for this stage. Metallic gold and silver may appear, adding a heraldic dimension to mandalas of Stage Seven (see plate 21).

Exercises

Before beginning your mandalas, stand, stretch, and breathe as suggested in the yoga movements (see appendix B, page 262). "Soul Awake" (see appendix C, page 282) is a stirring song that creates the energy associated with Stage Seven. A group can sing this song in rounds, creating a mandala of sound.

Goal-directed, quantifiable behaviors that rely on instruments of measurement are highlighted during this stage. In order to explore these qualities in your creative self-expression, some mandalas of Stage Seven require measuring, using a compass, and aligning a straight-edged ruler. If you find any of these skills a challenge, it is worth the effort to create these measured mandalas. They can exercise your math, logic, and thinking skills as a balance for your more comfortable ways of functioning.

Squaring the circle is a point of transition into the remaining stages of the Great Round. In Stages Seven, Eight, Nine, and Ten, there is less emphasis on *who you are* and more emphasis on *what you can do*. While experiencing these stages in real life people may ask you: "What are your skills? What can you do? When can it be done?"

Notice what it is like for you creating mandalas with straight as well as curved lines. Does your energy build in response to the challenge or is it tiring to focus? Does self-judging hinder your efforts? If so, use self-soothing skills such as breathing and relaxing and invite your inner critic to suspend its commentary while you concentrate on your task.

MANDALA OF FIRM FOUNDATION
Materials You'll Need:
Basic Art Materials (see page 36)
Coloring Mandala 7 (see appendix A, page 246)

During Stage Seven, you likely feel comfortable with yourself and your place in the scheme of things. This creates a firm foundation for identity. The harmonious balance between circles and squares seen in this mandala reflects the balancing of masculine and feminine energy you experience during this stage. Use bright sunny colors to fill in this design of circles and squares. Emphasize balance and symmetry in your color placement in order to align yourself with the qualities of Stage Seven.

SQUARING THE CIRCLE MANDALA
Materials You'll Need:
Basic Art Materials (see page 36)
Squaring the Circle template (optional; see appendix A, page 236)

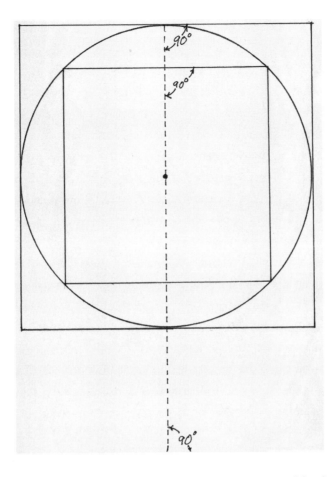

Squaring the Circle

When you square a circle, you draw a square outside a circle. The width of the square is the same as the diameter of the circle. Of course it is also possible to draw a square inside a circle (see the image above). Jung observed Squaring the Circle Mandalas in the dreams and artwork of his patients. He concluded that this motif is a naturally occurring symbol of wholeness.

Creating a Squaring the Circle Mandala can be a way to cultivate the connection between ego and Self. The creation of this mandala requires measurement, straight lines, and drawing the circle, so it calls for the use of drawing instruments. It is a balance of curved and straight lines. If you wish to bypass the use of drawing instruments as part of the creative process, you may refer to the Squaring the Circle template in appendix A.

Squaring the Circle Mandala is a centered, symmetrical design. Begin by choosing a center point and creating a circle on a piece of paper. Draw a straight, vertical (up and down) line through the center of the circle. Let the line extend past the circle an inch or two at both ends. Place the center of your protractor over the center of the circle. Let the protractor line up along the straight line you just drew so that the 0 angle is on the line near the top of the circle.

Using the protractor, measure and lightly mark points at 90 and 270 degrees. Line up your ruler between these points and draw a straight, horizontal (side to side) line through the center, extending both ends an inch or two beyond the circle.

Lay your protractor along the vertical line so that its center lies over the point where the line intersects the top of the circle. The 0 angle should be on the line. Measure and mark 90 and 270 degrees. Line up your ruler between these two points and draw a straight line. The middle of the line should touch the circle.

Using this same procedure, measure and mark points at 90 and 270 degrees on the bottom and sides of the circle by placing the center of the protractor over the point where the vertical line meets the bottom of the circle and over the points where the horizontal line meets the circle on both sides. Then connect each set of points as before, drawing the final three lines that will complete the square for your Squaring the Circle Mandala. Add colors, textures, and images to complete your mandala to your satisfaction. Now you have made this archetypal mandala your own.

SOLAR/LUNAR METALLIC MANDALA
Materials You'll Need:
Basic Art Materials (see page 36)
Aluminum foil, metallic wrapping paper, glitter, metallic paints, etc.
Cardboard, tagboard, or other stiff material

Stage Seven on the Great Round is most closely associated with light. During ancient times, the sun and the moon were the primary sources of light. Over time, mythologies assigned masculine qualities to the sun, while the moon has long been considered representative of the feminine. The Solar/Lunar Metallic Mandala invites you to express both your masculine and feminine qualities in the creation of this mandala.

Light is also symbolic of consciousness, which is intense, focused, and accessible during this stage. Stage Seven may also be associated with receiving a personal calling to perform idealistic deeds. Honor, pride, and a desire to serve motivate individuals to become like medieval knights on a mission. Therefore, it is appropriate to use clear jewel tones and the heraldic metals of gold (solar) and silver (lunar) as you develop this mandala.

Draw a circle on sturdy paper or cardboard. Create a mandala design based on the number 4 that includes both solar (masculine) and lunar (feminine) imagery. Try to equally balance the space given to these two qualities and include both straight and curved lines. In this way the balance of masculine and feminine qualities during Stage Seven—and within yourself—will be represented. Choose metallic paints or papers to complete your Solar/Lunar Metallic Mandala design.

MANDALA OF THE SACRED MARRIAGE
Materials You'll Need:
Basic Art Materials (see page 36)

Medieval alchemy, the forerunner of modern chemistry, was a quest to create gold or other precious substances from worthless ingredients. The arcane procedures often began with a base material—earth or even excrement—that was subjected to burning, dissolving, or mixing with other chemicals. One of the more important procedures was the *sacred marriage,* which brought together two very different previously refined compounds in a new combination that elevated the pairing to a qualitatively higher level of functioning.

In a process somewhat reminiscent of alchemy, marriage is the joining of two individuals who make a serious commitment to share their lives together. By doing this, they create something that has not existed before: a marriage. In order to have a successful marriage, each partner must tend to his or her own needs, respect and value his or her partner, and also cultivate the strength and health of the marriage. More than a little alchemy may be required to accomplish this!

Self-knowledge is an important factor in building a marriage. Also helpful is awareness of what kind of marriage you'd like to be in and learning what is necessary to accomplish it. The Sacred Marriage Mandala allows you to reflect on the relationships of other people you know and discover more about your own needs, preferences, strengths, and challenges as a marriage partner.

Begin with a circle. Reflect on couples that you admire. They may be real, imaginary, mythic, or from religious sources. Find or create images that represent this union and the individuals who comprise it. Arrange your images in the circle to form a symmetrical design based on an equal-armed cross. Complete your Sacred Marriage Mandala with a balanced combination of form, color, and texture.

Respond to your Sacred Marriage Mandala by answering these questions in your journaling:

What do I like most about this couple?

What qualities do the two partners bring to their marriage? (He is ___;
    She has ___, etc.)

What strengths in each partner support the relationship? (She is ___;
    he has ___, etc.)

What deficits in each partner challenge the relationship? (He/she lacks
    ___.)

How are the qualities of the partners reflected in me? (Try substituting
    "I am"; "I have"; "I lack" for "he/she is"; "he/she has"; "he/she lacks"
    in statements above.)

What does this couple tell me about my own relationship needs and
    preferences?

YOUR PERSONAL SHIELD MANDALA
Materials You'll Need:
Basic Art Materials (see page 36)

What matters to you? What is most important? What are your core values—the principles by which you live and give of the best of yourself? After reflecting on these questions, record your answers in your journal. Your Personal Shield Mandala allows you to proclaim your deeply held values and place them in a mandala that can be an enduring reminder of how you choose to live your life.

Draw a circle on a piece of paper. Divide it into four sections. In each section of your mandala place a symbol of one of your core values. For example, "justice" might be symbolized by a scale. "Beauty" could be represented by a rose. If some of your values are more important than others, give them a larger section of your mandala. When completed, take a look at Your Personal Shield Mandala and notice what it says about you. How do you carry your core values into the life you lead (or would like to lead)?

MEDICINE WHEEL MANDALA
Materials You'll Need:
Basic Art Materials (see page 36)

The Medicine Wheel is a mandala of the cycles of time and space originating among the Plains Indians of America. It is a structure that offers orientation to the physical world as well as to the inner symbolic world. The Medicine Wheel Mandala gives you an opportunity to orient yourself in relation to the four directions, to recognize the land where you are living, and to record personal associations that arise in relation to these.

On a large piece of paper, draw a circle 12" wide or larger. Add lines to represent the four directions: north, south, east, and west. Turn your mandala so that the north line points toward the compass direction north. Now try to put aside any information you have acquired about directions, power animals, and colors. Find the personal meaning of each direction for you: the color, meaning, animals, plants, or trees that fit for you and where you live. For example, my personal association with north is mountains because the land to my north rises into the Appalachians. I associate east with spring, so I pick the early-spring-blooming plum blossom to represent this direction on my Medicine Wheel. Place images and symbols of your personal associations on your Medicine Wheel Mandala.

TREE MANDALA
Materials You'll Need:
Basic Art Materials (see page 36)

Trees are ancient symbols of individuality. Each tree fulfills the potentials encoded in its seed as allowed by the environment where it takes root. Jung wrote of trees as a symbol of the Self, which functions like a seed, unfolding human potentials. And, again like a tree, human potentials ripen in accordance with conditions and opportunities in the environment.

Trees are also an apt symbol for the human body. They stand erect, firmly supported by a network of roots underground, with limbs and branches extending outward. Like movable roots, our feet and toes grip the earth and provide us a firm base for balancing the trunk of our body, which, in turn, supports our extended arms and our head resting upon our neck.

When you look up into the canopy of a single tree, you can see a mandala with limbs and branches radiating out from the center trunk. You can see a similar mandala when you look down at the root system that extends outward from the main trunk of a tree. And in the same way, we can look down at our body and see a center trunk from which extend the four appendages of arms and legs: we can see our body as a mandala.

The Tree Mandala gives you an opportunity to explore the diverse meanings of trees by creating a tree drawing inside a circle. Choose the type of tree and the view of the tree you want to depict, i.e., looking down from above the tree or seeing it straight ahead of you.

Draw a circle. Lightly sketch lines up and down and side to side through the center of your circle. This will provide some guidelines for your Tree Mandala. You may show either a bird's-eye view of your tree, or you can draw a person's view. However you choose to create your tree, let it cover the center of the circle.

Fill in your tree, its surroundings, and the mandala circle with color and form. When complete reflect on the qualities of your tree and its environment. Is your tree healthy? Does it have all it needs to grow? If not, what is lacking? What does it need to grow to its optimal size? Add to your Tree Mandala images of what your tree needs to fulfill its potential.

After reflecting on your Tree Mandala, consider how the state of your tree and its needs might tell you something about yourself. If your tree needs water, perhaps you, too, need more water, or some other vital nourishment. If your tree is not wellrooted, maybe you need greater stability in your life as well. If your tree is cramped inside the circle, you might consider how you can open yourself to new growth possibilities.

MANDALA OF THE FOUR QUADRANTS (FOR A SMALL GROUP)
Materials You'll Need:
Basic Art Materials (see page 36)
Piece of sturdy paper, approximately 36" x 36"

Creating a mandala with a group allows you to get to know each other better, to develop a sense of belonging in the group, and to enjoy a less verbal, right-brain activity together. Group mandalas can be useful for building a team, becoming aware of the dynamics of a group, and practicing cooperation for a shared goal. (For more on groups please see appendix D, page 286.)

The Mandala of the Four Quadrants is a group exploration of four aspects of something whole. Examples might be the four seasons, the four directions, the four times of the day/night (sunrise, noon, sunset, midnight), the four functions of thinking, feeling, sensing, and intuition, the four stages of life (childhood, adolescence, adulthood, elderhood), or any other fourfold division of wholeness. Let your group agree on the choice.

Draw a large circle on your paper. A pencil attached to a piece of string can be your compass. Divide the circle into four equal sections so that each quadrant has a space. To create a sense of ceremony, you might sing a song together as you all move around the circle. I suggest "Soul Awake" (see appendix C, page 282). When you identify the place that feels best to you, stand or sit there. Others will keep moving around the mandala until each person identifies the place that feels best for him or her to be.

Negotiate with others on how best to fill your shared space. For example, does your group prefer to work individually with each person having a space, or to work all together on the same shared space? Quadrants may have more than one person. Some quadrants may not have anyone. As with individually drawn mandalas, there is no *right* or *wrong* way of doing things.

When all members have found a space that feels right, draw or paint images in the mandala that symbolize your quadrant. When all group members are finished working on the mandala, talk together about the experience and the results of your work. Decide together what to do with the mandala after your time together. For example, one group I facilitated decided to seal their mandala in a large bottle and drop it into a river to float out to sea.

Reflecting on Stage Seven

Stage Seven is a time of energy, balance, and wholeness. Successful bridging of the opposites is featured. Mandalas of this stage have given you ways to explore masculine and feminine qualities, ponder your core values, and utilize your geometry skills to draw a perfect square outside a circle. Summarize your experience of Stage Seven, Squaring the Circle, by developing a mandala design on Mandala Card Seven.

MANDALA CARD SEVEN
Materials You'll Need:
Basic Art Materials (see page 36)
Cardboard, tagboard, or other stiff material
Collage images

Create a card of the size and shape desired. Place on your card a mandala design that includes a circle and a square or a cross. Let your design be balanced and symmetrical as it serves to symbolize you, a unique individual with many skills. Add other images, words, textures, or colors to complete your Mandala Card Seven. Let it dry flat, then store in a safe place.

STAGE EIGHT
Functioning in the World

Stage Eight aligns with the month of August, with early afternoon, and late summer. With this stage, we shift into the most outwardly active time in the Great Round. It is a stage notable for energetic and successful doing, creating, and communicating. The emphasis here is on functioning well both as an individual and in relationships with others. You are fully *functioning in the world.*

In the culmination of a process begun in Stage Three, you have attained individual consciousness: an ego. You have separated from the parental matrix and readily take responsibility for your own life. You can enjoy being with others, and you can be equally content spending time alone with yourself. Therefore, Kellogg has named this stage *Functioning Ego.*

You tend to be alert and capable of thinking clearly during Stage Eight. Typical emotions experienced during this stage include optimism, happiness, excitement, self-confidence, generosity, and enthusiasm. While in this stage, you have your feet planted under you and your head in the clouds. Patty Hutton's mandala (see plate 22) is a good image of this. Being firmly oriented to life's practicalities, you are free to devote your energy to creative work. You may feel attuned to the harmonious flow of right action during this stage of *functioning in the world.*

Stage Eight is a time of much activity directed toward clearly defined goals. During this stage you are *doing*: you are engaged with the world of people and things. You are actively implementing strategies, solving problems, or creating products that benefit yourself and others. Your efforts are well received because you offer the excitement of genuine creativity in a form that can be appreciated. You are riding high in the mainstream of life.

Working with others is highlighted here. We easily join with groups in order to accomplish our goals for this circling of the Great Round.

Diplomacy, respect, and empathy are constelled when functioning at our best during this stage. We can find skillful and respectful ways to explain our mission and ignite others with our passion. Of course this stage will be revisited again and again whenever you bring an inspiration from Stages Two, Three, and Four into full expression through your efforts.

Perhaps you will occupy an identified leadership position or be a team member who leads by quietly and effectively developing consensus. In Stage Eight you are performing your life's work. If you are fortunate, you will know this is so. Some of us, however, may not see the importance of what we are doing or how it meshes with who we are, until later in life. Here is Susan's story.

Susan took a job in a land surveyor's office because it was close to her house. She had two daughters in elementary school, and working close to home meant they could stop by her office and check in after school. Susan's primary goal at the time was fulfilling her role as a mother and contributing some income to the family's monthly finances. She enjoyed the work, but had no thought it would ever develop into more than a temporary job.

In the land surveyor's office she learned to scale a drawing, compute angles, and produce land plats with black ink. Her work had to be perfectly neat. When Susan moved on to other work as a writer, she set her drawing skills aside. Not until years later did she realize the importance of her drawing skills. She was asked to produce ink drawings for a book she was writing. Because of her job with the land surveyor, she had the skills to create the book. Many of her drawings were mandalas.

> This space seems to represent individuality. . . . [It] is significant in terms of body image. There is a sense of movement of the body in space. —Joan Kellogg

Intentions for Stage Eight

During Stage Eight your energy is high, your goals are clear, and you have a feasible plan of action for accomplishing them. Your mission is not simply the result of an intellectual exercise of assessing pros and cons. It is rooted in your unique being and the gifts you have to share with the world. In terms of observable results, Stage Eight is one of the most creative and productive. This stage is highly valued by our culture. Hopefully you do not share the commonly held mistaken notion that you should always function here.

Stage Eight Mandalas

Mandalas of Stage Eight convey balance, energy, and movement anchored by a strong center. The mandalas of this stage are often based on the number 5: five-pointed stars, flowers with five petals, or even tracings of hands. The paramount symbol for this stage is the five-pointed star, which signifies the *one* thing that you have chosen (consciously or unconsciously) to develop from the myriad possibilities of Stage Two.

The star may also refer to your physical body, with the five *points* of head, two hands, and two feet. Feet, essential for balance and movement, are equipped with five toes. Five also alludes to the significance of your hands, with their five fingers. Hands allow you to literally *take hold,* and so they are prominent during this stage when you are actively shaping things in order to bring your vision into the world. The mandala of Sue Kahn, a member of our mandala group (plate 23), shows this hand imagery.

Also typical in mandalas of this stage is the swastika, an ancient sun symbol. It is derived from the Sanskrit word *svasti* meaning "well being." The four *legs* of the swastika might have explained to the ancients the sun's ability to "walk" (move) across the sky. These four legs plus the center point of the swastika add up to the five-pointed design expected in this stage. The swastika has been negatively associated with Hitler, the Nazi regime, and the Holocaust. Your mandala work with the swastika can reclaim this symbol as a neutral/positive one despite its negative association. Swastikas suggest energetic movement and underscore the sense of being a center of power and effectiveness during Stage Eight.

Colors in Stage Eight mandalas tend to be bright, warm, and sun kissed. Gold, yellow, and orange are prominent. Clear shades of blue, turquoise, red, magenta, and green are also often seen. These are the colors of ripening field crops, orchard fruits, and vegetables in the kitchen garden.

Exercises

Before beginning your mandalas, take a few minutes to perform the yoga movements for Stage Eight (see appendix B, page 264). During the yoga pay attention to your body as a five-pointed form. Feel the extension you achieve with the yoga position. What is it like to claim your *stardom*?

Hands are an important motif for Stage Eight. Your hands make it possible for you to take hold of tools and use your skills with creativity. Some of the mandalas of this stage require careful use of drawing instruments. Are you willing to take all the steps outlined to create the Mandala of the Shining Star? Doing so is a practice in patience, following directions, and mastering skills. These are important qualities associated with Stage Eight. Turn to your journal to explore your responses to the exercises of *functioning in the world.*

MANDALA OF THE FUNCTIONING EGO
Materials You'll Need:
Basic Art Materials (see page 36)
Coloring Mandala 8 (see appendix A, page 247)

During Stage Eight your star rises as those around you take notice of your skills, abilities, and dedication. This five-pointed star mandala suggests a person standing firmly on both feet, arms outstretched, head held high. Such is the feeling of being in Stage Eight. Choose bright, solar colors to complete this mandala. As you color, bring your awareness to the areas of your body they might reflect. Star points with feet, hands, head. Star center with heart. How is it for you to consciously hold these connections between your mandala and your body? Explore this in your journaling.

MANDALA OF THE SHINING STAR
Materials You'll Need:
Basic Art Materials (see page 36)
Metallic paint (optional)
Five-Pointed Star template (optional; see appendix A, page 237)

Our bodies have five points: head, hands, and feet. Our hands and feet each have five digits. Therefore, the number 5 is closely associated with our physical body. One way to look at the five-pointed star is as a symbol of our physical presence. Since we actively grasp, shape, and create materials with our hands, the five-pointed star can also reflect our productivity. When we say someone is a *star,* we mean that they are expressing their talents and personal qualities in creative ways that get them attention as someone special.

The Mandala of the Shining Star is your opportunity to learn what it takes to make a star. Refer to the diagram on the next page as you create your mandala. You will need concentration, patience, and creativity (all the qualities that help someone become a star performer) to complete this project. Let the Mandala of the Shining Star be a way to claim your own star qualities.

Draw a circle. Sketch a vertical line (straight up and down) from the center point of the circle to intersect both the top and bottom of the circle. Now place a protractor on this line with the center of the protractor on top of the center point of the circle, and the 0 of the protractor on the line that intersects the top of the circle.

Beginning from this 0 point, measure and mark the following:

36 degree angle

72 degree angle

108 degree angle

144 degree angle

180 degree angle

216 degree angle

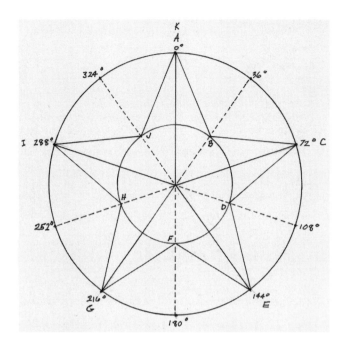

Diagram for drawing a
five-pointed star

252 degree angle

288 degree angle

324 degree angle

Draw a line from the 36 degree mark through the center of the circle
to the 180 degree mark, the opposite point on the circle. Continue connecting opposite points around the entire circle. When you are finished,
you should have ten lines running from the center point to the outside
of the circle.

Now using the center point of your first circle, draw a smaller circle.
(The distance between this circle and the larger circle will determine
the length of the arms of your star.) Now take a straight edge and align
it from the intersection of the first line with the larger circle (A) to the
intersection of the second line with the smaller inner circle (B). Draw
a line between A and B. Then move your straight edge to connect the
intersection of the second line with the smaller inner circle (B) and the
intersection of the third line with the larger outer circle (C). Draw a line

from B to C. Continue in this manner until you have defined your basic five-pointed star mandala.

Fill in your mandala star with bright, bold colors, metallic paint or paper, or other materials that reflect your active approach to sharing your talents with the world. You might want to hang your Mandala of the Shining Star on the door to your room to claim your star power.

STAR ME MANDALA
Materials You'll Need:
Basic Art Materials (see page 36)
Large piece of paper (big enough for you to lie down and stretch out on; rolls of sturdy brown paper for wrapping packages or for covering school bulletin boards are good options—you can tape together pieces of paper to create a large enough sheet.)

Since the time of the Renaissance, one has seen images of a five-pointed star, overlaid with the form of a human being, contained within a circle. Arms and legs are outstretched, and the head is held erect to fill each of the star points that fully extend to touch the circle. It is a stance that clearly proclaims, "I am here."

The Star Me Mandala allows you to explore this archetypal image through your own body experience, to create an image of your body in this powerful stance, and to encircle your body imagery within the mandala. You will be invited to reflect on your experience, to respond to your mandala, and to share your impressions. You will need the assistance of a trustworthy companion for body tracing and witnessing your Star Me Mandala.

Lie down on your back on the large piece of paper with arms and legs outstretched in star position. Feel how your body fills the space. Have a partner trace around your body. Sit up and take a look at your body tracing. How is it different from or the same as your felt experience of yourself lying on your back? Next, draw a large circle around your body tracing. Add color and form to complete your mandala. Talk about your experience and your mandala with your companion.

PROBLEM-SOLVING SWASTIKA MANDALA
Materials You'll Need:
Basic Art Materials (see page 36)

Swastikas are ancient symbols of the sun *walking* across the sky. They were coopted for the propaganda of the German Nazi party during World War II. The Problem-Solving Swastika Mandala allows you to reclaim this symbol for a new, positive use. The swastika within the circle becomes a structure for the thorough exploration of a personal concern. The exploration can increase your clarity about the matter and therefore support your decision making.

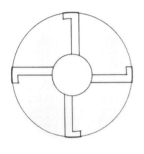

Swastika exercise

Draw a circle about 10" across and mark four equidistant points top, bottom, right, and left. Create a center circle about 3" across, using the same center point as the first circle. Start developing the swastika by aligning the center of the circles and the top point on the larger circle with a straight edge. Draw a line along the straight edge from the outline of the small circle to the top point on the larger circle. Draw a line parallel to this line, about an inch away, moving in a clockwise direction. Do the same with the remaining three points until there are four lines from the small circle to the larger circle. Beginning at the top point, add a "foot" extending an inch or more to the left along the circle. Do the same for the remaining three "legs." (See image at left.)

Place words or images in the center of the swastika to represent what it is that you want to explore more fully. Beginning on the topmost leg of the swastika and staying within the form of the leg and its attached foot, write or illustrate your *thoughts* about the subject. This may be self-talk, pros and cons, or the *logical* point of view of the situation. Then on the opposite leg and foot, write or illustrate your *emotions* about the topic. These could include any positive or negative feelings you experience associated with the concern.

Moving to the right leg of the swastika, explore your *sensory* information about the topic. What do you see, hear, taste, smell, or touch that gives you information about your concern? For example, include words and images reflecting what you have experienced or observed being done, spoken, or given that touches on the subject you are exploring. Finally, move to the left leg and explore information you receive through your *intuition*: dreams, uncanny *knowing,* hunches, and gut feelings about the situation.

You may wish to gain more insight and understanding by completing the following sentences in your journal or around your Problem-Solving Swastika Mandala.

With regard to my concern:

I think ___, therefore I conclude that ___.

I feel ___, therefore I am (not) willing to ___.

I have seen, heard, smelled, tasted, touched ___, therefore I experience ___.

I have a spontaneous understanding that ___, therefore I know ___.

Now review, with an open mind, the added information you have gained from considering your thoughts, emotions, sensory awareness, and intuition regarding your concern. Return to the center image of your mandala once again. Alter the image or words in the center as you feel necessary to express the totality or essence of your expanded outlook on your concern. Then complete the following sentence:

Based on my analysis of the information I have, it is best for me to ___.

MANDALA SERIES FOR HEALING
Materials You'll Need:
Basic Art Materials (see page 36)

This exercise was inspired by a mandala series developed by Michael H. Brown and cited in Rachel Norment's *Guided by Dreams* (2006, 81–83).

To begin, consider what needs to evolve or be healed at this stage of your life. Reflect on these areas: relationship with yourself, relationships with others, professional life, and spiritual life defined as the meaning and purpose of your life. Based on your reflection, formulate your goal for healing change. Now draw a circle on each of four sheets of paper. Number the sheets one through four. Set aside sheets two through four. Place sheet one with its empty circle on the table in front of you. Use it to create your first mandala. Now complete the following series of four mandalas that represent this goal:

<u>First mandala:</u> **Include images literally or concretely depicting you and your goal. Set this mandala aside. Reach for sheet two to create the next mandala.**

<u>Second mandala:</u> **Create an image symbolizing your goal. Continue as instructed above to create mandalas three and four.**

<u>Third mandala:</u> **Include images representing what needs to be done to attain your goal.**

<u>Fourth mandala:</u> **Create images that depict a source of help in attaining this goal.**

After drawing each mandala, write about it, stating what the colors and shapes mean and what the total image communicates to you. Then call the image up in your mind's eye and ask it what it has come to teach you. Write down what comes to you in this imaginary dialogue.

After you have completed work on the four mandalas, place them together where you can look at them. Reflect on your mandalas and the messages you have received from each one. Respond by writing about your experience in your journal. Summarize the guidance you have received for healing change.

MANDALA INVOKING YOUR CREATIVE ENERGY
Materials You'll Need:
Basic Art Materials (see page 36)

Our bodies generate all kinds of energy. Kinetic energy allows us to move our muscles. Nerve cells transmit electrical energy signals to our brain that enable us to think, feel pleasure and pain, and balance our body's chemicals. In the philosophies of the East, subtle energies such as *chi, winds,* and *kundalini* are also thought to circulate as a natural part of the body's functioning. These are significant contributors to the physical and spiritual health of the body. In her book *Mandala: Luminous Symbols for Healing,* Judith Cornell encourages the creation of mandalas in white pencil on black paper to invoke and give expression to the body's subtle energies. The Mandala Invoking Your Creative Energy is inspired by her work.

Draw a circle. Sit quietly and relax for a few minutes with your eyes closed before beginning your work. Reflect on the abundant energy within you that flows through your hands as you express your creativity. Invite that energy to guide your hands as you create your mandala. Open your eyes. Trace the outline of your hands inside the circle. Complete your mandala by adding forms and colors as you wish to represent your creative energy streaming through your hands. Annie Kelahan, a member of our mandala group, created a mandala in response to this directive (see plate 24).

WHIRLED PEACE MANDALA
Materials You'll Need:
Basic Art Materials (see page 36)
Pinwheel template (see appendix A, page 238)
Straight pin
Pencil with eraser
Cardboard, tagboard, or other stiff material

When experiencing Stage Eight, it often happens that we join with others to work toward worthy goals. Therefore, it is in keeping with our exploration of this stage to put our personal efforts toward making positive change in the world. The Whirled Peace Mandala is part of a worldwide effort to demonstrate support for peace. (Visit www.pinwheelsforpeace.com to learn more about this effort.) Creating the Whirled Peace Mandala is a way to express a personal view in favor of peace. Of course these instructions, like those for all the mandalas in *The Mandala Workbook,* can be adapted to your particular needs.

Diagram for making a pinwheel

Using the template, trace and cut out the pinwheel square. Include all lines as well as the center point in your tracing. On one side of the paper, write down your feelings about world peace. On the other side of the paper, use markers, colored pencils, paint, or other art media to visually express your feelings. On a piece of stiff material, trace around a coin to create a small circle. Fill the circle with a color or image that symbolizes world peace. Cut out the circle and set aside.

Following the lines traced on your square, cut in from all four corners, leaving about 2" of center uncut. Gently bend in (don't fold) one of the cut corners to the center point. Skip the next cut corner, and bend in the next one. Skip and bend in until four points meet in the center. Place your small circle over the center. Then stick the straight pin through the center of the small circle, all four points, *and* the back of the pinwheel. Stick the pin into the pencil eraser, leaving a bit of space between the eraser and the back of your pinwheel to allow it to move. Set up your pinwheel out-of-doors. As the wind turns your pinwheel, let your resolve to live peacefully be energized.

Reflecting on Stage Eight

Mandalas of Stage Eight have given you an opportunity to explore your power, creativity, and problem-solving abilities. This stage emphasizes cooperation, productivity, and practical skills for *functioning in the world.* Reflect on the qualities of Stage Eight, Functioning in the World, that were especially significant for your personal growth and self-awareness. Consider singing "Deep in the Song" (see appendix C, page 283) to spark your reflection and help you take the essence of Stage Eight into the development of Mandala Card Eight.

MANDALA CARD EIGHT
Materials You'll Need:
Basic Art Materials (see page 36)
Cardboard, tagboard, or other stiff material
Collage images

Cut out a card the size and shape desired for your Mandala Card Eight. Using drawing, painting, and collage, create a mandala incorporating a five-pointed star or swastika. Incorporate symbols of your personal experience of Stage Eight. Add images that suggest energy, creativity, and active engagement. Use words, textures, or colors to complete your card. Let it dry flat and then store it in a safe place.

Reaping Rewards

In the Great Round of the year, Stage Nine is the month of September, when harvesting crops is a major occupation. Productivity is also highlighted for those who do not work on the land. Stage Nine is a time when creative energy is coming to fruition. This stage is reminiscent of the afternoon and the just less-than-full gibbous moon.

Stage Nine usually coincides with early middle age. There is a real coming together in this stage as we shape our place in the world by our values and the work that we do. Projects dreamed of and actively pursued in previous stages come to completion during Stage Nine and we begin *reaping rewards*. Community recognition may come our way. Or we may enjoy the private satisfaction of having brought our vision into reality.

The creative energy that has characterized the last few stages begins to slow here. Like a runner who passes the finish line and begins to slack her pace, we ease up our efforts now. We find it possible to relax and reflect on our accomplishments. During this stage our thoughts may be of such clarity that we achieve an intellectual understanding of the world and our place in it. We will visit this stage again whenever we complete a project we have worked hard on.

During Stage Nine we are *reaping rewards*. Those of us in the middle years can take delight in our family and friends. We find enjoyment in our roles as parent, adult child, brother, sister, aunt, or uncle. Churches, businesses, and all sorts of groups find us the backbone of their organizations. We are members, leaders, and financial supporters who keep things functioning.

Greater spiritual understanding is possible during Stage Nine as clarity of thought converges with depth of feeling. These qualities, sometimes characterized as *masculine* and *feminine* ways of being, seem to come into balance and harmony during this stage. Perhaps you will arrive at spiritual insights that lend peaceful wisdom to your outlook. A sense of yourself as a spiritual being within your social roles can provide a comforting background to your activities. As an illustration, here is the story of Pat.

Pat came to the States a poor immigrant from Ireland where he had moved barrels on and off ships. He was husky and strong, a man's man who liked his beer at the end of the day. He found his way from New York to Chicago where he slept in the basement of the local Catholic church for awhile.

When an artisan came to repair a hole in the church's stained glass windows, Pat was there to help. The artisan saw that he had a talent for the work, and, equally important to the artisan who had to erect scaffolds, a strong back, too. So Pat accompanied the itinerant stained glass worker to his next job. Time passed; Pat became proficient in the craft of stained glass. He set up his own workshop where he produced windows for new parish churches. He married and had two children, a girl and a boy.

One Saturday morning he was overseeing the installation of his latest piece, a rose window, behind the altar of St. Teresa's Catholic Church. It had come together beautifully once the complicated design was transferred to glass. Still, he had had no way of seeing the full effect of the color until now. The carpenters edged the window into place and secured it with hardwood trim. Pat held his breath while they finished caulking. Then the carpenters stepped away and Pat could at last see his rose window with the morning light streaming through.

The beauty of it stunned him, and he put his hand on the altar to steady himself. Seated in a pew behind him, his daughter called softly, "Come look at it from here, Pop." Pat made his way, a bit breathless, to where she was and sat down beside her. He felt a surge of pride as he marveled at the masterpiece he had created, but the moment was also a spiritual awakening for him. Tears were running down his cheeks. His daughter slipped her arm through his and whispered, "It's beautiful."

"I know," Pat replied. "And so are you," he said as he patted her hand. From that day on, Pat's work in stained glass took on a different meaning for him. It became something like a prayer that he prayed with great devotion.

Like the rose window Pat created, we find that many traditions have produced the orderly, symmetrical mandalas associated with Stage Nine. The decorative motifs of Islamic art and many of the folk art designs of Eastern Europe, Russia, and India also display these characteristics.

Intentions for Stage Nine

A fully opened rose, glowing in the afternoon sunlight, conveys the quality of Stage Nine. This is a time of resolution—intellectually, emotionally, and spiritually—of the concerns prominent during earlier stages. The projects that you have put your best efforts toward accomplishing come to completion here. The task of Stage Nine is to enjoy your success to the fullest without confusing what you do with who you are. May you enjoy *reaping rewards.*

Stage Nine Mandalas

The mandalas of Stage Nine are lovely, balanced, and complex. Their equilibrium mirrors the coming together of many facets of life in a coherent pattern based on even numbers greater than 4. Creating the mandalas of Stage Nine can be a pleasurable blend of rational thought and feeling-toned color choices.

> [This space] speaks of present harmony and status, such as a full-blown rose might display seconds before all the petals fall. There is more of a feeling of being rather than doing. —Joan Kellogg

The construction of Stage Nine mandalas often requires planning and the use of a ruler, compass, and protractor. A structure of concentric circles is an important element of the grid that facilitates the creation of Stage Nine mandalas. This is overlaid with a pattern of lines radiating from the center. Once a pattern is established in one segment of the mandala, it can become a relaxing meditation to repeat the pattern in the remaining segments.

The mandalas of Stage Nine have a natural appeal for those who rely on their *thinking* and *sensing* abilities. Those who find measuring and exactitude challenging may prefer to produce these mandalas *intuitively*. When you take this approach you will *feel* when they are in right balance. However, it can be an important exercise in strengthening undeveloped parts of yourself to try the less familiar approach to creating the mandalas of this stage.

Colors typical of Stage Nine recall the seasonal transition from summer to autumn. As you observe in nature around you, so it is with mandalas of this stage: warm tones of red, blue, purple, orange, green, brown, and gold are seen. These colors recall the richness of harvest time.

Exercises

Before you begin creating your mandalas, consider singing "It Is Here" (appendix C, page 283) to help yourself relax and breathe. The yoga movements for Stage Nine (appendix B, page 265) help you gather your energy from high and low to better focus. Following these warm-up activities, assemble the materials you will need on a flat, well-lit surface. Rest your hands lightly upon your drawing instruments and take a few more deep, relaxing breaths. Then lift your hands and place them in your lap. Now you are ready to begin creating your mandalas.

The mandalas of Stage Nine are based on principles of geometry known to the ancient Indians, Arabs, and Greeks. The drawing and measuring tools you will use were invented thousands of years ago and are virtually unchanged. In the beginning, the skills you will master were considered sacred, even magical. Pay close attention to your process. Letting your measuring and circle and line drawing become a meditation can help you be patient and appreciate each step.

Notice how it is for you to take time to measure and construct your mandala form before coloring. Is it enjoyable to establish structure, or is it frustrating to the point that you just want to skip to the next stage? If your reaction is pleasure, then you probably rely most often on your thinking skills. The mandalas of Stage Nine will be your favorites. Enjoy.

If you get impatient with creating the necessary mandala grids, you may find that your feelings are a primary source of guidance for you. Stop and take a few relaxing breaths whenever you feel uncomfortable with the process. Choosing to work slowly and deliberately through each step of the development of these mandalas can exercise seldom-used personal abilities and lead to a justified feeling of accomplishment.

Turn to your journal to write about your experiences with creating mandalas of Stage Nine. What have you learned from the process of creating these mandalas? What have you learned about yourself?

YANTRA MANDALA
Materials You'll Need:
Basic Art Materials (see page 36)
Coloring Mandala 9 (see appendix A, page 248)

During Stage Nine we begin to see through the appearances of things and grasp the fundamental structures of reality. This mandala is based on a sacred Hindu design used for meditation to better grasp the processes of existence. The converging triangles represent the dynamic harmony of active and receptive qualities constantly generating the universe. Use rich, jewel-toned colors to fill in this mandala. As you do your coloring, reflect on the *big picture* of your life. Carry your thoughts and experience into your journaling.

BASIC MANDALA GRID
Materials You'll Need:
Basic Art Materials (see page 36)
Basic Mandala Grid template (optional; see appendix A, page 239)

Mandalas of Stage Nine resemble crystals. They have an even number of points, and their interior patterns are organized in concentric circles. In order to create these lovely mandalas with precision, one needs a grid. Please be aware that producing this grid requires thought and patience. Staying relaxed with the process can give you an enjoyable experience. Mastery of the grid is invaluable for creating all complex mandalas.

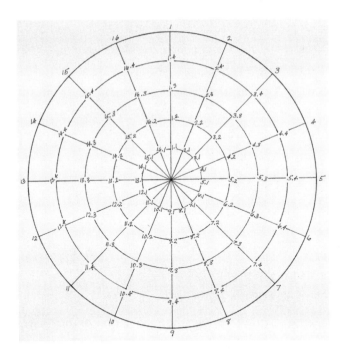

Basic Mandala Grid

Refer to the figure shown here as you create this mandala. Please note that the figure was created on a smaller scale than the one you will be creating. You may also make use of the template grid for a larger version that you can trace if you prefer. With your ruler as a guide draw straight lines from one corner of your 12" x 18" paper to the opposite corner. Repeat with the other two corners of your paper. Place the point of your compass at the intersection of these two lines. Draw a circle with a radius of 1". In the same way, from the same center point, draw four more circles with radii of 2", 3", 4", and 5".

Now draw a line perpendicular (at a 90 degree angle) to the bottom edge of your paper that starts at the top of the 5" circle, runs through the center point of your circles, and ends at the bottom of the 5" circle. Place your protractor's 0 measurement line on top of this line with the protractor's center point covering the center point of the circles.

Now create eight 22.5 degree angles by marking your drawing paper lightly with pencil at the following angle measurements on your protractor:

22.5

45

90

135

180

202.5

225

270

315

Line up your straight edge to connect points marked at 22.5 and 202.5. Draw a line between these two points that starts and ends on the 5" circle and runs through the center of the circles. Draw lines in the same way between 45 and 225, 90 and 270, 135 and 315.

Now rotate your protractor to the right so that the center point is over the center of your circles and the 0 line touches the line between points marking angles 22.5 and 202.5. Again make light marks on your paper at the following numbers:

45

90

135

180

225

270

315

(You should already have marks at 22.5 and 202.5.)

As before, line up your straight edge and draw lines that start and end on the 5" circle and run through the center point of the circles between points marking 45 and 225, 90 and 270, 135 and 315.

To follow instructions for the mandalas in this section, you will find it helpful to number in light pencil the intersections of lines and circles, as shown in the illustration. This completes a Basic Mandala Grid. Congratulations!

BASIC MANDALA GRID FOR IMPATIENT PEOPLE
Materials You'll Need:
Basic Art Materials (see page 36)
Basic Mandala Grid template (see appendix A, page 239)

This mandala grid is preferred by some. It allows you to use your skill for visually estimating distances in place of strict measuring with ruler, protracter, and compass. Those who rely on intuition or sensory awareness more than thinking may find this grid easier. Remember to take short breaks to breathe and relax as you create this grid. Notice what you like or dislike about the process, and carry these insights about yourself into your journaling.

As described in the previous exercise, mark the center point of your paper, draw circles, and establish a line perpendicular to the bottom of the paper that intersects the center of the circle and touches the top and bottom of the 5" circle. At the point where the line intersects the center point, measure and mark an angle that is 90 degrees to the line. Align your straight edge between this mark and the center point of the circle. Draw a line through the center of the circle, intersecting the perpendicular line at 90 degrees and touching opposite sides of the circle.

Number points where lines intersect the circle (1, 5, 9, and 13) as shown in the illustration for Basic Mandala Grid (see page 160). Using your eye, estimate and mark the midpoints on the circle between point 1 and point 5, point 5 and point 9, point 9 and point 13, point 13 and point 1. Draw lines connecting these points so that you now have a circle intersected by four lines through the center point.

Now repeat this process, finding and marking on the circle the midpoints between the points already on the circle, and connecting these points with lines through the center of the circle until you have a total of eight lines running through the center. Number the remaining points as shown in the illustration. This completes a Basic Mandala Grid.

MANDORLA MANDALA
Materials You'll Need:
Basic Art Materials (see page 36)

The word *mandorla* is Italian for "almond." A mandorla is created by the intersection of two circles. Mandorlas represent the coming together of two essentially different realms, such as heaven and earth, matter and spirit, life and death, or creation and destruction. As exemplified in Christianity, Jesus occupies the mandorla at the intersection of circles representing divinity and humanity.

What circles in your life would you like to bring together in a mandorla? What are your dilemmas? A split between mind and body, order and chaos, or good and evil? Perhaps you struggle with the choices of career or parenting, mountains or ocean, friends or family. Creating a mandorla can give you a way to graphically bridge qualities that seem miles apart in your thinking. It is quite possible that your creative self-expression will reward you with a new perspective. Remember to record your insights and what you learn about yourself in your journal.

Begin by measuring to find the center point of a piece of 12" x 18" paper. Draw a line horizontally from side to side of the piece of paper and through the center point. Measure along this line from the center to a point 2 1/2" from the center and make a dot. Measure 2 1/2" along the line on the opposite side of the center point and make a dot.

Set your compass for a radius of 4". Place the point of your compass on the dot you just marked on the line and draw a circle. Now place the point of your compass on the dot on the opposite side and draw another circle. You will now have two circles intersecting to create a mandorla. Complete your design with colors and forms that represent the two sides of your dilemma. For example, one circle might represent "body" and the other "spirit, soul, or consciousness." Let intuition guide your choice of colors and forms for the almond-shaped mandorla space. Reflect on what you see once your Mandorla Mandala is completed. Do some journaling about your mandorla. What does it have to tell you about your dilemma?

EIGHT-POINTED STAR MANDALA
Materials You'll Need:
Basic Art Materials (see page 36)
Basic Mandala Grid template (optional; see appendix A, page 239)

Creating mandalas as a meditation practice originated in the East and was transmitted and adapted by cultures of the Middle East and Europe. Knowledge of measuring and drawing geometric forms was once a closely guarded secret revealed to a special few. Now this knowledge is widely disseminated and has become a secular means to an end, such as the calculation of manufacturing materials, the rendering of architectural drawings, or the plotting of land to be bought or sold.

The Eight-Pointed Star Mandala involves you in creating a beautiful geometric form. You will be doing by hand what is usually calculated by computer now. In a way, you are resurrecting an ancient practice. Your motivations of creative expression and self-discovery are similar to those of ancient scholars who found divinity in numbers, lines, and angles.

For those of us who rely on impulse and intuition in creating mandalas, the orderly steps required for the Eight-Pointed Star Mandala can make us impatient. However, when you slow down and appreciate each step of the process, this creative project can be deeply rewarding. For those of us who have struggled with the less structured mandalas earlier in *The Mandala Workbook,* the Eight-Pointed Star Mandala can feel like a warm homecoming to a familiar way of working.

Whichever group you belong to, let yourself enjoy the process. Take a few moments to breathe and relax before beginning your mandala. Pause for relaxation as needed throughout your drawing process. Start by creating a Basic Mandala Grid in pencil as directed in the earlier Basic Mandala Grid exercises (see pages 159 and 162 and the template). Then, using your straight edge, draw lines between the following numbered points:

1 and 2.3

2.3 and 3

3 and 4.3

4.3 and 5

5 and 6.3

6.3 and 7

7 and 8.3

8.3 and 9

9 and 10.3

10.3 and 11

11 and 12.3

12.3 and 13

13 and 14.3

14.3 and 15

15 and 16.3

16.3 and 1

You should now have an eight-pointed star.

To make a more complex star, draw lines between these following points as well:

1.4 and 2.2

2.2 and 3.4

3.4 and 4.2

4.2 and 5.4

5.4 and 6.2

6.2 and 7.4

7.4 and 8.2

8.2 and 9.4

9.4 and 10.2

10.2 and 11.4

11.4 and 12.2

12.2 and 13.4

13.4 and 14.2

14.2 and 15.4

15.4 and 16.2

16.2 and 1.4

You can add yet another star to your composition by connecting:

1.3 and 2.1

2.1 and 3.3

3.3 and 4.1

4.1 and 5.3

5.3 and 6.1

6.1 and 7.3

7.3 and 8.1

8.1 and 9.3

9.3 and 10.1

10.1 and 11.3

11.3 and 12.1

12.1 and 13.3

13.3 and 14.1

14.1 and 15.3

15.3 and 16.1

16.1 and 1.3

Now to complete this lovely design, connect:

1.1 and 5.1

2.1 and 6.1

3.1 and 7.1

4.1 and 8.1

5.1 and 9.1

6.1 and 10.1

7.1 and 11.1

8.1 and 12.1

9.1 and 13.1

10.1 and 14.1

11.1 and 15.1

12.1 and 16.1

13.1 and 1.1

14.1 and 2.1

15.1 and 3.1

16.1 and 4.1

Congratulations! Your Eight-Pointed Star Mandala is complete. Now you can trace in ink or colored pencil the lines you want to keep and erase the pencil lines you do not need (see plate 25). Choose colors that represent something in your life coming into balance. Or you may intuitively choose colors and afterward reflect on what they symbolize for you. Journaling about your mandala design and colors can help you clarify insights about yourself and your life.

EIGHT-POINTED STAR MANDALA, VARIATION

Materials You'll Need:

Basic Mandala Grid template (see appendix A, page 239)

Cardboard, tagboard, or other stiff material, approximately 10" x 10"

Awl

Upholstery or tapestry needle and thimble

Colored cotton crochet thread, ribbon, yarn, string, embroidery floss,
    or other (twine, raffia, etc.)

Scissors

This variation on the Eight-Pointed Star Mandala allows you to use thread in the place of drawn lines. The process will become slow and craftsman-like, almost like needlepoint. Unlike in a drawn mandala, you will be able to pull out and replace threads you do not like. The completed mandala can be quite beautiful.

As you do your needlework, notice the feeling of pulling thread from the center to the edge of the circle. You will repeat these movements countless times to craft this mandala. Synchronize your breath with the movements from time to time. Breathe in as you push your needle through the center, breathe out as you pull it through a hole on the circle. Let your breathing carry you into intense concentration on your task. Notice what this is like for you. Perhaps you will write a few words in your journal as a record of your experience.

Begin by making a Basic Mandala Grid on cardboard. (See pages 159 and 162 for instructions.) Decide which mandala variation you wish to create. Then, at the appropriate numbered points, punch holes through the cardboard with an awl. Thread a needle with colored thread and tie a knot at one end. Pull the thread up through one of the holes from the back of the mandala and push it down through the hole you wish to connect to. Continue to connect points as described in the Eight-Pointed Star instructions for the mandala you are making. If necessary, punch more holes and add lines of thread to create your desired Eight-Pointed Star Mandala design.

SOLOMON'S SEAL MANDALA
Materials You'll Need:
Basic Art Materials (see page 36)
Basic Mandala Grid template (see appendix A, page 239)

The intersecting triangle design of the Solomon's Seal Mandala probably owes its origin to the ancient yantras of India. In mystical Judaism the design signifies the reunion of God and his spouse, the Shekina. Triangles suggest vectors of movement. The interpenetration of upper and lower triangles signifies the active coming together of equal and opposite movements into perfect balance. The moment is one of stillness, such as that following the crystallization of natural elements.

If you are attracted to this mandala, reflect on the energetic processes at work in your life that might be represented by the triangles coming together. Carry this awareness into your creation of the mandala form. By doing this, you can experience in the moment a connection between your graphic expression and your inner process. The mandala can then become a vehicle to assist you in arriving at inner balance and harmony.

First, create a Basic Mandala Grid on paper as described in the exercises on pages 159 and 162 (or use the template). Measure and mark a midpoint between points 3 and 4 and label it 3.5 (see Solomon's Seal Grid on next page). In the same way, measure and mark midpoints between points 6 and 7 (6.5), 11 and 12 (11.5), 14 and 15 (14.5). With your straight edge draw lines between the following points:

3.5 and 9

9 and 14.5

14.5 and 3.5

Now draw a line between points

1 and 6.5

6.5 and 11.5

11.5 and 1

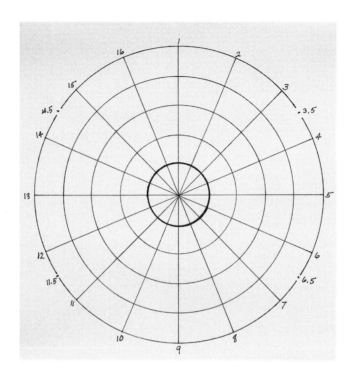

Solomon's Seal Grid

Draw lines between these points:

1 and 9

3.5 and 11.5

6.5 and 14.5

These lines intersect and mark the midpoints of the lines forming the Solomon's Seal Mandala. Connecting these points you may draw another Solomon's Seal fitting inside the larger one you just drew. Now trace over the lines you want to keep in your completed mandala. These may include the 1" and 5" radius circles as well as your finished Solomon's Seal design. Erase the pencil grid lines and add color to your Solomon's Seal Mandala with the medium of your choice.

SUBLIME FLOWER MANDALA
Materials You'll Need:
Basic Art Materials (see page 36)

This ancient mandala pattern is seen in Eastern, Middle Eastern, and European art and craft. The design emerges almost magically from simple sweeps of the compass and produces a flower with twelve petals, which naturally relates it to the archetypal twelve-pointed mandalas of the zodiac, the Buddhist Wheel of Life (see figure 8, page 15), and the Great Round (see figure 12, page 25).

Creating the Sublime Flower Mandala is easily done with a compass that holds its adjustment. Take a few moments to breathe deeply and relax before beginning your mandala. You might want to sing "It Is Here" (see appendix C, page 283).

Using your compass, draw a circle about 10" across on paper. Keeping your compass adjusted to the radius of the circle, place the point of your compass anywhere on the circle. Draw an arc inside the circle that touches the circle in two places. Moving clockwise around the circle, place the point of your compass at the next spot where an arc intersects the circle. Draw another arc as you did the first one.

Continue clockwise in this way until all points on the circle are touched by two arcs. You will have a six-petaled flower. Now measure the space between petal points and mark a dot on the circle exactly halfway between two petals. Place the point of your compass on that dot. Draw an arc, as above, that touches the circle at two points. Moving clockwise, draw arcs as before until you have completed a twelve-petaled flower. Add colors of your choosing. This example was created by Sue Kahn (see plate 26).

What is it like for you to create this ancient mandala form? How was it to use a compass as your primary instrument to generate the design? What are your associations to the colors you used in your mandala? Respond by writing in your journal.

MANDALA OF YOUR HIGHER POWER
Materials You'll Need:
Basic Art Materials (see page 36)

Stage Nine in the archetypal mandala cycle is a time when we often experience intellectual and spiritual realizations. Perhaps we are able to accept or deepen our understanding of traditional religious concepts during this time. It may be that we achieve clarity about our non-traditional beliefs as well. You may have a sense of your Higher Power already. If not, then journaling about God, your wisdom figures, or other sources of guidance in your life may help you gain ideas for this Mandala of Your Higher Power.

Taking another approach, you may wish to let the process of creating your mandala be your exploration. In this case, follow spontaneous inspiration for what belongs in the center. Some of us may prefer the center to remain empty, beyond symbolizing. Be open to whatever appears in the center of your mandala as helpful information about your spirituality. Share your mandala with your spiritual director or a trusted friend. Journaling will help you explore your insights further.

Using your compass, draw a circle with a radius of approximately 1". (The circle will then be 2" across.) Place the point of your compass at the same center point and draw a circle with a radius of approximately 4". Create a symmetrical design from the 4" circle as directed in the Sublime Flower Mandala, but as you draw your arcs, skip over the inner circle and continue the arc on the other side so that there are no lines inside the inner circle.

Before proceeding, lay down your materials and sit quietly for a few moments. Relax and breathe. Close your eyes, if you wish. Invite God or your Higher Power to give you an image, a line, a sound, a color, a feeling, or a movement in your imagination to help you begin your mandala. When you feel ready, open your eyes, and place the essence of what you received, as best you can, in the inner circle.

Add color to enhance your mandala. When it is completed, allow some time to reflect on the Mandala of Your Higher Power. You might pose this question to your Higher Power, as represented in the center of your mandala: "What is your guidance for me in this moment?" Your journal is an appropriate place to carry on this dialogue in writing. When your dialogue is completed, you might also write in the petals the names or concerns that you wish to surrender to the care of your Higher Power. Share your mandala with your spiritual director or a trusted friend.

MANDALA OF CRYSTALLIZATION MOMENTS
Materials You'll Need:
Basic Art Materials (see page 36)

Using journaling, explore memories of your significant accomplishments, moments when your efforts came to fruition. These may be something like graduation, winning an athletic competition, or launching a successful business. Moments that are important to you may go unacknowledged by others: guiding a child safely through a difficult adolescence, caring for a sick loved one, or creating a thriving vegetable garden on a once barren plot of land. Take note of any random memories that present for your attention. You may not have realized what an important accomplishment it was.

This mandala gives you a way to honor what you are proud of having done. Select six or eight of your most important crystallization moments. You may have felt a satisfying sense of accomplishment at the time, or you may only now realize the significance of what you did. Draw images or select magazine pictures to represent each one. After drawing your mandala circle, arrange these symbols near the outer edge such that each one is given an important place. Add other lines, forms, and colors as needed to complete your design. Once your mandala is finished, return to your journal and respond to these statements:

I am most proud of myself for ___ .

I now realize that I value ___ .

I learn from this mandala that I am a person who ___ .

More and more I accept that I am ___ .

I look forward to more ___ .

Reflecting on Stage Nine

Stage Nine, Reaping Rewards, is a time of resolution when creative energy is slowing. Projects come to completion, spiritual awareness is highlighted, and the promise of early stages of the Great Round is fulfilled. As a way of bringing your exploration of Stage Nine to a close, create Mandala Card

Nine including imagery that expresses your understanding of this stage of crystallization, when things come together.

MANDALA CARD NINE
Materials You'll Need:
Basic Art Materials (see page 36)
Cardboard, tagboard, or other stiff material
Collage images

Cut a card in the shape and size you prefer. Using drawing, painting, or collage, place on your card a mandala that resembles a Solomon's Seal, a six- or eight-petaled flower, or a design of interlacing lines with six or more even-numbered points. You may add other images, words, textures, or colors to complete the design that expresses the feeling of *reaping your rewards*. Let your card dry flat, then store in a safe place.

Letting Go

Stage Ten is the gateway to the last stages of the Great Round. The bright, solar, yang energies of the upper half of the Great Round begin to give way to dark, fluid, lunar, yin forces. The stage is aligned with the month of October on the Great Round of the year. During this month nature sees to it that things begin to soften around the edges: flowers drop their petals, colorful leaves fall from trees, and fruit decays in preparation for releasing its seeds. As creatures of nature, we, too, are required to let go when a cycle of life is nearing completion.

You may welcome the ending. Perhaps you are bored with the way things are in your life. The attainments that justified your pride in the stage earlier no longer interest you. Or maybe you are really done with a demanding relationship or have accomplished all you can in a work position. Perhaps something beyond your control disrupts life and forces your path in a different direction: a natural disaster, a job loss, a diagnosis, or the death of a loved one. Whatever ushers in Stage Ten brings with it the undeniable awareness that all things must come to an end—including you.

Stage Ten may be encountered earlier in life when illness, depression, or deep disappointments challenge us. We are shaken loose from our assumptions about who we are and what we can expect from life. For some of us this may be experienced as a moment of sheer terror. For others it may be an exhilarating call to adventure. Stage Ten marks an end to the enthronement of ego as the center of consciousness. We become aware of something beyond ourselves exerting powerful influence on our psychic life. We are *letting go.*

In Stage Ten, you may have the sense that an adventure is about to begin, and there is something in you that welcomes a change when *letting go.* However, you cannot respond to the call without also experiencing a time, even if only briefly, of shock, grief, and disorientation. The order that was your life must be disengaged, unraveled, released. Stage Ten is your invitation to this important inner work.

You may find yourself out of step with the world. You may wish to turn back the clock to recapture the past. However, life goes on and you cannot stop the flow. During Stage Ten you experience yourself moved around by inexorable forces beyond your control. Strange, frightening, and disreputable messengers may find their way to your door. You may have dreams or fantasies of humiliation, mutilation, or death. This is a challenging time when additional support is welcome. Some will turn to friends and family. Others will turn to spiritual resources for comfort. Here is what Tina did.

Tina brought a piece of knitting with her to the group. She told us that she had wanted it to be a sweater, but it had not turned out well. Therefore, she was unraveling it. She began pulling the sweater apart and rolling the yarn into a ball. Tina took this unraveling as a metaphor for her experience of Stage Ten. She was *letting go* of her sweater, releasing the hours of labor and the idea that the project should have a certain result. She was deconstructing the sweater in preparation for a new beginning: another knitting project. "I like thinking that nothing is really lost in *letting go*. It is just transformed."

> This space represents the death of outmoded conscious contents and the pain of change. —Joan Kellogg

In psychodynamic terms, this stage concerns the dethronement of the ego as the center of identity. This stage prepares the psyche for experiencing its true center, which Jung called the *Self*. The Self encompasses the wider realm of the unconscious as well as the territory of ego consciousness. At first, the Self can be perceived as a threat from the viewpoint of the ego. With acceptance of the primacy of the Self, your personal identity can become aligned in such a way that you feel held, supported, and companioned by the deep psychic center of the Self.

The traditional holiday celebrations around the end of October offer community support during Stage Ten of the Great Round of the year. Halloween, All Saints, the Celtic Samhain, and the Mexican Day of the Dead celebrations reinforce community ties and manage taboo energies associated with death and dying. A similar role appears to be assigned to the Hindu Goddess Kali who accompanies devotees when their life journey turns dark. Annie Kelahan's mandala (see plate 27) incorporates the archetypal imagery of Kali's downward-pointing triangle.

Stage Ten is exemplified in myths and fairy tales as the first step into deepening wisdom. A hero or heroine encounters a dark, wild, dangerous being that blocks the path, chases, or runs away, enticing the hero or heroine to leave the familiar and follow a path toward the unknown. Such tales as *Little Red Riding Hood* and *Alice in Wonderland* provide examples of young heroines snatched into another reality (the belly of the wolf), or falling into a topsy-turvy world. The abduction of Persephone by Hades, Lord of the Underworld, and the descent of the Mesopotamian goddess Inanna to her sister's domain of the Below also describe encounters with transformative dark mystery.

> To round itself out, life calls not for perfection but for completeness; and for this the thorn in the flesh is needed, the suffering of defects without which there is no progress and no ascent. —C. G. Jung

Intentions for Stage Ten

With Stage Ten you begin your descent into darkness, the unknown, the unconscious, and, eventually—on your last turning of the Great Round—death. Consciously directed energy begins to wane with this stage, and the unconscious becomes more active. Your assumptions about life are challenged, and you are cracked open to experience new vistas, undreamed-of realities, and ways of being you have been far too busy to notice in the previous few stages. The task is to face the shadows, to listen to the trickster, and, in short, to surrender and let the former order disintegrate. Stage Ten is a time of *letting go.*

Stage Ten Mandalas

Mandalas of Stage Ten incorporate symbols of coming to ground, sinking, going below. They may include a gate or an entrance to a cave. Downward-pointing triangles and the Christian cross of crucifixion are seen here. *X*'s both small and large, as in the skull and crossbones, a symbol of danger to life, are typical. The wheel motif, suggesting martyrdom and the relentless passage of time, may also appear in mandalas of Stage Ten. Designs can be free-form and spontaneous, conveying a sense of loosening structure. The mandala of Edna Bacon, a member of our mandala group (plate 28), shows an example of this imagery.

Colors of this stage tend to be dark, autumnal, and earthy. Brown, indigo, shades of red, old gold, and dark green are associated with this stage. These colors may be combined with intense yellow, orange, and red. You will recognize the traditional colors of Halloween here. Stage Ten mandalas communicate powerful emotions such as anger, fear, suffering, and grief. Sometimes they convey a sense of eeriness, foreboding, or powerful mystery.

Exercises

Before beginning your exploration of Stage Ten mandalas, perform the yoga movements suggested (appendix B, page 267). Also, singing "I Will Let Go" (appendix C, page 284) is recommended. These activities will help you relax, center, and become firmly grounded. You might also consider lighting a candle to set this time apart as special.

As you work on the mandalas of Stage Ten, notice what it is like to let go, to face the unknown, to address difficult life events. How is it for you to let sand sift through your fingers, to burn your mandala creation, or to contemplate the worst thing that could happen? Is this a process with which you are familiar? Do you accept or reject surrendering to mystery as a natural part of life? In your journal, explore your responses to this stage and these mandalas.

MANDALA OF SACRIFICE
Materials You'll Need:
Basic Art Materials (see page 36)
Coloring Mandala 10 (see appendix A, page 249)

Stage Ten, Letting Go, requires a sacrifice. The parting with what was can feel like a bittersweet pause at a crossroads, an urgent summons into alien territory, or even the ultimate surrender of crucifixion. You are being separated from that which is no longer needed. Celtic crosses like the one in this mandala dot the landscape of Scotland. Tall, silent, enduring stone, they stand against the sky washed by the winds and rains of countless seasons, reminders that even though things change, there is a part of you that lives on. Use sunset colors for coloring this mandala.

MANDALA OF LETTING GO
Materials You'll Need:
Basic Art Materials (see page 36)

The turning cycle of life brings in the new, and takes away that which is no longer needed. Sometimes we are glad to let go. At other times, we do not feel ready to release what we had. The process keeps moving, and it carries us with it. We are taught that *letting go* is a natural part of living.

What are you letting go of? Is your favorite season coming to an end? Has a choice neighborhood restaurant closed? Are you selling your house, your car, your horse?

Are you being asked to sacrifice something: your comfort, your dignity, your job? Whom are you letting go of? Is someone leaving, growing up, or moving away? Has a relationship come to an end? Has someone died? The Mandala of Letting Go gives you a way to acknowledge what is passing. The mandala is a safe container for the feelings stirred up by *letting go.*

Draw a circle. Ground and center yourself by singing "I Will Let Go" (appendix C, page 284). Sketch within your circle an *X* or an upright Latin cross. Let these crossing lines be a starting point for your mandala. Allow it to unfold spontaneously as you reflect on your emotions in response to life's requirement that you let go of something or someone.

When your Mandala of Letting Go is completed, set it up so you can look at it for awhile. You might want to light a candle or some incense nearby as a way of honoring what you have expressed in your mandala. When you feel ready (minutes, days, or weeks later) put your mandala away in a safe place, or intentionally release it by burning. Your *letting go* is a commitment to living.

BURNING WHEEL MANDALA
Materials You'll Need:
Raffia, straw, vines, and/or dry fallen twigs
Stick or pole, approximately 3' long
Small bits of paper, leaves, or other flammable materials (optional)

The wheel with eight spokes is an ancient symbol of the sun as the ruler of time. It still appears in the iconography of Hinduism and Buddhism. Frazer (1950) documents the use of burning wheels in Eastern Europe and the islands of Great Britain for marking the turning of the year at the solstices. Country people would tie straw to a wagon wheel, set it on fire, and roll it down a hill as part of their seasonal celebration. At the winter solstice the burning wheel would have been a way of observing the important shift from increasingly long nights to lengthening days and shorter nights.

The turning of the seasons provides an apt metaphor for the cycles of life. In Stage Ten we begin the end of a cycle, whether it is a decade birthday, a farewell to the last child off to school, or our retirement from a busy career. The complex feelings that such transitions stir sometimes are best expressed in symbolic actions. In the spirit of marking the cycles of life, here are instructions for creating a Burning Wheel Mandala. Please observe necessary safety precautions.

Braid raffia or grass and connect the ends to create a circle. Using four raffia braids or dry sticks, form eight spokes and attach them to the circle. Add sticks, strands of raffia, straw, or dry leaves and vines to embellish the wheel. Continue in this manner until you have created a wheel with eight spokes. You may want to interweave bits of paper with written statements of gratitude, regret, gains, and losses related to your transition.

Push a pole through the center of your woven wheel. Before lighting fire to your Burning Wheel Mandala, determine that you are in a locale where fire is allowed by local authorities. Then carefully prepare a place where fire can be safely contained with fire tamping materials if necessary (for example, running water, loose dirt, or a fire extinguisher). Once these safety precautions are put in place, you may set fire to your Burning Wheel Mandala. As it burns, reflect on *letting go.*

GHOST CATCHER MANDALA
Materials You'll Need:
Basic Art Materials (see page 36)

Change means moving into the strange, unpredictable territory of the unknown. Some of us feel safe only in familiar situations where we have a sense of control. Naturally, the shift required by *letting go* will be beyond our control. We may attempt to prepare for the change by thinking of all the possible outcomes.

Some of us seem to focus on the negative possibilities more than the positive ones. Of course this creates fear, anxiety, and worry that can be difficult to contain once they get launched. The Ghost Catcher Mandala provides a way to bring shadowy possibilities into the light of full attention. Then we have the opportunity to take actions that claim and integrate the energy we have leaked out into thoughts about phantom possibilities.

What are your fears, your anxieties, and your worries? Turn them over to the Ghost Catcher Mandala. Draw a strong circle and place inside it images representing your personal list of *things that go bump in the night.* You may want to reinforce your circle to firmly contain your fears. Consider placing an *X* over the fearful images inside the circle.

Create a positive statement based on what you now feel or what you see in your mandala, and write it next to your Ghost Catcher Mandala. For example: "Now I know that my fear is manageable," "I like seeing my fears contained in the circle," or "Now I see that I can do ___ and feel fine." Once your mandala is completed, put it in a box or folder where you can store it. Get it out to look at and possibly add to, when you find yourself beginning to worry.

TREASURED BODY PART MANDALA
Materials You'll Need:
Basic Art Materials (see page 36)
Full body photo or drawing of yourself

All of us have lost parts of our bodies. As children we lost our baby teeth, got haircuts, and cried over skinned knees and elbows. As adults we may have had wrinkles, fat, breasts, kidneys, lungs, wombs, or gall bladders surgically removed. The surrendering of bits of our flesh is no small thing and often rouses a maelstrom of emotions both positive and negative. We seldom have a place to honor our feelings and say goodbye to the body part. The purpose of the Treasured Body Part Mandala is to create such a place.

Draw a circle. Add a downward-pointing triangle inside the circle. Place the picture of you inside the triangle. With color or symbol, indicate the surrendered body part on your image. Add more colors or lines as needed to complete your mandala. Write the story of separating from your body part. Share your story and mandala with a trusted friend, loved one, or therapist.

MANDALA GATEWAY TO THE WORST THING THAT CAN HAPPEN
Materials You'll Need:
Basic Art Materials (see page 36)

When we are faced with change, our imagination can create ominous possibilities that press in on us at an unconscious level. Bringing these fears out in the open often helps us grasp there is less to fear than we thought. This Mandala Gateway to the Worst Thing That Can Happen can be a way to contain and manage your fears. Maureen commented that creating a gate she could open or close over the image of her worst fear helped her feel more comfortably in control.

Draw a circle. Reflect on a change that you are required by life to make. Allow your anxieties about the change to come fully into your awareness. Ask yourself, "What is the worst thing that can happen from this change?" Illustrate this negative possibility in the mandala circle. Now create the image of a gate and place it over the circle containing negativity. Your gate may be open or closed, solid or revealing. Let the gate be as strong as you want it to be to give you a feeling of safety. Design your gate so that you can open or close it when you wish. You may even want to write this affirmation in or around your mandala circle: "I have effective ways to manage the stress of change and *letting go*."

MANDALA FOR THE LOST AND GONE
Materials You'll Need:
Basic Art Materials (see page 36)
Photographs of missing friends, loved ones, and pets (optional)
Symbols of a house, a home country, a former work position,
    or lifestyle (optional)
Representations of a relationship (optional)

The autumn month of October is a time of festivals that observe the end of the growing season and the increasing darkness of longer nights. The Celtic holiday of Samhain, which evolved into All Hallow's Evening, or Halloween, marked a time when contact was possible between the world of spirits and the world of the living. On this occasion the family gathered around their hearth in quiet celebration, welcoming the visiting spirits of dead family members.

Mexican culture honors the memory of deceased family members with *El Dia de los Muertos*, the Day of the Dead. A celebratory atmosphere prevails at all night gatherings of families and friends. There they remember the lives of loved ones while creating altars holding their photographs, marigold flowers, and gifts of favorite food and drink that the dead generously share with the living.

Moving through Stage Ten, we are required to let go as we near the ending of one of the many cycles of a lifetime. *Letting go* naturally brings up memories of what we have lost, and who has gone. So there may be grieving to be done or revisited. There may also be celebration and gratitude to express as well. Creating a Mandala for the Lost and Gone can be a way to witness and honor the places, animals, and people we are missing.

Draw a circle and create a Latin cross as a background motif. Superimposed on the cross place a cutout heart or circle. Let these be the background for photos or other mementoes of your lost and gone. Add color and form to create a suitable surrounding for what you wish to honor in this mandala. Take time to let yourself feel what you feel. You might want to journal or talk with someone about what is shown in your Mandala for the Lost and Gone.

When you have completed your process with the Mandala for the Lost and Gone, you may want to wrap it carefully in tissue paper and place it in a safe storage container such as a box or an art folder. Perhaps you will wish to display it in your home, on your altar, or in a scrapbook of memories. Or you might prefer to release your mandala by burning, burying, or dissolving it in salt water. Let your heart guide your choice.

MANDALA FOR FACING IT
Materials You'll Need:
Basic Art Materials (see page 36)
Mask-making materials
Glitter, feathers, ribbon (optional)

We all have situations, people, or things about ourselves that we would rather not face. It is a form of denial that can impede our personal growth and rob us of information we need in order to make responsible choices. The Mandala for Facing It gives you an opportunity to explore hidden and projected parts of yourself. This can be an informative step toward self-knowledge and reclaiming disowned parts of yourself.

Begin with making a list of situations, people, and emotions you do not want to face. Perhaps it will include a particular person or a feeling such as fear, anger, or loss. You might list a house, a job, a birthday, a disability, or an addiction. Give yourself praise for having the courage to create your list. Select one item from your list for your Mandala for Facing It.

Draw a circle on cardboard or other stiff material. Sketch a Latin cross in the circle. Use this as your beginning point to create a face by centering the nose on the perpendicular line, with the mouth and chin below. Place the eyes on the horizontal line.

Now represent the item you chose from your list as a face. If you selected a person, use eye color, hair color, and other details to give the face in your mandala a general resemblance to the person. For other items, such as a house or a job, impose the image over the face sketch. For example, if you want to face housing issues, you might create a face where the eyes are also the windows of the house. For emotions, you might show the face expressing that emotion (see plate 29).

When your mandala is complete, prop it up where you can see it. Now you are literally *facing it.* To go further, open your journal and engage in an imaginary dialogue with your Mandala for Facing It. Complete several sentences that begin, "You are ___." Next, replace "You are" in the statements with "I am." End your experience by writing several times in your journal "Now that I have faced ___ I can ___."

MANDALA MASK FOR LETTING GO
Materials You'll Need:
Basic Art Materials (see page 36)
Mask-making materials: cardboard, plaster tape (follow instructions
**   on the box)**
Feathers, glitter, ribbon (optional)

Sometimes we get caught up in playing a role that no longer serves us. You might be an outgoing clown in social situations, yet long to be quiet and genuine with people. Perhaps you feel your job requires you to be very busy and brusque when you really prefer to be a relaxed, outgoing person. Possibly you find yourself behaving impulsively, or being compulsively dependent, when inside you know you are level headed, competent, and independent. Perhaps you are a new parent, and now know that it is time to set aside your rebellious adolescent identity in order to begin fulfilling your responsibility to your son or daughter. The Mandala Mask for Letting Go allows you to explore your roles through creative self-expression within the protective mandala circle.

Draw a circle, and let this be your starting point for a face mask representing the role you wish to let go. Be sure to include facial expressions or other graphic representations of the emotions that are part of your role. Is there a particular hairstyle for the role? Show it in your mandala mask.

Are there certain implements or fields of knowledge associated with the role? Include a reference to these as well in your mandala.

When your mandala mask is completed, witness and respond to your work. Share it with trusted others or journal about it. You might consider a ceremonial release of your mask by burning it, burying it, or adding something to your mandala that changes it for the better. Symbolic actions such as these can help your unconscious get the message about your desired change.

KALI YANTRA
Materials You'll Need:
Basic Art Materials (see page 36)

The Hindu goddess Kali both brings destruction and lovingly receives its victims. We are most familiar with images of her as a dark, terrible deity naked except for her grisly necklace of severed heads. However, there is a life-affirming side to her as well. It is thought that Kali is so inured to destruction, chaos, and suffering that she can be present with and *hold* anyone, no matter how horrible their experiences.

Hindu tradition exemplifies her in a yantra, a sacred diagram that is like a mandala. The downward-pointing triangle dominates the Kali yantra. In some versions, five triangles nest in smaller and smaller dimensions surrounding a center dot representing the bindu, the point of beginning and of return. Creating this mandala inspired by the Kali yantra can be a way of coming to terms with the flux and flow life presents as you experience Stage Ten.

Draw a circle and create a Basic Mandala Grid as described in the exercises on pages 159 and 162 (or use the template in appendix A, page 239). For the innermost triangle, make marks on the innermost circle of the Basic Mandala Grid halfway between points 3.1 and 4.1, and halfway between points 14.1 and 15.1. Connect these two points with each other and with point 9.1 to create a downward-pointing triangle.

Using your ruler, measure and mark points approximately 1/2" outside each line of the triangle. Now draw lines parallel to the sides of the small triangle to create the next larger triangle. Continue in this way until you have drawn five downward-pointing triangles.

Anchoring your compass on the center point of the Basic Mandala Grid, draw a circle enclosing these triangles, but not touching their points. Now draw three more circles about 1/2", 1", and 1-1/2" larger than the first circle, again using your compass and the same center point. Finally, you may draw flower petals evenly spaced in the area between the largest outer circle and the circle just inside it.

Use colors and materials that seem appropriate to you to complete your design. Perhaps you will make intentional choices of colors. You may also simply let intuition or chance guide you. In traditional Kali yantras, dark blues, black, and reds often appear.

MANDALA MASK
Materials You'll Need:
Basic Art Materials (see page 36)
Cardboard, tagboard, or other stiff material big enough to cover face
Images of a helpful person or animal
Paints
Glue, glitter, string

Putting on a mask is an ancient practice for taking in a bit of the strength and power of the being depicted in the mask. This makes sense because as the creator of the mask, you already have these qualities. Your mask is just a reminder that you do.

What person or animal would you most like to have accompany you on this journey through Stage Ten, Letting Go? In Tibetan mandalas, fierce deities are sometimes invoked as defenders, guides, and companions. Would you choose such a being? Or would you prefer a wise elder: a Merlin or Hecate? Perhaps your choice would be a pure soulful young girl such as Dante's Beatrice for your ultimate guide. You might consider a loyal dog, a raven, wolf, eagle, or horse as your companion. Use this mandala project to create an image of the companion you would like to have for this part of your journey.

Draw and cut out from cardboard a circle that is bigger than needed to cover your face. Within the circle, draw, color, or paint the face of your preferred companion. Add color in the circle, outside the mask face, to suggest the atmosphere of Stage Ten.

Make holes for eyes, mouth, and nose. Add holes to attach string or ribbon so you can secure the mask to your face. Perhaps you will enjoy wearing your mask for some friends, playing the role of the being in your mask, or looking at your reflection in a mirror.

KINESTHETIC MANDALA OF LETTING GO
Materials You'll Need:
Basic Art Materials (see page 36)
Bowl filled with sand

Movement is significant in creating and experiencing mandalas (see the yoga movements in appendix B, page 267). Exploring materials while creating mandalas can give us insights into and provide balancing or restorative information about our inner psychological reality. Movement experiences with materials form the basic building blocks of our concepts about the world. The Kinesthetic Mandala of Letting Go allows you to experience the gesture of letting go.

Place the bowl filled with sand before you. Take up a handful of sand and try to hold onto it, letting none leave your hand. Now spread your fingers and let go of the sand. Feel it flowing out of your hand. Repeat. Notice what it is like to try to hold, and then to let go of, the sand. Respond to your experience by writing in your journal or sharing with a trusted partner. You may want to experiment with making patterns in the sand as you let go, or adding bits of paper or other materials to signify something non-physical that you are letting go. When your Kinesthetic Mandala of Letting Go is finalized, it is time for one more experience of letting go: pouring the mandala into your garden, a nearby body of water, or a boggy spot in the path you walk each day to collect your mail.

Reflecting on Stage Ten

Stage Ten mandalas have allowed you to come face to face with hidden parts of yourself, let go of unnecessary roles, and find suitable companions for this part of your journey through life. As you complete your exploration of Stage Ten, take a short break for refreshment before proceeding to the next step: treat yourself to a drink of water, a cup of tea, or some slow, easy stretches. If you lit a candle, this would be a time to blow it out.

Following your break, reflect on what you have experienced working on these mandalas. Focus on surprises, realizations, gratitudes, or regrets that surfaced during your creative exploration. Respond by describing in your journal what you did and how it affected you. When you have completed your journaling, become aware of the most important aspects of Stage Ten for you. Carry these into developing Mandala Card Ten.

MANDALA CARD TEN
Materials You'll Need:
Basic Art Materials (see page 36)
Cardboard, tagboard, or other stiff material
Collage pictures
Storage box

Cut out a card the size and shape you would like. Continuing to develop your personal deck of cards, create a mandala design on your card expressing the qualities of the theme of Stage Ten: *letting go.* Your design might incorporate a gateway, a crucifixion scene, an *X,* or a downward-pointing triangle. Add images, words, textures, and colors to complete your card. Allow to dry flat. Store in a safe place.

Falling Apart

Stage Eleven coincides with the month of November in the Great Round of the year. Plants have gone dormant and cold weather has forced living creatures to seek shelter in the warmth. Some even settle into hibernation for the cold season. This stage recalls the darkness of evening and the fragile waning moon. During Stage Eleven, conscious, solar, yang energy so prominent at Stages Seven and Eight dissolves into dark yielding yin energy associated with the unconscious.

This stage may be a time when you are disoriented by changed circumstances. Perhaps a bout of poor health that depletes your energy puts you here. You might be the unfortunate victim of a catastrophe. Or perhaps it is the Self, nudging you toward fulfilling your potential, that pushes you here. The challenge of Stage Eleven is to accept that your ego is not the true center of your psyche. Within the mystery that is yours, a deeper center of order asserts its primacy. It mandates your *falling apart.*

Through Stage Eleven we descend into the *matriarchy* once again.

Psychologically we may find that Stage Eleven erases every ounce of pride and pretense, so that we become truly humble and broken open. Only in this way can we be received by the boundless ocean of love some experience as God. It may be comforting to remember that this is a natural—even necessary—process that makes possible the miraculous regeneration of the new. Our faith in a deeper order often blossoms in the midst of this time of transition. A broken heart can open to love, compassion, and wisdom.

Kellogg has named Stage Eleven *Fragmentation.* During this stage, your world seems to be falling apart. The person you took pride in being at Stage Seven, Squaring the Circle, is confronted with emotions, behaviors, and qualities you would rather not own. The resistance you feel comes from your ego, the conscious part of you that prefers the illusion that it is in control. Encounters with your shadow in dreams, relationships, or on the streets challenge you to accept that the good person you are is also capable of unsavory human behaviors. Egocentricity is purged as treasured beliefs are unmasked as servants of personal gain. This discovery is part of a natural process that teaches humility, wisdom, and compassion toward yourself and others.

During Stage Eleven you may feel lost, abandoned, angry, wild, sad, unsure, and out of control. You have little energy to give to day-to-day tasks. Life seems chaotic—and often it is—because you are less capable of remembering to pay your bills, keep up with appointments, and maintain relationships during this stage. You may have little appetite, or you may crave comforting junk food instead of healthy nourishment. Bright light may feel intrusive. Sleep rhythms can become disturbed as well. Jennifer's story is informative.

Jennifer was nearing forty when her family confronted her with the chaos her abuse of prescription drugs was causing. Her brother and parents brought to her attention that her day-to-day functioning was increasingly erratic. Jennifer was a freelance writer who worked at home. It had been a month or more since she submitted anything to her editor.

Some days she kept her six-year-old son home from school because she could not get out of bed to drive him. There was little food in the house, other than cereal, chips, and sodas. Laundry had not been done, and the house was a mess. Jennifer's ex-husband had voiced his concerns for the safety of his son and was initiating an attempt to gain sole custody. Clearly, Jennifer's life had fallen apart.

She admitted herself to a hospital for drug treatment while her parents kept her son. Once Jennifer's head began to clear, she was horrified and ashamed of what her life had been like. She had to endure days of painful soul searching, feelings of loss, and confusion. Gradually the treatment restored her physical and mental health, and she became able to go on with her life, clean and sober.

There were relapses when Jennifer again found herself falling apart. Reality was hard to face during those times. Her ex-husband was awarded custody of their son. However, each time she found herself falling to pieces, the lessons of earlier visits were helpful. She became capable of catching her addiction sooner and getting the help she needed. Talking to a supportive friend, Jennifer could honestly say:

> I used to fear the falling apart that comes with addiction. Don't get me wrong. I wouldn't wish it on anybody. It's just that . . . Now, more and more I know I can manage whatever happens.

Accepting destruction as an ordinary life occurrence allows us to join with nature as it takes its course. Like a pastry chef who slices up her pie and shares it with a group of friends, the sacrifice of one's prize creation can become a sacramental gesture of giving nourishment. Rather than waiting for the natural process of decomposition to destroy her handy work, she cuts it apart while it can still be of use to others. The destruction of her pie also frees the chef from past accomplishments, and makes space for something new to come in.

So it is that Stage Eleven is also a time of release from strictures that hamper full expression of your potentials. Some of your most admirable qualities have been hidden away in the interest of developing skills that allow you to earn a living or to be respected by your family and peers. When it seems that you have lost much that you value, hidden strengths and abilities surge into view. Stage Eleven can also be a time of heightened creativity when you find it easier to forgo the self-imposed requirement to make something *beautiful.*

Mythologically this passage is mediated by dark, powerful monsters that rip and devour. Mystics call this time the *dark night of the soul,* when faith is put to the test. Biblical stories of the suffering of Job and of Jonah swallowed by the whale exemplify this stage in which one feels overtaken by the forces of entropy for an uncertain period of time in fear, darkness, and confusion. Through the experience, one is transformed, most often for the better, although it is a dangerous passage from which not everyone returns.

Intentions for Stage Eleven

Stage Eleven is our ego's most challenging stage. It can be experienced as a time of purification. The phrase *Let go and let God* becomes deeply meaningful here. Stripped of pretense, we are better able to let in and integrate unconscious material. We have an opportunity to surrender and learn to trust the Self as our true center.

Stage Eleven Mandalas

The mandala circle serves as a safe container for the powerful and confusing emotions that often accompany this stage. Within the structure of the circle, mandalas of Stage Eleven tend to have a fractured, chaotic, disjointed appearance. They may look like a pie, with each slice a different color. Or mandalas may look like a crazy quilt that has no center, sense of order, or harmony. However, because of fearless abandon to the art-making process, the mandalas you create here can also have a fresh, lively, and even playful quality, even though often seeming a bit askew. Kaaren Nowicki, a member of our mandala group, created such a mandala (see plate 30).

Destruction as part of the creative process is seen in mandalas of this stage. Susanne's broken mirror mandala (see plate 31) and Diana's eyeglasses mandala (see plate 32) are good examples. Breakage is a safe outlet for strong feelings and allows an externalization of the chaotic mental state that so often accompanies Stage Eleven, Falling Apart.

Colors tend to range from dark and muddy to overly bright, garish, and even fluorescent. A sense of disintegration is sometimes revealed in mandalas by the layering of colors that results in a disorderly mess, unpleasant to the eye. The mandalas of this stage often include the colors we do not like and never choose. This is indicative of the fact that personal qualities rejected and repressed often make their presence known during Stage Eleven. This is not all bad. Mandalas created without a plan in "ugly" colors can reveal vitality, raw beauty, and unsuspected art talent.

This pie without hub [Stage Eleven mandala] is significant as a sign of dismemberment, each piece of oneself at odds with all other pieces. The absence of the hub implies a fractured ego. —Joan Kellogg

Exercises

Begin your creative session by exploring the free-form movements suggested in appendix B (see page 268). Singing the song "Falling Apart" (see appendix C, page 284) also supports your attunement to Stage Eleven. Assemble your materials and light a candle to mark the beginning of your creative session.

Mandala projects for this stage invite you to tear up materials, abandon order, and shatter glass. You are even encouraged to devour one of your mandalas. What is it like for you to be destructive? We are encouraged to pursue the things we like as a way to find happiness. What do you learn about yourself by focusing on colors and people that you dislike? How do you feel about chaos after the mandalas of Stage Eleven?

MANDALA OF FRAGMENTATION
Materials You'll Need:
Basic Art Materials (see page 36)
Coloring Mandala 11 (see appendix A, page 250)

During Stage Eleven life can seem shattered, with no hope of returning to the way it was before. Yet there are diamonds among the shards, if you can see them. Your challenge here is to let the chaos be and to remain calm and patient despite the turmoil. Have faith: the Great Round is ever turning, and this time does not last forever. Pick bright, clashing colors for this mandala. Let go of trying to make the finished mandala look anything other than ugly. How is this approach different or the same from what you usually do? Make a few notes about this in your journal, if you like.

MANDALA OF TEARING APART
Materials You'll Need:
Basic Art Materials (see page 36)
Old cards, letters, school papers, etc.

The Mandala of Tearing Apart allows you to experience the duality of destruction and creativity. In order to make something new you must also destroy something. A jar of paint is consumed to make a painting. A bag of clay is emptied to make pots. Before making an omelet you must first break the eggs. Another word for this process is *transformation.*

Draw a circle on a piece of colored construction paper. Choose another sheet of construction paper in a different color and tear it into pieces. (You might also tear up old cards, letters, school papers, sheet music, or credit card slips). Arrange the torn and broken pieces in a design inside the circle, but do not glue down. When your design is completed, pick up the paper, and jostle it. Glue down the torn paper pieces in the random design that emerges. Respond to your jostled design. How do you like it? What was it like to incorporate random activity into your design? (See plate 30.)

Now tear apart your mandala and hold all the pieces in your hands. Notice what feelings this stirs up for you. How is this like or not like other experiences you have had of Stage Eleven, Falling Apart? Put the torn pieces down and write your response to the Mandala of Tearing Apart. Now write positive messages on each torn piece. For example, *life is a blessing, an ending is a beginning, hope comes in through a broken heart.* Collect the pieces in a special bowl. Any time you feel the need for encouragement, draw out a piece and read what is written on it.

MANDALA OF YOUR LEAST FAVORITE COLOR
Materials You'll Need:
Basic Art Materials (see page 36)
Black construction paper, 12" x 18"
Assorted paper scraps in many colors, patterns, and textures
Glue
Glitter

We all have personal qualities that have been tucked away from awareness in our unconscious. These comprise our *shadow.* Perhaps we were born into a family that already had a talented athlete, so our athletic ability is not recognized and falls into our shadow. Some families prefer outgoing displays of emotion as a means of working through issues, so they may unintentionally inhibit their children from developing their natural think-ing ability. Thinking then becomes a quality of the child's shadow.

Our shadow is like a mirror image of our ego, the person we know ourselves to be. In order to live out all our potentials, recognizing the tal-ents and capacities concealed in the shadow is part of our journey toward wholeness. By discovering and integrating the personal qualities of our shadow, we regain energy that was bound up in keeping these things hid-den from ourselves. The Mandala of Your Least Favorite Color is a gentle approach to learning something about the hidden shadow self.

Draw a circle on the black paper and set aside. Choose your least favorite color from the assorted paper scraps. With your journaling ma-terials, engage in a dialogue with this color.

Addressing the color, begin by writing:

You are ___.

You make me feel ___.

You remind me of ___.

Next, take the part of the color, and write as if you *are* the color responding to what has just been written.

You are ___.

You make me feel ___.

You remind me of ___.

Now switch back to being yourself in the dialogue and respond to what the color has *said.* Continue going back and forth until you feel your conversation is at a natural stopping point.

Now tear into pieces the paper that is your least favorite color. Ar-range all the pieces of your least favorite color inside the circle on black paper. Do not throw any pieces away. You may layer the pieces to fit all of them into your circle. You may add other colors in and around your circle to create a design you like. Be sure to use all the pieces of your least favorite color. Glue or tape your pieces in place.

The feelings you express about your least favorite color often reveal something about your shadow. For example, if you say to your color, "You are too strong" or "too smart" or "too bright," the qualities of strength, intelligence, and charisma are probably part of your shadow. By including all the pieces of your least favorite color in the circle of your mandala, you are graphically bringing them closer to your conscious identity.

In order to further integrate the shadow contents represented in your mandala, re-write the statements beginning "You are ___" to read "I am ___." This will help you take back some of the projections that have been pushed out of your ego into the shadow.

MEMORY MANDALA
Materials You'll Need:
Basic Art Materials (see page 36)

We have all had experiences of things falling apart. Perhaps a car we were counting on for work transportation suddenly quit running. Or a tight deadline for a project was missed because you caught the flu. Maybe a decade birthday causes you to become unraveled in ways you never expected, and you find yourself dissolving into tears for unknown reasons. Yes, we have all survived *falling apart,* and we are here today, wiser for having done so.

There are skills we have learned about navigating this segment of the Great Round of life. Past experiences are a rich source of information about ways we can take care of ourselves, and the Memory Mandala helps you discover what you already know about this. However, many of us may still believe that *falling apart* is a catastrophe. It is not. It is just another natural step in the cycle of living a full life: no better or worse than any other.

Draw a circle on white paper and set aside.

Now turn to your journal. After a few deep, relaxing breaths, reflect on times when things fell apart for you: a destructive storm cut off your electricity, you lost your college scholarship, your spouse asked you for a divorce. In your journal write about one of these times. What was it like for you? Describe the energy you had (or did not have) during that time.

Now set aside your journal and turn to the circle. Using your drawing materials, express that energy of *falling apart* with colors and lines inside your mandala circle. You may draw and fill a second or even a third circle with the energy. When the energy subsides, go to the next step.

Reflect on your past experience as you witness your mandalas. Let yourself recall any good that came from the *falling apart*: finding a book that changed your life for the better, developing a friendship you would not have had otherwise, learning about a previously undiagnosed illness. Returning once again to your journal, remember and write about the gifts, discoveries, and new growth that came from your experience of *falling apart.*

In and around your mandalas add colors and forms to reflect the personal growth you experienced during your time of fragmentation. As the layers of media thicken, you might also be able to scratch patterns in with a blunt tool, as well as drawing, painting, or collaging them.

Once again turning your thoughts to the same past experience of *falling apart,* remember ways that you comforted and cared for yourself. Whom did you call on? What books, poems, or Biblical passages gave you hope? What activities helped you release pent-up energy? How did you take care of your needs for healthy food, rest, and companionship? Returning to your journal, write about whom and what was helpful then.

Remembering that the experience of *falling apart* is natural during some stages of life, what can you do now in your creative and spiritual practices to refine your skills for the next visit to this stage? Perhaps you could select comforting music and have it on hand. Is there a tree you know of that could be a comfortable place to lean for awhile? Are there meditation, yoga, or dance techniques you find especially grounding? What works best for you? Write a list of all these actions and activities for nurturing yourself.

Add the nurturing activities to your mandala in written or graphic form. Having reminders of soothing, self-nurturing activities can itself be helpful because sometimes it is hard to think during Stage Eleven,

Falling Apart. But why wait until you fall apart? Choose at least one self-nurturing activity every day from your list and enjoy doing it as a way to take good care of yourself.

MANDALA OF PEOPLE I DISLIKE
Materials You'll Need:
Basic Art Materials (see page 36)
Magazine images of people

Most of us like to think well of ourselves. Early in life we repress behaviors our loved ones do not like. We cultivate behaviors of which they approve. In this way our ego takes shape as what is *good* in us and our shadow becomes the depository of what is rejected as *bad.* This is a necessary trade-off that allows us to live in civilized society. However, some of the qualities relegated to our shadow do not need to be there. They can be recognized and gradually integrated into our ego.

Stage Eleven, when things fall apart, is challenging to our ego, especially if we pride ourselves on being competent, reliable, and clear headed. When we fall apart, we are forced to learn that we are also incompetent, unreliable, and confused. Our proud ego falls apart temporarily. Falling apart can be a step toward wholeness.

When we can tolerate the truth about ourselves and integrate shadow qualities into our conscious ego identity, we can become wiser, more tolerant, humble, and more resilient. The Mandala of People I Dislike is an exploration of your personal preferences. It may also help you learn more about your shadow.

Draw a circle on a sheet of construction paper in a color you find unpleasant. Look through magazines to find pictures of people who irritate you. They will probably reflect qualities of which you disapprove, looks you find disgusting, or behaviors that are alien, bizarre, or unlawful. Arrange your images into the circle and glue them in place. Reinforce your drawn circle to make it a strong container for your unpleasant Mandala of People I Dislike.

Study the people in your mandala and write in your journal as if you were speaking openly to each person in turn. Finish the phrases, "I don't like the way you ___," "I am disgusted that you ___," "It bugs me that you ___," "Why can't you ___ like other people?"

According to Jungian psychology, we often project our own unsavory characteristics onto others as an unconscious mechanism to avoid seeing them in ourselves. If you wish to go further in processing this mandala in order to take back some of your projections (with the goal of growing toward greater wholeness), follow these directions: replace "you" in your journaling with "I." Read your revised phrases aloud to yourself. Then write more in your journal about what it is like to hear these statements applied to you. When you can admit to even a tiny bit of truth in your "I" statements, you are reclaiming some of your projected energy and enjoying an expansion of consciousness.

CRAZY QUILT MANDALA
Materials You'll Need:
Basic Art Materials (see page 36)

Crazy quilts are a time-honored art form for using up the dregs, the fragments, the leftovers and castoffs of clothing and fabric. They are constructed from random pieces with the only pattern being that there is no pattern. The Crazy Quilt Mandala honors the thrift and creativity of people who made something warm, useful, and beautiful out of things that had fallen apart. It is a good teaching example of what is possible for us in our growth process when we fall apart.

On a sheet of white paper draw a circle and randomly divide it into wedges or sections by drawing lines from side to side (you need not run lines through the center point of the circle). Color each section differently. Experiment with colors you would not ordinarily use or that clash, in your opinion.

When your mandala is complete, cut or tear it into random pieces. (Pay attention to how it feels to destroy your mandala.) Using all the pieces of your deconstructed mandala, create a new design using a piece of black paper as a *quilt* background. You may add other materials to your design if you wish. Let your design suggest the form of a circle.

Give your artwork a title and record it in your journal. Then write your response to the artwork and the process of bringing it into being. Construct a poem from your journal writing. One way to do this is to begin your poem with the title of your artwork and use words from your journaling that catch and express the essence of your art-making process. Add the poem to your artwork.

VARIATION
Use cloth scraps instead of paper.

MANDALA OF BROKEN MIRRORS
Materials You'll Need:
Basic Art Materials (see page 36)
Broken or breakable mirror (smaller than the surface you wish to cover)
Ceramic tile pieces (optional)
**Plywood piece, tabletop, wooden tray, or other surface suitable
    for mosaic (in a size you can work with comfortably)**
Combination mastic and tile grout
Hammer
Cloth or sturdy plastic bag
Protective hand and eye gear
Metal rim/wooden frame to edge your piece

When things fall apart, we can be left feeling broken. It can be a great comfort to have something outside ourselves that mirrors our inner experience of fragmentation. Creating the Mandala of Broken Mirrors gives you an opportunity to take ownership of the process of destruction and to claim the equally powerful response of creativity. The Mandala of Broken Mirrors can be a metaphorical action for recalling and bringing order into the memory of a painful event from the past (see plate 31).

Draw a circle on the surface on which you will apply the mosaic and set aside. Wearing protective hand and eye gear, place the mirror in the bag and tap it with the hammer to break it into random fragments. Pieces of approximately 1" square or larger are easiest to work with. Next, apply mastic/grout on the mosaic surface according to the directions on the package. Arrange the broken pieces of mirror in the grout to create a circular design. Continue adding pieces until the entire surface is covered. (You may wish to fill the background with a different material, such as stones or ceramic tile.) Allow to dry. Add a metal rim or wooden frame to finish the edges of the piece. Apply grout according to directions to fill in all cracks and spaces.

Look at your fragmented reflection in the Mandala of Broken Mirrors. You will see yourself, and yet not the usual reflection you are accustomed to seeing. This strange new likeness can be a mirror of your experience of personal growth. You have changed, but feel disjointed until you get used to your new way of being. This mandala is a reminder that the circle holds: you are here, just growing and changing.

VARIATION

Use old dishes, teacups, ceramic tiles, jewelry, eyeglasses, and other cast-off and broken things that signify what you are releasing or surrendering at this time. (See plate 32 of Diana Gregory's mandala of her old pairs of glasses.)

FALLING APART MANDALA
Materials You'll Need:
Basic Art Materials (see page 36)

Music creates an atmosphere that guides us into a state of being and stays with us through our experience. Music offers us the reassurance of sound, melody, and rhythm. We can then carry forward our music experience into creative self-expression with art media. This is the logic behind the Falling Apart Mandala.

Draw a circle. Sit quietly, singing Maureen Shelton's "Falling Apart" (see appendix C, page 284). From the feeling stirred by the song and your singing, move into self-expression with your art materials. Set your hands free to express what this stage of separation, confusion, and transformation is like for you.

When your mandala is complete, place it a few feet away from you and witness it without judgment. In your journal describe what you see, and what it was like to sing and create your Falling Apart Mandala. Store your mandala in a safe place if you want to keep it. If you choose to let it go, release it with intention and ceremony.

SCRATCH ART MANDALA
Materials You'll Need:
Basic Art Materials (see page 36)
Sharp stick, plastic fork, or similar scratching tool

When emotions are strong, we may need a mandala that helps us both contain and express our feelings. This mandala is a variation of a favorite elementary school art-making project.

Draw a circle. Then, using crayons or oil pastels, fill the circle with a jumble of brightly colored shapes. Bear down on your crayon or oil pastel to cover the paper inside the circle. Next, take black crayons or oil pastels and completely cover the brightly colored shapes inside the circle. Now with your scratch tool, scrape a random pattern of lines through the black layer to reveal the colors underneath.

When your mandala is complete, witness it by looking at it without judgment. Then respond to your mandala in your journal. Address the question: "What was it like for me creating this mandala?"

MANDALA OF ABIDING ORDER
Materials You'll Need:
Basic Art Materials (see page 36)
Two photos or drawings of large circular flowers, approximately 4" to 8"
    across, one smaller than the other
Cardboard, tagboard, or construction paper

When we embrace the view that life is comprised of ever-repeating cycles of beginnings and endings, we have a sense of enduring order beneath apparent fragmentation, chaos, and falling apart. Paying attention to the natural cycles of life around us, we see evidence of this ancient viewpoint. Beneath the decomposing plant is another ready to sprout. The Mandala of Abiding Order is a meditation on this way of looking at life.

Draw a circle. Cut out the larger of your two flowers and glue it inside the circle. Now cut out the smaller flower. Cut it into square pieces (approximately 1/2" to 3/4" in size). Transfer these pieces onto the larger flower. Arrange pieces in such a way that the background flower is discernable, while leaving about 1/2" in between pieces of cut-up flower. When your arrangement is complete, the first flower should be visible between the pieces of the second flower. Now glue the loose pieces in place. In your journal, respond to the fragmentation and perfect order in your mandala.

PIZZA MANDALA—WITH EVERYTHING (A GROUP MANDALA)
Materials You'll Need:
Pizza dough
Tomato sauce
Cheese
Pizza toppings of your choice, such as sundried tomatoes, olives, onions, sausage (cooked and crumbled), green and red peppers, mushrooms, artichoke hearts

The theme of the agricultural cycle is to harvest and transform plants so that human beings can digest them. The process of eating is a destructive act that allows our bodies to live, be nourished, and create energy. Mythic stories of the self-sacrifice of the Mesoamerican gods of maize and corn elevate taking in food to a sacrament. The Christian Mass is also considered a sacramental meal.

The Pizza Mandala is a light-hearted approach to the intentional ingestion of food. This project is also an opportunity to create and consume a mandala. You and your group can make of this an amusing group activity, an enjoyable bonding experience, or an intentional symbolic sharing of the fruits of the group experience.

Cut up the ingredients. Use plenty of onions. Shedding a few tears will season the Pizza Mandala nicely. Spread tomato sauce on pizza-dough round, then top with ingredients. During preparation, you may enjoy sharing your associations to the ingredients. Do they remind you of something you are letting go of now? Bake the pizza in a 400 degree oven for 15 to 20 minutes or according to your recipe's directions. How does it feel to surrender your mandala to the oven for transformation? Cut up, share, and enjoy the Pizza Mandala with your group. What is it like to eat your creation?

Reflecting on Stage Eleven

Stage Eleven has been an exploration of the theme of *falling apart*. You have experienced this through your mandalas with broken mirrors, shadow work, and crazy quilt designs. Entropy as a part of nature's life cycle informs the qualities of this stage. If you lit a candle at the beginning of your creative session, blow it out before continuing with your review of Stage Eleven. Enjoy a stretch or a cup of tea. These activities help mark your transition from creating to reflecting.

As you review your experiences with the mandalas of Stage Eleven, what stands out as especially significant? What have you learned about yourself from the process? What is the essence of your understanding of Stage Eleven, Falling Apart? Let your reflections provide a starting point for developing your Mandala Card Eleven.

MANDALA CARD ELEVEN
Materials You'll Need:
Basic Art Materials (see page 36)
Cardboard, tagboard, or other stiff material
Collage images

Make a card in the size and shape you prefer. Utilize collage, painting, or drawing to develop your imagery for your Mandala Card Eleven. Include a mandala that conveys your experience of *falling apart*. Your design might resemble a piece of shattered glass, a pie cut into wedges, or a scramble of chaotic lines. Add more images, words, textures, and colors to complete your card design. Allow to dry flat. Store your card in a safe place.

Opening to Grace

Stage Twelve coincides with December, the darkest month of the year. Indeed, the longest night of the year, the winter solstice, takes place during this month. Many cultures have special holidays that bring light into the darkness: Christmas, Hanukkah, and Diwali are a few. This stage is reminiscent of midnight darkness lit only by phosphorescent plants, glowing insects, and reflective animal eyes. In terms of a human lifetime, Stage Twelve resonates with the wisdom of old age.

Stage Twelve invites you to lean into the ground of your being, the Self, trusting in this source of continuing support during the ups and downs of your personal journey. Touching into a sense of order beyond that created by your ego allows an *opening to grace.* Paradoxes that were once disturbing are resolved through non-rational means. Your inner contradictions are transformed into a new, more complex identity.

This stage marks the blissful coming together of a fragmented ego in a new alignment. During this stage your ego is a transparent locus of consciousness. You are self-aware, but fully grasp the importance of your relationship to a Higher Power. You can accept that the ego functions as an expression of the dynamism of the Self, your inner wisdom. You embrace the ego's inability to know everything about who you are and accept trustworthy mystery as your companion.

When you find yourself in Stage Twelve, you may feel like a new person and an old soul. As a result of the realignment of ego and Self during this stage, powerful energy is channeled by the ego. Peak experiences are not unusual during Stage Twelve. Instead of feeling invaded by light as in Stage Eleven, you may experience yourself as radiating light.

Stage Twelve is a time of release from the intense emotions of Stage Eleven, Falling Apart. A review of the past is often part of the process.

Looking anew at past events can realign their pattern of meaning and allow a great *Ah hah!* to emerge where there was only pain, confusion, and anger before. During Stage Twelve we can experience joy, relief, love, and forgiveness.

We may come to an appreciation of all the experiences that have made us the person we are in this moment. Perhaps we can look back over a period of time and see the turning of the Great Round through it all. This helps us understand the enduring order beneath the flux and flow of ordinary reality. Once fully integrated, the qualities of Stage Twelve allow us to feel calm acceptance and readiness for whatever is to come next.

Kellogg calls this stage *Transcendent Ecstasy*. Some experience this stage during sexual orgasm. Others come to this enlightenment after hard struggles with their dark, hidden selves. Those recovering from addictions understand this path. Women speak of having an ecstatic feeling after natural childbirth. Near-death experiences, and perhaps death itself, belong in this stage as well. Christian mystics describe this state as *union with God.*

Once experienced, there is a desire to savor this stage again. Practices such as fasting, ritual food and drink, sweat lodge, vision quest, and extended periods of prayer, meditation, chanting, singing, and dance may be viewed as ways to access the heightened awareness associated with Stage Twelve. The experience may also occur spontaneously, triggered by a stunning sunset, by suddenly appreciating a loved one's uniqueness, or even by sensing an evocative fragrance. Mandalas often arise spontaneously in response to the experience of *opening to grace.*

> This space is like a volcanic ecstasy or bliss; hence, it has an active, rather than receptive, orgasmic nature, an exploding diffusion of boundaries where one becomes and generates light rather than being invaded by it. —Joan Kellogg

Intentions for Stage Twelve

Stage Twelve seems to be nature's way of preparing us to die a good death. Most often, however, it announces our rebirth: we take the essence of this turning and carry it like a seed into the next circling the Great Round. The task of Stage Twelve is to humbly accept the gifts of *opening to grace.*

With this stage the turning of the Great Round is complete. Here we can look back and grasp the essence of this journey through the stages. While Stage Twelve is a completion, it is also preparation for a new beginning that commences with Stage One on the next turning of the Great Round. And so the Great Round continues in the mandala that is our life.

Stage Twelve Mandalas

Mandalas of Stage Twelve tend to have simple, luminous forms against a dark background. They often display glowing flowers, glistening trees, or fountains of light. Chalices or other vessels filled with light are also seen. Patty's mandala (plate 33) is an example. Human figures with arms held wide in ecstasy may appear in mandalas of this stage. Birds in flight, effortlessly breaking through the mandala circle, are typical. Illumination pouring down from above, suggesting an intense light source outside the circle, is another motif of Stage Twelve mandalas.

Colors tend to include darks—indigo, black, purple—and pastels such as pink, peach, blue, yellow, light turquoise, and lavender. White may be applied over colors, giving a lustrous *pearlized* effect that, according to Kellogg, is often associated with mandalas reflecting a spiritual experience. The mandalas of Stage Twelve are lovely, uplifting, and awe-inspiring.

Exercises

In preparation for creating the mandalas of Stage Twelve, take some relaxing breaths and perform the meditative yoga movements suggested (appendix B, page 270). You might want to light a candle or incense before you begin your creative session. Go slowly through the mandala exercises, allowing yourself time to savor them and enjoy your experience with the stage of *opening to grace.* Take note of what you like or dislike about the mandalas of this stage. What is hard or easy for you about Stage Twelve? Are you comfortable with ecstasy? Why or why not?

MANDALA OF RECEIVING GRACE
Materials You'll Need:
Basic Art Materials (see page 36)
Coloring Mandala 12 (see appendix A, page 251)

During Stage Twelve of the Great Round, you drink from the cup of wisdom. You grasp the pattern of your life in all its infinite beauty. Past and future merge into the eternal Now. Here, by the grace of God, not by willing or effort, you come to know the Mystery of Life. Explore the use of iridescent pastel colors against a dark background when coloring this mandala. Do some journaling about your mandala and what it means to you.

MANDALA OF OFFERING UP
Materials You'll Need:
Basic Art Materials (see page 36)

After the *letting go* and the *falling apart* of the previous stages comes a peaceful time when we can truly release what is beyond our control. We can forgo the emotional debt owed to us by another. We can entrust what we do not understand to a Higher Power. We are ready to offer up whatever we cannot hold.

Perhaps being born into a privileged life leaves you with a burden of guilt when you hear how poor many in the world are. Guilt can be good when it sensitizes us to the needs of others and motivates us to help. However, sometimes guilt can lead to feeling helpless and overwhelmed, and we become frozen in indecision. Offering up such guilt to your Higher Power (for of course we are not responsible for where we are born) can clear your energy to be open to the right thing to do.

A mandala to signify surrendering your guilt to your Higher Power for safekeeping might include, for example, a white bird in flight (symbol of your Higher Power) carrying away a purple heart (your guilt) against a background of rainbow colors (your cleared energy). This is just an example. Use your own symbols to give this exercise personal meaning.

After your mandala is completed, and you have had ample time to process its imagery through journaling or witnessing dialogue with a trusted other, you may consider a ritual of offering it up. Perhaps you will transform your mandala into prayer flags or place it in your garden where the elements will reclaim it gradually.

ECSTATIC MANDALA
Materials You'll Need:
Basic Art Materials (see page 36)
Black drawing paper, 12" x 18"
Glitter

Ecstasy is a natural human experience. It is described as a feeling of transcendence, a sense of being one with all, of merging into cosmic consciousness. Most people have had such experiences at some time in their lives. Descriptions in Western cultures tend to be in religious terms: a visit to heaven or being in the presence of a revered being such as Jesus. The state of ecstasy can also occur as a runner's high, as the result of a strenuous vision quest, or in association with natural childbirth. In Jungian terms, ecstasy can be thought of as an intimate connection between ego and Self.

The Ecstatic Mandala gives you an opportunity to reflect on your personal experience of transcendence. Draw a circle. Black paper contrasts beautifully with the pastel colors typical of Stage Twelve (pink, blue, yellow, green, lavender, and peach). Colored chalks and pastels work best. Take a few deep, relaxing breaths, and perform the suggested yoga posture in appendix B (see page 270).

Let yourself remember an experience of natural ecstasy from some time in your life. Perhaps it came to you after a hard, dark, painful period. Or it might have been a delightful surprise, a moment of grace like a stunning sunset. Your moment might have come when you were a child swinging, rolling down a hill, or whirling to the point of intoxication. You might find that singing the song "Let It Sing" (see appendix C, page 285) will help stir your memory.

Recall as much as you can the light, texture, taste, sounds, and emotion of your experience of ecstasy. Perhaps you will write in your journal for awhile as you explore your memories. Let an image, color, or line emerge as a starting point for your Ecstatic Mandala. From this beginning let your mandala unfold. You may find that you need glitter, simple drawings, or cutout magazine images in your mandala. Staying as close to your sensory memory of ecstasy as possible, continue working until your mandala is completed. Step back and look at it. Reflect on what you carry from that numinous experience that informs your life in the present moment.

MANDALA OF LIGHT AT THE CENTER OF DARKNESS
Materials You'll Need:
Basic Art Materials (see page 36)
Black, white, or colored paper, 12" x 18"
Glitter or glitter glue

Stage Twelve is a time of *opening to grace.* A deeper resolution of our inner conflicts is possible here under the aegis of the Self. This is a time of completion, fulfillment, and synchronicities. The paradoxical language of Western mystics describing their encounters with God can inform us about the qualities of this stage. They speak of "darkness beyond light," "a dazzling darkness," and "darkening [that] gives light" (Grant 1985, 223–31). The Mandala of Light at the Center of Darkness is a guided exploration of the mystery at the source of the feeling of transcendence.

Select your paper and draw a circle. Then relax and breathe. In your imagination, focus on absolute darkness without form. You may close your eyes if you wish. Continuing to breathe and focusing on what you see in your mind's eye, notice a tiny point of light appearing in the darkness.

Allow the point of light to grow and shine brightly in the darkness. Observe as the light takes on a discernable shape. Fix this image in your memory and gently open your eyes. Carry your image of light into your Mandala of Light at the Center of Darkness. Use drawing or painting to show, as best you can, your interior image of light. (Some people find they must go a bit outside the circle when creating this mandala.) When complete, place your mandala on a home altar. Turn to your journal to write about your mandala, the experience of creating it, and about what it brings to your altar.

MANDALA OF THE SACRED CHALICE
Materials You'll Need:
Basic Art Materials (see page 36)

A sacred chalice is a footed cup holding liquids for ritual imbibing, for pouring libations, or for collecting blood from ritual sacrifices. The Holy Grail was a legendary sacred chalice thought to have been used by Jesus at the Last Supper for a ritual of sharing wine with his disciples. Some consider the chalice a womb symbol as well. A chalice, like a mandala, is a container for sacred energy. The Mandala of the Sacred Chalice serves as a container for the essence of your experience of the Great Round.

First, draw a circle. Then sit quietly and reflect on your experiences throughout the cycling process described thus far in this book. Let a sense of the richness of your experience come into your awareness. In your circle draw the image of a chalice. In your chalice, translate the richness of your exploration in the Great Round through activities described in this book into an object or symbol that signifies the experience of greatest value to you during this process of discovery.

In your journal, respond to your artwork by answering these questions: "What does this mandala tell me about myself, my values, and my life journey?" and "What am I taking with me from this experience into the next turning of the Great Round?"

MANDALA OF TRANSIENT BEAUTY
Materials You'll Need:
Basic Art Materials (see page 36)
Colored powder (spices, herbs, coffee, dry tempera paint, glitter, etc.)
Womandala Bag from Stage One (optional; see page 50)

Stage Twelve is an ecstatic realization of the completion of a cycle. It is a looking back over the previous stages to appreciate the overall experience. It is also a time to realize that the cycle keeps moving: we are experiencing that things are not permanent. Though nothing is ever really lost, change is never ending. The Mandala of Transient Beauty is an exploration of the ongoing change that is life.

Write on a piece of paper a word, a phrase, or a sentence or two describing the essence of your experience of Stage Twelve, Opening to Grace. Kindle a safe fire and burn the piece of paper with your words written on it. Collect the ashes and mix them with a colored substance you find pleasing: a spice, dry powdered tempera, colored sand, face powder, baby powder, or glitter. Place the mixture on a piece of black paper.

Shape the material into a mandala using only your hands. Let the image in your mandala resemble a fountain of light, birds taking wing, or a sacred flame. When complete, step back and appreciate your accomplishment. Respond to your creation by writing about the process and what the image represents for you. Write about how it is to know that your mandala is transient and will not last long.

To complete work on your Mandala of Transient Beauty, choose how you wish to transform it. You might carry it to your compost pile and add it to the mix there. You could tip your mandala into a special pot for keeping or let the wind at the top of a hill carry the bits away. Or you might funnel the mixture of ashes into the Womandala Bag you created for Stage One. In this way, the remains of the Mandala of Transient Beauty will be a seeding of your next journey through the stages of the Great Round.

DANCING YOUR BODY MANDALA

Dancing is a time-honored way of expressing ecstasy. We can create ecstatic mandalas through the dances we perform and the movements we make. Jung commented that some of his patients preferred to express their mandalas as dance movements. Dancing Your Body Mandala is a way to explore creating a body-centered mandala.

Go to a place where you feel safe and where you are able to move freely. Choose music that makes you want to dance. Begin by performing the yoga movement suggested for this stage (see appendix B, page 270). When you feel ready, start the music. Take a standing position and focus on your body's center point, just behind and a little below your navel.

Let an urge to move begin deep within your center and flow out through your limbs as spontaneous movement. Do not push yourself. Tuning in to the sense of your body as a mandala, move as your body wants to move. If you lose attunement to your center, stop. Relax. Breathe until you feel connected to your center again. Then tune in to yourself as a mandala. Allow the music to support you as you move. Enjoy.

MANDALA OF THE WINTER SOLSTICE
Materials You'll Need:
Basic Art Materials (see page 36)
Wreath of grapevine or evergreen
Holiday ornaments (optional)
Florist wire
Wire cutters

Stage Twelve coincides with the month of December. The winter solstice, the shortest day and longest night of the year, takes place around December 21. Take a few moments to reflect on what this event means to you. Perhaps you will revisit memories of the events of the past year. This turning of the year may usher in a busy holiday season for you. Or it may be your custom to retreat into spiritual contemplation during this part of the year. You may simply be glad to have the promise of light in the form of lengthening days to come after the solstice.

Ask yourself: "What do I want to observe, celebrate, or honor during this season?" "How do I choose to do it?" "With whom?" "When?" Write your answers in your journal. Resolve to share your preferences for celebrating the season with your family and friends and negotiate to get to do what you would find meaningful.

Now let this personal exploration be the basis for the creation of your Winter Solstice Mandala. Attach decorations to your wreath that show what is important to you. These could include photos, flowers, ribbons, favorite verses, fruit, or ornaments of straw, bread dough, clay, glass, wire, paper, and wood. Display your wreath where you can look at it often during the darkest time of the year. You might want to place it on a tabletop so that you can add candles for lighting on the evening of the winter solstice.

MIND'S EYE MANDALA

Only your imagination is required for the Mind's Eye Mandala. This is a mandala you construct in your mind's eye as you read the guided imagery suggestion below. You might like to make an audio recording of yourself reading the guided imagery or invite a trusted friend to read it aloud while you visualize. Pause between sentences to allow optimal visualization. Eastern religions create mandala visualizations as an important part of their spiritual practice. The Mind's Eye Mandala was originated by me and has no connection with spiritual practices of any faith tradition.

Begin by settling into a comfortable sitting position. Relax your body. Take some deep breaths in and out, relaxing more with each out-breath. Prepare to read or listen to guided imagery for creating the Mind's Eye Mandala. If you would like, close your eyes.

Imagine that you are comfortably seated on a soft cushion placed on top of a mountain. There is a warm shawl around your shoulders. On your tongue there is the taste of honey. You are breathing in and out, relaxed, alert, focused. Fresh cool air touches your face and fills your lungs.

Looking around, you see a long view of mountains and valleys of rich green forests, mossy boulders, and lively streams bounding down rocky ravines. In the far distance, rising above the horizon, you notice a tiny speck. As you watch, it becomes larger, moving toward you. Now you can see that it is a creamy white, pink, and golden Peace Rose, opening its velvety petals as it comes floating nearer to you.

The flower, as large as the biggest hug, comes to a pause a few inches in front of your face. Emitting a delicate fragrance, its golden center radiates light as the petals are gently ruffled by the breeze. As you breath in, the flower's scent enters your body as a feeling of peace. Continuing to breathe naturally, imagine that with your next inhalation, your breath carries the rose into your heart center. There, the rose with its glowing aureole of petals radiates love in the form of light.

Allow the light to enter, ease, and release any tightness, pain, or discomfort you might be feeling. Now, if you wish, imagine the light bathing all your organs in radiant healing energy, touching each and every cell in your body, bringing you health and wholeness. Rest in this peaceful light for a few moments.

Now imagine that the light filling your body converges once again in your heart center. As it comes together, notice that it is forming a mandala of many colors. Observe with your mind's eye as it takes form. Does it fix on a design? Or does it continue to shift like a kaleidoscope? There is no right or wrong way. This is your mandala, created by you, just for you.

When you feel you have completed your Mind's Eye Mandala, send it in your imagination to the place where you want it to be. Perhaps you will send it someplace you can call on it later. Or perhaps you will prefer to release it permanently. It is up to you. Notice as it fades from view. Say a silent goodbye as it passes out of sight.

Now gently return your attention to your body. Notice the surface on which you are seated. Feel how your body is firmly supported. Gently rotate your shoulders, move your feet and hands, and slowly open your eyes. Breathe normally as you glance around your room. When you are ready to bring your Mind's Eye Mandala experience to a close, clap your hands together.

Reflecting on Stage Twelve

Stage Twelve is the grace-filled conclusion of the stages of the Great Round. This stage marks the end and the preparation for the next beginning. Opening to the ecstasy, harmony, and wholeness of Stage Twelve challenges us to accept the gifts of the moment. What are your memorable experiences of this stage? Carry these into creative expression as you develop your Mandala Card Twelve.

MANDALA CARD TWELVE
Materials You'll Need:
Basic Art Materials (see page 36)
Cardboard, tagboard, or other stiff material
Collage images

Cut out a card in the shape and size you prefer. Stage Twelve is the last in your series of mandala cards. The theme is *opening to grace.* With collage materials, drawing, or painting, create Mandala Card Twelve. On your card develop a mandala that includes a chalice, a fountain of light, or celestial birds. Add other images, words, textures, or colors to complete your card design. Allow card to dry flat. Store in a safe place.

Stepping to the Center

You have created mandalas for the Twelve Stages of the Great Round. Now it is time to fulfill the mandala of the Great Round by looking back over your process and all that you have created. Just as adding the center point to a circle establishes a sense of order and sets in motion the dynamic connections between center and circumference, this chapter offers activities that bring together the experiences and insights gained from exploring stages separately. This work may stimulate new insights, even as it creates closure with your process of exploration. Perhaps it will help you appreciate that the Great Round itself is a mandala.

In completing our process of the Great Round, we are *stepping to the center,* a place of integration. Here you can see the patterns in your experiences, take stock of your strengths and your challenges as shown in your mandalas, and appreciate the accomplishment of your exploration of the twelve stages. There are more suggestions for mandalas to express and contain your experience. And in doing the activities in this chapter, you will be seeding yourself for future turnings of the Great Round.

Exercises

Before beginning, collect the mandalas you created based on suggestions in the earlier twelve chapters of this book. Assemble your Basic Art Materials. You may want to light a candle or incense to mark the opening of a time of reflection, exploration, and creativity. Relax and prepare by performing the Yoga Mandala of the Great Round (see appendix B, page 271), which moves you kinesthetically through all twelve stages. Moving beyond Stage Twelve, we find ourselves in a time of reflection about the entire cycle of the Great Round. This, too, is an important step in the cycling process. Taking stock of the experience can truly bring your Great

Round to completion. Keep your journal nearby to respond in writing as you explore the exercises suggested below.

MANDALA OF LOOKING BACK
Materials You'll Need:
Basic Art Materials (see page 36)

Think back to the beginning of your journey. What were your hopes, fears, and intentions embarking on the twelve stages in *The Mandala Workbook*? Next, reflect on where you are now. Then respond to the following questions in your journal or discuss with a trusted friend:

What was my intention (what did I expect) going into this process?

What has surprised me?

What has disappointed me?

What has hurt me?

What am I grateful for?

What have I learned about myself?

What have I learned from others and about others?

What have I learned about mandalas?

What will I take with me from this exploration of the Great Round?

From your journaling identify the essential gift(s) for you of the past days, weeks, or months you have spent creating mandalas with the guidance of this book. Write these in a list, a sentence, or a poem. Now draw a circle and create a mandala that incorporates words, poems, or images expressing the gifts you have received.

MANDALA OF THE GREAT ROUND MANDALAS
Materials You'll Need:
Your mandalas from the Twelve Stages of the Great Round
Journal for writing

Gather the mandalas you have completed for the Twelve Stages of the Great Round. Arrange them together in a large, composite mandala. Choose the place for your mandala layout with care: will it be a room with good light, your favorite spot in the garden, or perhaps even a computer-generated collage of your mandalas scanned into your PC?

Place Stage One at the bottom of your arrangement and then go clockwise around so that Stages Two, Three, Four, Five, and Six are on the left of the large mandala circle. Stage Seven belongs opposite Stage One. Stages Eight, Nine, Ten, Eleven, and Twelve are arranged along the right side of the large mandala circle.

Take time to appreciate the colors, lines, and symbols that you have used. Notice where a motif or color first appears and how it re-appears in a slightly different form in later mandalas. This shows your growth process. Respond to your Mandala of the Great Round Mandalas by writing in your journal or inviting a friend or friends to witness your process along with you.

EXPLORING YOUR OPPOSITES
Materials You'll Need:
Your mandalas from the Twelve Stages of the Great Round
Journal for writing

Arrange your mandalas in the layout described in the preceding exercise. Now let us examine the layout of your mandalas in a way that highlights the dynamic relationship between opposite stages of the Great Round. In this exposition we can see that the opposite stages reflect the ends of a continuum. For example, Stage One exemplifies darkness, the unconscious, and formlessness or non-ego. Opposite is Stage Seven, the experience of intense light, consciousness, and individuality. The axis between Stage One and Stage Seven is actually a continuum of gradations of light and dark, conscious and unconscious, individuality and formlessness or non-ego.

This connection means that each stage implies its opposite. For example, experiencing Stage Ten, Letting Go, naturally suggests qualities of Stage Four, Beginnings, as well. In a similar way images of springtime can be aroused by our experience of the dark days of fall.

The Self is both the source and the final destination of the dualities of the stages. As we transit through the stages of the Great Round, we come to know the stages as qualities of the ego. The middle point encompassing the dualities of the continuum is the Self. Living from the center, one has the ability to be fully present in the ego stage of the present moment while holding awareness of the opposite stage. Ultimately, one is capable of seeing through the duality to the overarching wholeness of the Self.

Arrange mandalas from each of the Twelve Stages into these six pairs:

Stage One and Stage Seven (dark/light, feminine/masculine, body/mind)

Stage Two and Stage Eight (potential/manifest, formless/formed, fluid/solid)

Stage Three and Stage Nine (moving/still, shifting/crystallized, growing/ grown)

Stage Four and Stage Ten (beginning/ending, birthing/dying, new me/old me)

Stage Five and Stage Eleven (unity/fragmentation, tight/loose, centered/un- centered)

Stage Six and Stage Twelve (conflict/tranquility, agony/ecstasy, initiation/ completion)

These pairs represent opposite stages on the Great Round. Examine your mandalas and respond to the following questions:

Which mandalas resulted in the pairing that is most interesting to you? Describe why and how you find these mandalas so meaningful together.

What surprises you most as you examine these pairings of your mandalas?

What can you now see looking at this arrangement of your mandalas?

Write out the titles you gave your mandalas, in the pairing order given above. This is your poem entitled "Exploring the Opposites." Read your poem aloud. What do you notice as you read your poem? Perhaps you can turn to your journal to respond or write more poetry inspired by your mandalas.

Are there other mandala pairings you would like to explore? What are they and what do they tell you about yourself and your process?

MANDALA OF THE GREAT ROUND OF THE YEAR
Materials You'll Need:
Basic Art Materials (see page 36)

The twelve-month year comprises a Great Round. Since ancient times this round has been a mandala used for explaining the passage of time, for tracking the changes in the sun's light, and for accounting for the cycles of plants and animals. Creating this mandala can be a useful year-end reflection. It can help you review the previous year in order to prepare for the new year.

On a large piece of paper draw a circle. You may want to divide it into twelve sections, one for each month. Reflect on the past year of your life. Go month by month, noting major events, turning points, name changes, achievements, losses, regrets, gratitudes, and wisdom. In your mandala find a way to honor all that you have lived during the past year. Share your mandala with a trusted friend or loved one.

LITURGICAL YEAR MANDALA
Materials You'll Need:
Basic Art Materials (see page 36)

The Liturgical Year Mandala allows you to focus on the spiritual experiences of the past year. On a piece of paper (approximately 36" x 36") create a circle. You may structure the mandala with months or with markers of the liturgical year of your faith tradition: the seasons, holy days, fast days, feasts, saint's days, solstices, and other observances.

Review your spiritual biography for the year and place symbols in your Liturgical Year Mandala to express your challenges, rewards, and insights during this time. In the center of your mandala, place the symbol of your personal guide, or your Higher Power, as you understand him or her now, after the year's lived experience. Place your mandala near your home altar as a guide for contemplation.

MANDALA OF THE TWELVE ASTROLOGICAL SIGNS
Materials You'll Need:
Basic Art Materials (see page 36)
Books on astrology (optional)

The zodiac is a mandala created as a map of the heavens. Observations of the constellations led to the development of its twelve astrological signs. This archetypal map of the Cosmos is one of the sources for the Great

Round. Creating the Mandala of the Twelve Astrological Signs is an opportunity to explore your responses to these ancient potentials.

On a piece of paper (approximately 36" x 36") draw a circle. Divide it into twelve segments. Represent an astrological sign in each segment, expressing your impression of the qualities of each sign in its segment. You may wish to consult a book on astrology for your mandala. The European signs are Aries, the ram; Taurus, the bull; Gemini, the twins; Cancer, the crab; Leo, the lion; Virgo, the virgin; Libra, the scales; Scorpio, the scorpion; Sagittarius, the archer; Capricorn, the goat; Aquarius, the water carrier; and Pisces, the fish.

When your mandala is complete, reflect on the way you have expressed each astrological sign graphically. Considering the zodiac as a venerable expression of the cycle of the Great Round, explore your visual impressions, thoughts, and feelings about each sign. Which ones are you attracted to? Which ones repel you? What do your responses tell you about yourself and your journey? Write in your journal or discuss with trusted others.

MEDICINE WHEEL MANDALA
Materials You'll Need:
Stones (at least thirteen; approximately 4" to 6")
Feathers, flowers, colored sand, poems, candles, and more as you wish

Orienting to the four cardinal directions is a human activity that has been an important basis for creating mandalas. Knowing one's physical whereabouts helps with psychological orientation as well. Even now, such orientation to physical space can be nurturing.

Inspired by the Native American custom, this Medicine Wheel Mandala can be a lasting outdoor mandala for all seasons. Choose a flat, open, yet secluded area outside. Place a stone to mark the center of your Medicine Wheel Mandala. Determine where magnetic north is. Facing north while standing over the center stone, place a stone a foot or two from the center stone.

Stones placed to your right and left as you stand in the center facing north will mark east and west. Put a stone opposite north to mark south. In each of the spaces between the stones marking a cardinal direction, place two evenly spaced stones. You will now have a circle of twelve stones and a single stone marking the center.

You may wish to use traditional Native American associations to the directions. East represents springtime, south is summer, west is fall, and north is winter. Perhaps you would like to place a special marker near the spot where your birthday falls on the wheel. Add feathers, flowers, colored sand, poems, or candles to embellish your Medicine Wheel. Your Medicine Wheel Mandala might also become a special place for honoring birthdays of family and friends and acknowledging the passing of the seasons of the year. Placing markers on the wheel to mark the time of death for those who have recently passed away could be a comforting ritual.

The Medicine Wheel Mandala can also be a quiet place to meditate and get your bearings both physically, with reference to the clearly defined cardinal directions, and psychologically, by being held in the balanced wholeness of the fourfold circle.

MANDALA OF CARDS
Materials You'll Need:
Basic Art Materials (see page 36)
Cards created for the Twelve Stages of the Great Round
Storage box for Mandala Cards

For each stage of the Great Round you have created a mandala card. Now gather them together to form your completed deck of twelve cards. You might consider laminating your cards to reinforce them. Choose a special box, bag, or folder for their permanent storage and decorate it appropriately. Place your mandala cards inside for future use. Here are some suggestions:

1. Arrange your cards in a Great Round circle, beginning with Stage One at the bottom of the circle and moving clockwise. Reflect on

what you see in your Mandala of Cards. Respond by writing in your journal.

2. Choose a card at random from your deck of mandala cards. Reflect on the stage it represents and let this guide your reflection or stimulate your creative process.

3. Spread your mandala cards face down on your altar or a table in your meditation space. Pose a question or concern and pick a card at random from your deck to stimulate your thinking and imagination as you explore the question.

4. Place a different card from your deck of mandala cards on your altar each day, week, or month as an aid for focusing your meditation.

WOMANDALA BAG REPRISE

During Stage One you created the Womandala Bag and placed inside it a symbol of your intention for your journey of the Great Round. Now open your Womandala Bag and do one of the following:

1. Respond to the bag and its contents by writing in your journal. Re-read your intention and reflect on how it has come to fruition.

2. Develop a poem that expresses the whole of your journey that began with the creation of your Womandala Bag and the intention(s) you set in motion then. What are the lessons from this journey?

3. Place a new intention in your bag as a seed for your next journey of the Great Round.

GROUP CLAY MANDALA
Materials You'll Need:
25-pound bag of clay
Paper and pen or pencil
Table covered with sturdy paper or poster board

Art therapist Edna Bacon, a member of our mandala group, led us in this Group Clay Mandala experience. Edna attributed her inspiration for this mandala to the work of M. C. Richards. This was an enjoyable and enlightening activity for us to share together. May it be so for your group as well.

Distribute a double handful of clay to each person seated at the table. Roll your clay into a snake and have each person in the group do the same. Then connect the ends of all the clay snakes until you have formed a single large circle of clay. Rest your hands on the portion of the clay circle in front of you. Relax and breathe deeply. Close your eyes if you wish.

Reflect on the various stages of your journey as a member of the group. Remember where you were at the beginning of your journey and where you are now. Allow your hands to gently work with the clay, letting the energy that comes through your fingers manifest as indentations or texture. The only rule: do not break the circle. Open your eyes. Continue shaping your segment of the circle. Negotiate with neighbors where your portion of the clay circle touches theirs.

When the group comes to a comfortable stopping place, clean your hands and reach for paper and pen or pencil. Writing on a separate piece of paper or on the paper table covering itself, find a word or phrase that describes your section of the circle. Write down this word or phrase. Leaving your written word in your space, shift one place to the left, having all group members do the same.

Witness the clay in your new place and respond in the same way with a word or phrase written on the paper there. Continue shifting to the left, noticing the clay circle in front of you, and writing a word or phrase in response, until you are once again in the place where you started. Now each person takes a turn reading what they and others have written. Listen to these spoken words as a spontaneous poem voicing the countless interconnections among the members of the group.

Together as a group, choose a place to break the clay circle. Then working as a team, wind the circle, now one long snake, gradually into a tightly coiled spiral sculpture. While pinching the coils together upon the flat tabletop, protect the individuality of each person's section of the circle as much as possible. Once the piece is coiled, take a few moments to appreciate your group's mandala.

Decide together what to do next with your creation. It could be taken through the steps of clay production to become a finished piece. Each group member might take a piece of the wet clay mandala with them as a memento of the group. Or the clay might be respectfully returned to its container, to be available for future clay work.

Our group elected to carry our Group Clay Mandala to a special place outside where winter rains would cause it to melt into the earth. After placing it on the ground under a huge oak tree, we decorated it with pine cones, sticks, and bits of grass. Then stepping back, we joined hands in a circle around the Group Clay Mandala, shared a few words and poems, said our goodbyes, and gave each other hugs to mark the end of our group.

ENSO
Materials You'll Need:
Black ink or paint
Paper
Large flexible brush

Enso is a Japanese word meaning "circle." Enso paintings are associated with Zen Buddhism. The enso signifies enlightenment, the universe, and the circle of life. It is thought that the quality of the enso reflects the personality of the artist. An enso is a unique expression of you during a never-to-be-repeated moment. It seems a fitting conclusion to *The Mandala Workbook* (see image on next page).

Arrange your art materials for painting. Stretch and relax your body, then sit quietly with your materials in front of you. Take some deep relaxing breaths, focusing on the sensation of breath coming in and breath going out. When you feel ready, pick up your brush, dip it in ink or paint, and paint a circle in one stroke. This is your enso.

Reflecting on the Stages of the Great Round

The activities of Completing the Circle have given you opportunities to explore more deeply the mandalas inspired by *The Mandala Workbook*. You have learned ways to make use of your personalized deck of mandala

Enso

cards. This chapter has also offered guidance for creating several mandalas that encompass the whole of the Great Round. And you have created an enso, an empty circle that expresses who you are at this moment in time. In creating the enso, you link with the empty circle of Stage One and the next turning of the Great Round. What will it bring you this time around?

The Mandala Workbook has guided your exploration of mandalas for insight, healing, and self-expression. The exercises offered were inspired by the rich and varied uses of mandalas in cultures both ancient and modern. Through movement, drawing, painting, fiber art, mosaic, clay work, cooking, singing, and imagination you have created images of wholeness. The Twelve Archetypal Stages of the Great Round have given structure to your journey and brought the mandala exercises into one great mandala. And so it is that by arriving at this paragraph, you are completing the mandala that is *The Mandala Workbook.* May this experience continue to inform your life journey in positive ways.

Mandala Templates and Coloring Mandalas

This section includes full-sized illustrations of grids required for mandalas of Stages Seven, Eight, Nine, and Ten. These are intended to augment the smaller illustrations accompanying the text of these chapters. You may use the larger illustrations as a reference for your drawing. Or, if you are very impatient, you might prefer to trace the grids shown here as a first step in your creation of the mandalas that require these structures.

Also included are coloring mandalas meant as a warm-up exercise to each of the twelve stages.

Squaring the Circle

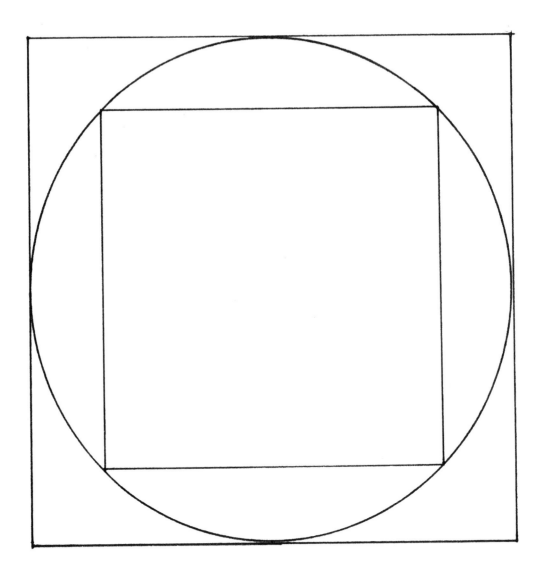

Five-Pointed Star

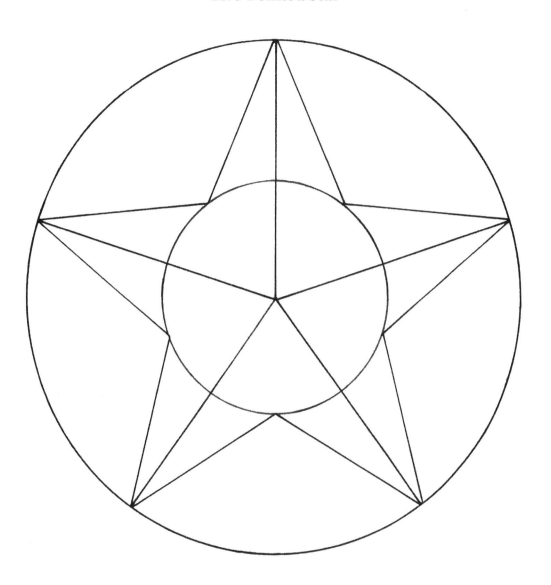

Pinwheel

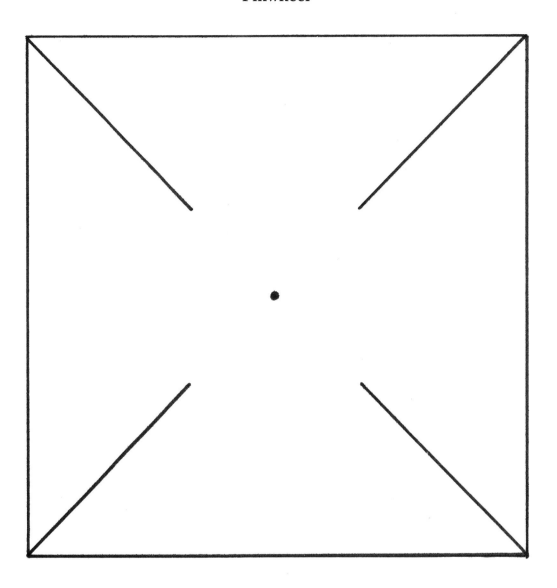

Basic Mandala Grid

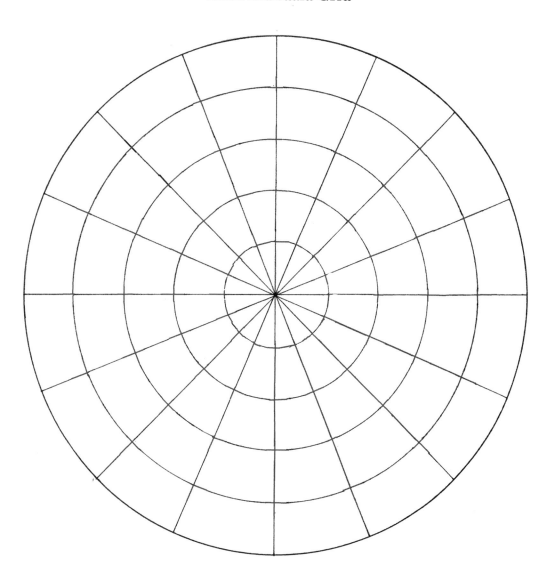

Coloring Mandala 1

Coloring Mandala 2

Coloring Mandala 3

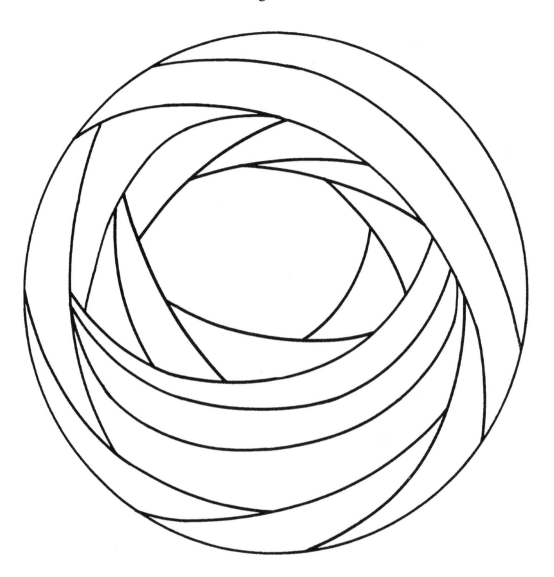

Coloring Mandala 4

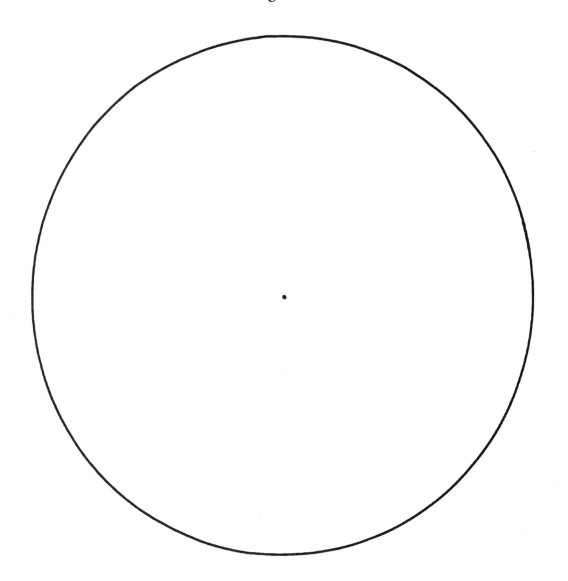

Coloring Mandala 5

Coloring Mandala 6

Coloring Mandala 7

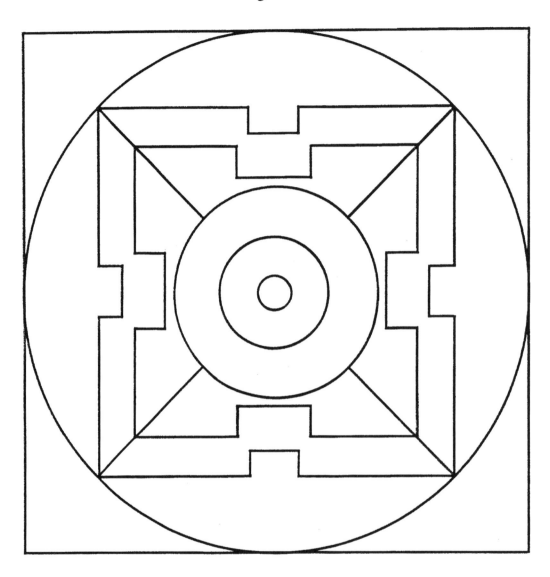

Coloring Mandala 8

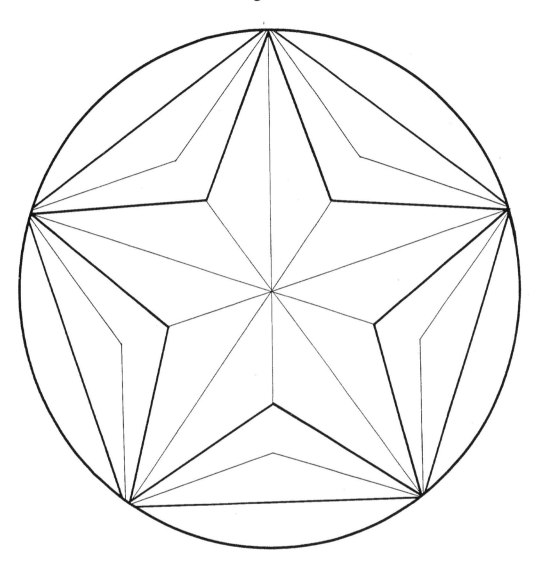

Coloring Mandala 9

Coloring Mandala 10

Coloring Mandala 11

Coloring Mandala 12

Yoga for the Great Round

These yoga movements were developed by Patty O'Keefe Hutton, a member of our mandala group. The yoga movements are helpful for relaxing, centering, and balancing prior to self-expression with art media. They also evoke the quality of energy associated with each stage, and so they can be a helpful first step into exploring a stage of the Great Round. Also, a number of the yoga movements create kinesthetic mandalas that offer a body-centered exploration of the stage with which they are associated.

It is suggested that you study the yoga movements so that you can perform them in preparation for a session of creating mandalas. Drawings illustrate the yoga movements. Written instructions accompany the drawings.

A compilation of the yoga movements, the Yoga Mandala of the Great Round, is also offered. It allows you to experience the yoga movements for all twelve stages of the Great Round in a seamless flow. This creates a kinesthetic experience of the Great Round and so allows you to integrate your experience of these archetypal stages in your body.

Stage One, Resting in the Darkness

CHILD'S POSE

Begin on your hands and knees, taking a moment to connect with your breath. Inhale deeply and on the exhale lower your hips down toward your feet, while your head moves to or toward the floor (see figure a). This should feel like a resting pose, so use any variation that helps you feel comfortable. (You can widen your knees; place your hands, your fists, a pillow, or a block under your forehead; or you can do this pose seated in a chair with a pillow on your thighs.) Once you are settled, close your eyes and begin *resting in the darkness.*

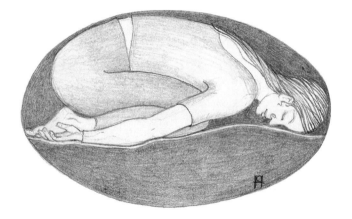

Find your breath. Notice where it goes when you are curled up like this. Do you feel your breath in your back? Does it move throughout your whole body? Use your breath to release, to relax, and to sink deeper into your Child's Pose. Take twelve deep breaths here, wrapping yourself around the gift of breathing.

Stay connected to your breath while you explore the qualities of Stage One. Perhaps you will meditate on what it is like to be waiting, receptive, hibernating, and unformed potential. You might imagine yourself as a seed: patient, quiet, gathering energy. Take your time allowing this energy to fill you.

When you are ready, ever so slowly, begin to rock in your Child's Pose. Let your hips sway from side to side a little, then a little more. Then, when it feels right, allow your hips to gently fall to one side, so that you can come into a fetal position for a few breaths. When you feel ready, taking all the time you need, bring yourself gently back up to a seated position.

Stage Two, Floating into the Light

HAPPY BABY POSE

Starting in Child's Pose (see figure a), roll gently onto your left side. Tucking your knees up close to your chest and placing your hands under your

Figure b. Happy Baby Pose

head like a pillow, enter the cozy space of the fetal position (see figure b, top). (To find more comfort in this pose, use a pillow under your head or between your knees.) When you have found your most restful position, breathe into it. Notice how the breath moves you when you let it.

Imagine you are lying comfortably in bed during those last dreamy moments before fully waking, grateful for the sensuous pleasure of being in your body. This is the feeling quality of Stage Two. When you are ready, languidly roll onto your back.

Bend your knees so that your thighs come as close to your torso as they can and lift your feet up toward the sky. Now reach up and grasp your feet with your hands. You can modify this position by rolling a towel lengthwise, grasping the ends in each hand, and letting the soles of your feet push up on the towel in a sort of upside-down jump rope position. Using the weight of your hands, playfully pull down on your feet, bringing your knees wide and in toward your body, into Happy Baby Pose (see figure b, middle). Breathe twelve breaths here as if you are a contented infant. Let your breathing be slow, deep, and trusting. Find in yourself the qualities of Stage Two: fluidity, openness, peacefulness, being one with nature, receiving blessings, loving, optimism, and curiosity. Can you sense that you are being rocked upon the waters of a gentle world?

When the time feels right, softly roll over onto your right side and into the fetal pose (see figure b, bottom). Rest until you are ready to float up into a seated position. Knowing yourself as loving and infinitely loved, connect with your breath to ponder the infinite possibilities of Stage Two, Floating into the Light.

Stage Three, Turning Toward the Journey

HIP ROTATION

To begin, softly ease yourself into Child's Pose (see figure a), roll to a fetal position on your side for a few moments, and then leisurely roll onto your back. Let yourself sense within a desire to move. This is where the journey begins in Stage Three.

Figure c. Hip Rotation

Interlace your fingers and place them behind your head. Breathe deeply and on the next exhale, bring your left knee up toward your chest, letting your right leg stretch out and touch the floor. (A pillow under the extended leg will take pressure off your lower back.) Begin to rotate your raised knee clockwise in a tiny circle (see figure c).

Slowly and by small increments, expand the circle outward in a spiral, letting your breath inform the movement, until you create a big, sweeping circle with your knee. Circle six times with your knee. (If you should hear a *thunk* in your hip, do not worry. So long as it does not hurt it is completely normal.) Gently extending your leg, continue the spiraling movements until you have swung your leg in its largest circle six times. Notice how the energy quickens!

The quality of Stage Three is much like this movement: becoming active, waking up with growing awareness of a sense of energy, life force, and heightened consciousness. Can you imagine yourself floating on the ocean doing this movement?

Once you have completed the sixth circle with your leg extended, gradually slow the movement down until you can change the direction of your spiraling. After six sweeping rotations in the opposite direction, begin to bring your foot in close to your body so that you can return to spiraling with your knee. Then let your knee make smaller and smaller spirals until you find your smallest circle, and finally come to a stop. Lower your foot to the floor and slowly stretch your left leg down beside your right leg. Do you notice a difference in how your right and left hips feel? Sensing such differences is also a quality of Stage Three.

Now bring your right knee up toward your chest and repeat the yoga movements on the right side. When you have finished, let both legs gently drop onto the floor, stretch them out side by side, and rest. While you are resting, envision the energetic spiral mandalas you have already created with your movement and intention in the air above you.

Stage Four, Embracing the New

HERO POSE AND UPPER SPINAL FLEX

From Child's Pose (see figure a), inhale and roll the spine up slowly, vertebra by vertebra, until you are sitting on your heels. (If you feel any strain in your knees or ankles you can place a pillow under your thighs, between your legs, or under your ankles. If none of these modifications work, feel free to come into any comfortable seated pose.) Try to keep your toes pointing back behind you so your weight rests on your feet and ankles. Place your hands on your thighs. Allow your back to lengthen from tailbone through the crown of your head by relaxing, lifting your chest, and dropping your shoulders (see figure d).

Now you are in Hero Pose, a good place for beginnings. Actively engage with your breath, and as you do, begin the slightest of spinal flexes:

Figure d. Hero Pose

as you inhale, let your chest expand outward; as you exhale, pull your belly in and round your back. Breathe deeply, twelve slow and conscious breaths as you open and activate something new in the spine. Imagine you are holding within your center something tender and new. You do not even have to know what your *something new* is! For now, let it be enough to nurture, bond, protect, affirm, and embrace whatever is growing within. You might breathe into it as something sweet and precious, residing just under your heart.

When you are ready, continue your relaxed breathing but allow the spinal flexing movements to become smaller and smaller until these movements cease. You are now resting in your center. Take a moment to breathe in the loving embrace of stillness.

Stage Five, Claiming Selfhood

FORWARD BEND, MOUNTAIN POSE, AND ARM CIRCLES

Beginning in Hero Pose (see figure d), come forward onto your hands and knees, and gently shift your feet flat onto the floor. Slowly straighten your legs, keeping your hands on the floor if possible. (If you feel any discomfort in your lower back you can widen your stance, bend your knees, and/or allow your hands to rest on your ankles or calves.) This posture is

Figure e. Mountain Pose and Arm Circles

a Forward Bend. Relax and take this opportunity to release anything that you do not need for the experience of Stage Five.

Now begin to curl your spine upright, straightening your back vertebra by vertebra, inhaling as you move. When you come to a standing position, let your arms hang relaxed as you exhale and roll your shoulders up, back, and down. Take a few deep breaths here in Mountain Pose (standing actively on the earth with your head in the sky). Picture yourself standing in the center of a target, fully balanced on your standpoint. Now imagine a target growing out from your heart center.

On the next inhale, extend your arms out to the side, parallel to the earth, with your hands in fists. Exhale, extending the pinky fingers of both hands out to the sides (see figure e). This will activate your heart meridian, a source of courage. Begin making very small circles with your whole arm, with the pinkies of both hands extended as if they were crayons and you were coloring in the center of a bull's-eye. Then expand the circle a bit to create the next ring of the targets. Make two more rings, each a bit larger than the last. Now make your widest circles, inscribing them six times. Slow the movement and then reverse the direction for six large circles. Then make the next-smaller-size circle, and finally complete the bull's-eyes. Inhale deeply here in the center, then exhale and allow your arms to float back down to your sides.

Take a moment to re-connect with your breath in Stage Five. Stand right where you are, *claiming your selfhood* and establishing your identity. If you feel any pressure here, remember that this stage is helping you to grow. Take courage.

Stage Six, Igniting the Inner Fire

MOUNTAIN POSE AND ANGEL WINGS

Start in Mountain Pose, standing with feet together, arms at your sides, grounded through your feet into the earth, while reaching toward the sky with the crown of your head. (If you have lower back issues, place your feet shoulder width apart or a bit wider until you feel comfortable.)

Figure f. Mountain Pose and
Angel Wings

Drop your shoulders and take a moment to feel the aliveness inside your
body. Become aware of your breath. Notice how your body feels on the
in-breath, and then again on the out-breath.

Bring your hands consciously into a prayer position (hands palm to
palm and finger tips over your heart). Take a few deep breaths here, going within. Inhale and lift your hands straight up to the sky, opening your
heart center as your chest expands with the breath. Exhale as you bring

your hands wide and down, creating a big circle around your heart. At the bottom of the circle, bring your hands once again into prayer position as you lift through the center of your body on the inhale and create your widest circle on the exhale (see figure f).

This is the Angel Wings rotation. Repeat this flowing movement six times, ending with your hands at your heart. Now reverse the direction of your circle, bringing your hands down with the exhale then circling wide and up with the inhale. Repeat your Angel Wings rotation six times in this direction as well.

While breathing into this movement reflect on the opposites that exist within you: left and right, up and down, inhale and exhale, hard and soft, open and closed, yin and yang. Now recall any issue you feel conflicted about. Use the movement and the breath to gather both sides of the issue in to your center. As you move and breathe, allow yourself to experience the contradictions, holding the dilemma softly within. Breathing in, we open and receive. Breathing out, we allow what is to be as it is.

End with your hands in prayer position over your heart. Take a moment in the silence to become aware of the complex and amazing being that you are, standing in your own truth and making your way.

Stage Seven, Squaring the Circle

THREE-PART HEALING BREATH

Begin in Mountain Pose (see Mountain Pose and Angel Wings in Stage Six), lifting through the top of your head, grounding through the bottom of your feet, relaxing downward with the hands and the shoulders. Find yourself in a place of balance and power. Take a moment here to imagine yourself on top of the Great Round, feet firmly planted, as if you are standing on top of the world. When you feel firmly grounded, begin the Three-Part Healing Breath.

This yoga practice involves breathwork linked with movement. The breath is made up of three deep, strong inhales followed by one releasing exhale. With the first in-breath, move your arms up and extend outward

Figure g. Mountain Pose and
Three-Part Breath

in front of your body. Without exhaling, move on to the second in-breath, and let the arms reach out to the sides. Still without exhaling, breathe in and let your arms reach up over your head. Now your lungs are full of good energy. Balance here for just a moment. Then exhale completely, sweeping your arms forward and down, releasing and dropping into a forward bend, letting your fingers almost touch the floor. (Sound is highly recommended on the exhale!) Then begin again, inhaling up to a standing position, keeping your back as straight as is comfortable, and ending the first inhale with your arms out in front again (see figure g). Continue, repeating the whole sequence twelve times.

As you move and breathe through this process, use the breath to activate your courage and imagine that your energy is as bright and intense as the noonday sun. Feel yourself filled with firmly balanced power. Acknowledge your ability to learn, to plan, and to love. From this point of power you are ready and willing to take a stand on what you know within yourself to be true. Feel the confidence that comes with knowing that you are equipped with all the tools and skills you need. Use this healing breath to release anything that you no longer need for your life journey and open yourself to receive whatever you will need to live a life according to your own values.

Stage Eight, Functioning in the World

MOUNTAIN POSE AND STAR POSE

Stand in Mountain Pose (see Mountain Pose and Angel Wings in Stage Six), tall in your body, creating a link between the earth and the sky. With your feet holding onto the earth, focus on this important connection for a moment. Now, feel the pull of gravity from your waist down to your feet and the pull of the stars from your waist to the top of your head. Hold this pose with intention and energy for a few deep breaths.

Inhale deeply and on the next exhale, step your right foot out to the side about a leg's length. Turn your toes in toward each other, finding a comfortable wide-angled stance. On the next inhale, let the breath lift your arms up until they are parallel to the earth with your palms facing down. Let your gaze be steady before you as your chin tucks in slightly (see figure h).

Now you are in Star Pose. Take twelve powerful breaths here, feeling your body reach out in five different directions: down through the legs, out through the arms, and up through the top of your head. In Stage Eight you find yourself standing firmly on your own two feet, arms reaching out to touch the world. Possessing a clear sense of self, you reach out to others, taking pleasure in the work of co-creating. Breathe into this wonderful pose and feel the expansiveness of your body and your being as you open yourself to life. This pose is said to honor the Goddess Tara,

who removes all obstacles from the paths of sentient beings, according
to Tibetan Buddhism and Hinduism. While standing in this pose, take a
moment to honor the bright star that is your very own self as well.

Stage Nine, Reaping Rewards

THE GREAT STRETCH WITH WIDE-ANGLE FORWARD BEND
Begin in Mountain Pose (see Mountain Pose and Angel Wings in Stage
Six), with your hands in prayer position (touching palms and fingertips
over your heart). Close your eyes for a moment and breathe deeply until
you feel relaxed, balanced, and clear. On the next inhale, extend your hands
up toward the sky as far as your arms will reach, keeping hands together,

Figure i. The Great Stretch with
Wide-Angle Forward Bend

into the Great Stretch (see figure i). Breathing into this pose, notice the
effort and aliveness in your body as you stand tall on the earth. Now, step
your right foot out to the side, bringing your arms out to your sides and
parallel to the earth. Now exhale, folding over into a Wide-Angle Forward
Bend. Then let hands drop down with fingers almost touching the floor.
Inhale back up to your Great Stretch, bringing your feet together again
and allowing the breath to fill your lungs and lift you up. Continue this
movement twelve times, aligning your movement with your breath.

As you move, imagine you are embodying the energy of *reaping rewards* during Stage Nine. This complex and harmonious movement balances you as you reach up to the heavens and then bow down to the earth. Envision yourself standing poised at the pinnacle as you reach up and then releasing all attachments as you bow forward. When you are ready, let this movement come to a satisfying close. As you rest in stillness, allow yourself to experience the sense of fulfillment, accomplishment, and enhanced self-esteem that comes with a job well done.

Stage Ten, Letting Go

THE DANCER

In Stage Ten you will find yourself stepping out in a way that can feel unsteady, reaching beyond your comfort zone, and possibly even losing your balance. To experience this state through yoga, begin in Mountain Pose and then move into the challenging balance pose called the Dancer. (Feel free to position yourself near a wall or chair for support. Just remember, losing your balance or being a bit shaky is very appropriate during Stage Ten.)

From Mountain Pose, shift your weight onto your left foot and find your balance. Inhale, and lift the right leg up and back behind you (here's where that chair might come in handy) while reaching back with your right hand to grasp (if possible) the inside of your right foot. Find your balance. If you are comfortable and would like to risk stretching further, reach out in front of you with your left hand, keeping it parallel to the earth with the palm facing down. Allow your torso to arch forward as you lift the back hand and foot into a graceful arch, opening your heart (see figure j).

When you have found the pose that you can maintain with a bit of concentration, hold it for six deep breaths. Then inhale and lower the back foot, bringing your spine up tall and allowing both hands to float down. Shake out your feet a bit and then find your balance on your right foot. Inhale, lifting your left foot up and back, repeating the process for six breaths on the other side. Then softly return to standing.

Figure j. The Dancer

Anything can happen in Stage Ten. You might wonder, "What now?" or "Is that all there is?" Your customary ways of being may feel empty and meaningless. Maybe an adventure is just about to begin. Who knows? Perhaps you will encounter spirit guides or a dark/wild/dangerous being blocking your path, just like in the fairy tales. Will you be asked to make a sacrifice? You could surrender to losing your balance. You may even choose *letting go*.

Stage Eleven, Falling Apart

FREE FORM YOGA OR THINGS FALL APART POSE
Stage Eleven calls for something a little bit different, so this will be a very un-yogic yoga pose in which we allow things to fall apart. First, create

a safe space within which to move, possibly placing a pad, blankets, or pillows around you. Start either sitting down or lying on the floor as you begin to imagine yourself breaking free, dissolving into formlessness, or having no center at all. What movement would embody that for you?

Remember, this is the stage where you are called to surrender to separation, face a loss of meaning, and encounter your shadow self. The movements you create do not have to look any certain way and they certainly do not have to look pretty. This movement is for you alone. Allow it to emerge organically as you delve into the crazy quilt of Stage Eleven. Take your time exploring this moving meditation on the transformational energy of fragmentation (see figure k).

When you are ready, bring your movements to a close, ending in any comfortable position. Breathe deeply and remind yourself that you no longer have to *hold it together*. Release and relax any muscles that are still trying to hold on. Breathe deeply, experiencing this place of purification as you gently remind yourself that quite often the *dark night of the soul* makes possible a miraculous regeneration of life.

Stage Twelve, Opening to Grace

EASY POSE WITH OPEN ARMS AND TWIST

Sit with legs comfortably crossed in Easy Pose, or any seated pose you prefer. Take some conscious breaths. Notice where the breath moves in your body and gently bring your hands into prayer position. Bow reverently to the faithful beating of your own unique heart. Raise your arms upward, creating the shape of a chalice (see figure l). Imagine you are being filled by light from an ineffable loving source somewhere above you. Notice how your consciousness can become alert, active, and diffuse as you allow yourself the sense of being suffused by the light.

Inhale facing forward and then exhale into a gentle, slow twist toward the left. Inhale slowly back to center and then exhale and twist gently to the right. Continue to twist gently to the left and right. With your deep knowing of the rightness of the Cosmos, you can reach beyond the circle, open to the energy that flows so freely. You can sense that you are at one with all, uplifted, and filled with feelings of joy, harmony, and reverence. As you gently twist with your arms upstretched, it is as if you are making an entrance in an open horse-drawn carriage, a gondola, or a dark convertible. A homecoming! You gently rotate from the waist, fully open to the gifts of wisdom that come from completing a turning of the Great Round.

Allow the movement to become smaller as you find your way to *center*. Exhale and let your arms float down to your sides, bringing them together and up once again into prayer position at your heart. Take a few deep breaths here. Honor yourself and your journey, as you acknowledge that getting to the place of true center comes through *opening to grace*.

Figure I. Easy Pose with Open Arms and Twist

Yoga Mandala of the Great Round

Revisit your journey with this flow of movement through the Twelve Stages of the Great Round: a Yoga Mandala. As usual, make adjustments, use props, or opt out of any movement that hurts you or does not feel comfortable or steady. If you want more information about movements, refer back to the in-depth instructions in this appendix.

Begin by sitting in Easy Pose with legs comfortably crossed and your hands in prayer position at your heart. Take a moment to connect with your breath, bringing consciousness to this present moment. Set an intention for your Yoga Mandala practice as you deepen your breath, listening within to sense the aliveness in your body.

STAGE ONE, RESTING IN THE DARKNESS

Take a deep breath in. On the exhale, release your hands down and lean forward onto your hands and knees. Adjust yourself so you feel comfortable and then on the next deep exhale, drop your hips back down toward your heels, allowing your head to gently drop toward the floor into Child's Pose. Take twelve deep breaths here.

STAGE TWO, FLOATING INTO THE LIGHT

Ever so tenderly and gently, roll to the left from Child's Pose into a fetal pose. Breathe three deep relaxing breaths here and on the next exhale, roll onto your back. Adjust yourself, bringing your knees toward your chest and grasping your feet with your hands into Happy Baby Pose. Take twelve deep breaths here. On the last exhale, roll over into a fetal position on your right side. Take three relaxing breaths.

STAGE THREE, TURNING TOWARD THE JOURNEY

From your fetal position on the right side, roll once again onto your back. Interlace your fingers behind your head. Bring your right leg down onto the floor and your left knee up toward your chest. Begin creating tiny circles with the left knee. Expand the motion until it begins to spiral outward, slowly increasing the size of the spiral. When you get to the outer edge of your spiral, circle six times and then change the direction, circling six times in this new direction before beginning to spiral inward, making the spiral smaller and smaller until your knee becomes still in the center of the spiral. Now, stretch the left leg down, bring the right knee up and repeat the knee spirals on this side. When you have finished, roll into a fetal position on your left side. After a deep breath here come back up into Child's Pose.

STAGE FOUR, EMBRACING THE NEW

From Child's Pose, inhale yourself up onto your hands and knees. Take one deep breath here and on the exhale sink back onto your ankles into

Hero Pose. Place your hands on your thighs, taking a few deep breaths. Begin a subtle spinal flex: as you inhale, let your chest expand outward and as you exhale, pull your belly in and round your back curving your spine as you engage the abdominal muscles. Repeat this flex twelve times, linking the movement with the breath. When you bring the movement to a close, find your center of balance and breathe into the energy that is moving through your body.

STAGE FIVE, CLAIMING SELFHOOD

Now, lean forward onto your hands and knees. Gently move your feet underneath you with knees bent. Take a deep breath and on the exhale begin to straighten your legs, bringing yourself into a forward bend. Take three deep breaths here and then on the next inhale, roll your spine up vertebra by vertebra until you exhale into standing. Find your Mountain Pose. Bring your arms up parallel to the ground with your hands in fists. Extend your arms, and moving your whole arm with pinky fingers extended, begin to draw targets on either side with your pinkies. When you reach the largest circumference of your target, circle six times, change direction and circle six times in the other direction before making the circles progressively smaller until you find the bull's-eyes at the center again. Release your hands and on an exhale, allow them to float back down to your sides. Settle into Mountain Pose.

STAGE SIX, IGNITING THE INNER FIRE

Bring your hands up into prayer position at your heart and take three deep breaths. On the next inhale bring the prayer position up above your head, opening, and circling the arms wide and down on the exhale. Repeat this heart opening movement six times and then reverse the direction: bring your hands together and down the centerline of your body on the exhale and then out and circling wide and up on the inhale. When you have finished, bring your hands into prayer position at your heart and take three long, deep, relaxing breaths.

STAGE SEVEN, SQUARING THE CIRCLE

Exhale your arms down and to your sides. From here we will engage in the three-part healing breath, taking three strong breaths in for every exhale. On the first inhale bring your arms out in front of you with palms facing down. On the second inhale, bring your arms out to the sides with your palms facing down. On the third inhale bring your hands parallel over your head with the palms facing one another. Pause here for a moment. Feel the breath filling you and then exhale forward and down to a forward bend, releasing energy and sound on the exhale. Repeat this sequence twelve times. Pause on your last forward bend. Take three deep breaths here and then on an inhale, roll your spine up to standing. Settle into Mountain Pose.

STAGE EIGHT, FUNCTIONING IN THE WORLD

From Mountain Pose step your right foot out to the side at a comfortable wide-angle stance. Point your toes in toward each other a bit as you lift up through the head. Inhale your arms up parallel to the floor. Feel the energy moving in the five directions of your Star Pose. Hold this position for twelve breaths. Then, on an exhale, let your arms float down and on the next inhale step your right foot back to center. Take a few breaths in your Mountain Pose as you feel the expansion that these movements bring.

STAGE NINE, REAPING REWARDS

Bring your hands to your heart in prayer position. As you inhale, lift the prayer position as high as you can comfortably reach, coming into the Great Stretch. Exhale your left foot out to the side as you bow forward, bringing your arms up and parallel to the ground. Inhale back up to the Great Stretch and back down into Wide-Angle Forward Bend twelve times, continually linking the movement to the breath. End in your Wide-Angle Forward Bend, working your feet back together until you are in a Forward Bend. Take three deep breaths here and then inhale, rolling your spine back upright, giving yourself a big shoulder roll when you get to the top of your rise.

STAGE TEN, LETTING GO

Find your balance in Mountain Pose and then shift your weight onto your left foot. Inhale your right foot up behind you as you reach back with your right hand to grasp the inside of the right foot. Breathe into this balance pose, inhaling your left arm out to the front, and arching forward, lifting the back foot and hand. Hold this pose for six breaths. When you are ready, exhale the back foot down and bring your spine upright. Allow both arms to float to your sides. Stretch out your feet a bit and then bring your weight onto your right foot, repeating this pose on the other side, holding that posture for six breaths as well. Once you have come back to your Mountain Pose, take a few deep breaths, once again sensing the aliveness that results from moving the body in new ways.

STAGE ELEVEN, FALLING APART

From Mountain Pose, find a safe way to crumple down into sitting and from there possibly crumple a little more, until you are lying on your mat. Wherever you begin (sitting or lying or somewhere in between), experiment with movements that feel to you like Stage Eleven, Falling Apart. Use your imagination and listen to your body. Play with movements that might express, for you, formlessness, fragmentation, or chaos. Go within to access your own inner knowing of these states. When your movements naturally come to a close, curl onto your right side into a fetal pose, take three deep breaths, and then inhale and push yourself up to sitting.

STAGE TWELVE, OPENING TO GRACE

Finding a comfortable seated position and breathe for a few moments. Find your center, a place of balance, poise, and relaxation. Then, on an inhale, lift and open your arms above your head in a graceful curve that is reminiscent of a chalice. Let your arms be very active as you lift them up and open through the front of your body. When you are ready, begin to gently and slowly twist from side to side, inhaling as you come to face forward and exhaling to either side. Repeat twist to both sides twelve times. Bring the movement to a close and release your hands down to your lap. Breathe here for a few moments in humility and gratitude for the grace you have received.

To bring this Yoga Mandala cycle to a close, gently roll down to your back. Place your hands about a foot beyond the sides of your body with your palms facing up and allow your feet to relax and fall open to the sides as well. This is the Corpse Pose, a position that allows your body to integrate this series of movements. Just breathe in and out. Rest from your efforts as you take in the essence of the Great Round through your body and breath.

This concludes the yoga movements for the Great Round. Performing one or all of these simple movements prior to creative self-expression can increase your relaxation, improve your physical well-being, and enhance your ability to focus. You might even enjoy adopting these simple movements as your regular routine of self-care. This will bring into your life the benefits of creating mandalas with body movement.

Songs for the Great Round

Maureen Shelton, a member of our mandala group, wrote these songs in response to her exploration of each stage of the Great Round. At each meeting she taught us a new song that we sang at the beginning of our gathering. Singing these songs helps align your energy with the stages you are exploring. I suggest you sing them or listen to them before or during your exploration of each stage. You can listen to Maureen's recordings of these songs on her CD available at www.mandalaCD.com. Her voice is pure healing sound.

Singing the songs at other times is also enjoyable. They can serve as encouraging affirmations during the stages of your life.

Stage One

In the Darkness Deep

I am warmed by all that will be, I am warmed by the love of all that has been, I am rest-ing, in the dark - ness deep. I am warmed by the spi - ral of wis-dom, I am warmed by the won-der of the sleep-ing stars, I am rest-ing in the dark - ness deep. I am warmed by the spi - rit of grace. I am warmed by the whisp-er that all is well, I am rest - ing in the dark - ness deep. I will fall in-to form in right tim - ing. I will fall in - to form in right time - ing, out of dark - ness in - to the light

Stage Two

We Are One

All is____ well, all is____ well, the well is____ deep.____

Drink your____ fill. One, we are one. One, we are____ one.__

Stage Three

Breath of God

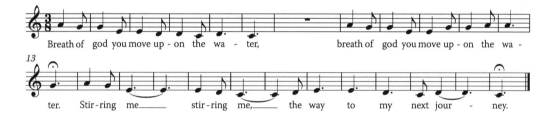

Breath of god you move up - on the wa - ter, breath of god you move up - on the wa -

ter. Stir - ring me____ stir - ring me,____ the way to my next jour - ney.

Stage Four

Grace Notes

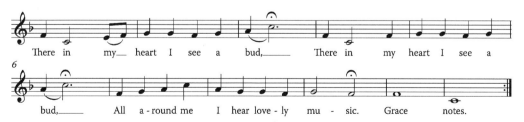

There in my____ heart I see a bud,____ There in my heart I see a

bud,____ All a - round me I hear love - ly mu - sic. Grace notes.

Stage Five

Make My Way

Stage Six

Hope of Sky

Light_____ my soul, il - lu___ mine_ me.___ Help me hold the depth of my roots,_____ and a hope of sky.___ And a hope of sky.

Light_____ my soul, il - lu___ mine me,___ help me hold the depth of my roots,_____ and a hope of sky,___ and a hope_____ of sky.

Stage Seven

Soul Awake

Oh my soul a-wake and sing your song, oh my soul a-wake and sing your song, the path is there for you to

take. Oh my soul__ a wake. Oh my soul a-wake and sing your song, oh my soul a-wake and

sing your song, the path is there for you to take. Oh my soul__ a - wake. Oh my soul a-wake and

sing your song. Oh my soul a-wake and sing your song. The path is there__ for you to take, Oh my soul__

Oh my soul a-wake and sing your song, oh my soul a-wake and sing your song. the

__ a-wake. Oh my soul a-wake and sing your song. Oh my soul a-wake, and sing your song, the

path is there for you to take. Oh my soul__ a-wake. Oh my soul a-wake and sing your song.

Soul Awake (continued)

Stage Eight

Deep in the Song

Stage Nine

It Is Here

Stage Ten

I Will Let Go

Stage Eleven

Falling Apart

Stage Twelve

Let It Sing

I greet you in the name of joy, great_____ joy. I greet you in the

name of joy, great_____ joy. The song_____ is here, oh_____

__ is here. Let it sing._____ Let it sing._____

Let it sing.

Let it sing._____ Let it sing.

Using *The Mandala Workbook* with a Group

Creative work in a group is enjoyable for a number of reasons. Having a group with agreed-upon times to meet affords structure that helps individuals focus on their creative self-expression. Groups offer the companionship of others sharing experiences similar to yours. Group members give support to one another as they witness each other's experience, creativity, and personal growth.

Having respectful listeners can help individuals discuss and arrive at insights about the personal meaning of their mandala-making experiences. The opportunity to witness the process of others can be inspiring, informative, and demonstrative of a wide range of possibilities for responding to life's challenges. So individuals benefit from the shared experience, creativity, and wisdom of the group. The group then becomes yet another mandala to explore.

The Mandala Workbook can provide a structure for your group gatherings. There are several mandala exercises that are designed for groups, such as the Pizza Mandala of Stage Eleven or the Group Clay Mandala of Stage Twelve. Working on individual mandala exercises together during the group time is also worthwhile.

Your group might agree on exploring one chapter per week or month—reading at home and then gathering together to create your individual mandalas, as our mandala group did. Or your group might select a particular mandala activity for a special occasion, such as the Stage Seven Personal Shield Mandala as a way to send off a group member on a personal travel adventure. If your group has a focus of inner child work, the Baby Me and Little Me mandalas from Stages Four and Five could be rewarding.

Whatever use your group makes of *The Mandala Workbook*, some attention to organization before beginning your group can be helpful.

Designate a group facilitator (or form a committee or simply take the lead in starting a group for yourself and a few others). The facilitator role can rotate to others as agreed upon.

The facilitator is responsible for tending the group's organizational needs such as:

Suggest meeting dates

Arrange place and time of meetings

Provide a group roster if group requests it

Organize presentation/discussion/sharing of chapter material (ask for volunteers or otherwise designate responsibility)

Suggest following some or all of these group guidelines

Invite discussion of guidelines

Group Guidelines

Decide together as a group on the guidelines that you want to adopt.

When you commit to the group, make a good faith effort to attend all meetings.

Let your group facilitator know ahead of time when you cannot attend a meeting.

Remember to initial, date, and title your work. (Journal about it if time allows).

Decide about disposition of artwork (take it home, store in art space, in folders, photograph, etc.).

Leave time at the end of the group so those who want to can talk about their experience and share their mandalas.

Respect the confidentiality of group members. Do not talk about them and/or their creative work outside group.

Take responsibility for getting what you want in your group: the more you contribute, and let others know clearly what you want and need, the more you will get out of the experience.

When addressing the group try to use "I" statements instead of questions, e.g., "I am curious about this symbol (color, material, etc.)" or "I'm wondering what this was like for you," instead of "What's this?" or "That means ___."

Own your projections onto others' artwork by saying, "If this were my mandala it would be telling me that I am ___" instead of "That sure looks angry!" or "You must be very sad now."

Remember: These guidelines are not *required.* It is up to your group to decide together what works best for you. Exploring *The Mandala Workbook* with others can be rich, rewarding, and fun. May your group itself become a lovely mandala.

References

Arnheim, Rudolf. *The Power of the Center: A Study of Composition in the Visual Arts*. Berkeley and Los Angeles: University of California Press, 1986.

Artress, Lauren. *Walking a Sacred Path*. New York: Riverhead Books, 1995.

Brauen, Martin. *The Mandala: Sacred Circle in Tibetan Buddhism*. Translated by Martin Willson. Boston: Shambhala Publications, 1997.

Campbell, Joseph. *The Hero with a Thousand Faces*. New York: World Publishing Company, 1971.

Cash, Thomas F., and Thomas Pruzinsky, eds. *Body Image: A Handbook of Theory, Research, and Clinical Practice*. New York: Guilford Press, 2002.

Chicago, Judy. *Through the Flower: My Struggles as a Woman Artist*. Rev. ed. Garden City, N.Y.: Anchor Books, 1982.

Cleary, Thomas. *I Ching Mandalas: A Program of Study for the Book of Changes*. Boston: Shambhala Publications, 1989.

Cooper, Donald. Personal communication with author, 2008.

Cornell, Judith. *Mandala: Luminous Symbols for Healing*. Wheaton, Ill.: Quest Books, 1994.

Craighead, Meinrad. *Crow Mother and the Dog God: A Retrospective*. Petaluma, Calif.: Pomegranate Communications, 2003.

Cyriaque, Jeanne, ed. "Shoutin' in Briar Patch." *Reflections: Georgia African American Historic Preservation Network* 4, no. 1 (2003): 2–3.

Eliade, Mircea. *Rites and Symbols of Initiation*. 2nd. ed. Translated by Willard R. Trask. Dallas: Spring Publications, 1994.

Fincher, Susanne F. *Creating Mandalas: For Insight, Healing, and Self-Expression*. Boston: Shambhala Publications, 1991.

———. *Coloring Mandalas 3: Circles of the Sacred Feminine*. Boston: Shambhala Publications, 2006.

————. "Mandalas and the Gestalt of Self." *The International Gestalt Journal* 30, no. 2 (2007): 65–78.

Fox, Matthew, ed. *Illuminations of Hildegard of Bingen.* Santa Fe: Bear and Company, 1985.

Frazer, James George. *The Golden Bough: A Study in Magic and Religion.* New York: Macmillan Publishing, 1950.

Gibson, J. J. *The Ecological Approach to Visual Perception.* Hillsdale, N.H.: Lawrence Erlbaum Association, 1986.

Gimbutas, Marija. *The Language of the Goddess.* San Francisco: Harper & Row, 1989.

Goldwater, Robert, and Marco Treves, eds. *Artists on Art: From the XIV to the XX Century.* New York: Pantheon Books, 1945.

Grant, Patrick, ed. *A Dazzling Darkness: An Anthology of Western Mysticism.* Grand Rapids, Mich.: William B. Eerdmans Publishing Company, 1985.

Harding, M. Esther. *Psychic Energy: Its Source and Its Transformation.* 2d ed. Princeton, N.J.: Princeton University Press, 1973.

Hilsinger, Serena Sue, and Lois Brynes, eds. *Selected Poems of May Sarton.* New York: W. W. Norton & Company, 1978.

Holy Bible: Containing the Old and New Testaments. Cleveland: The World Publishing Company, n.d.

James, William. *The Varieties of Religious Experience.* New York: Macmillan Publishing, 1961.

Jayakar, Pupul. *The Earth Mother: Legends, Goddesses, and Ritual Arts of India.* San Francisco: Harper & Row, 1990.

Johnson, Mark. *The Body in the Mind: The Bodily Basis of Meaning, Imagination, and Reason.* Chicago: The University of Chicago Press, 1987.

Jung, C. G. *Memories, Dreams, Reflections.* New York: Random House, 1965.

————. *The Archetypes and the Collective Unconscious.* 2d. ed. Princeton, N.J.: Princeton University Press, 1969a.

————. *Four Archetypes.* Princeton, N.J.: Princeton University Press, 1969b.

————. *Mysterium Coniunctionis.* Princeton, N.J.: Princeton University Press, 1970.

———. *Mandala Symbolism.* Princeton, N.J.: Princeton University Press, 1973.

———. *Dreams.* Princeton, N.J.: Princeton University Press, 1974.

———. *Psychology and the East.* Princeton, N.J.: Princeton University Press, 1978.

Kagan, Jerome. *The Second Year: The Emergence of Self-Awareness.* Cambridge, Mass.: Harvard University Press, 1981.

Kast, Verena. *The Dynamics of Symbols: Fundamentals of Jungian Psychotherapy.* Translated by Susan A. Schwarz. New York: Fromm International Publishing Corporation, 1992.

Kellogg, Joan. Lecture at Atlanta Art Therapy Institute, Atlanta, Georgia, 1983.

———. *Mandala: Path of Beauty.* Williamsburg, Va.: Mandala Assessment and Research Institute, 1984.

———. "Color Theory from the Perspective of the Great Round of Mandala." Unpublished manuscript, 1986.

———. and F. B. DiLeo. "Archetypal Stages of the Great Round of Mandala." *Journal of Religion and Psychical Research* 5, 38–49.

Kluckhohn, Clyde, and Dorothea Leighton. *The Navaho.* Rev. ed. Garden City, N.Y.: Doubleday & Company, 1962.

Lawal, Babatunde. "Embodying the Sacred in Yoruba Art." In the exhibition catalog for High Museum of Art in Atlanta, Ga., and Newark Museum in Newark, N.J., 2008.

Lerner, Jonathan. Personal communication with author, 2008.

Lonegren, Sig. *Labyrinths: Ancient Myths and Modern Uses.* Glastonbury, Somerset: Gothic Image Publications, 1991.

Neumann, Erich. *Art and the Creative Unconscious.* Princeton, N.J.: Princeton University Press, 1974.

Norment, Rachel. *Guided by Dreams: Breast Cancer, Dreams, and Transformation.* Richmond, Va.: Brandylane Publishers, 2006.

Patterson, Alex. *A Field Guide to Rock Art Symbols of the Greater Southwest.* Boulder: Johnson Books, 1992.

Perera, Sylvia Brinton. *Descent to the Goddess: A Way of Initiation for Women.* Toronto: Inner City Books, 1981.

Richards, M. C. *Centering: In Pottery, Poetry, and the Person.* Middletown, Conn.: Wesleyan University Press, 1964.

Rose, Joshua. "Full Circle." Exhibit at Zane Bennett Contemporary Art, Santa Fe, N.M. Artist's statement posted at www.zanebennetgallery .com, 2008.

Seftel, Laura. *Grief Unseen: Healing Pregnancy Loss Through the Arts.* London: Jessica Kingsley, 2006.

Stein, Murray. *Jung's Map of the Soul: An Introduction.* Chicago and LaSalle, Ill.: Open Court, 1998.

Steindl-Rast, David, and Sharon Lebell. *The Music of Silence: Entering the Sacred Space of Monastic Experience.* New York: HarperCollins Publishers. 1995.

Storm, Hyemeyohsts. *Seven Arrows.* New York: Ballantine Books, 1972.

Tucci, Giuseppe. *Theory and Practice of the Mandala.* London: Rider & Company, 1961.

Wosien, Maria-Gabriele. *Sacred Dance: Encounter with the Gods.* New York: Thames & Hudson, Inc., 1974.

Index

Page references to figures are in **boldface** type.

Adolescent Me Mandala (exercise), 120
alchemy, 133
Ancestors Holding Mandala (exercise), 90–92
angel wings, 260–62, **261**
Archetypal Parents Mandala (exercise), 117–19
Archetypal Stages of the Great Round of Mandala,
    25, 26, 30–31, 252–70
    reflecting on, 232–33
    Stages 1–6 vs. Stages 8–12, 128, 225
    See also specific stages
arm circles, **259**, 259–60
art, progression from mandala to human figure, **17**
art materials, 36
astrological signs, 228–29
Aztecs, 14
    Sun Stone, **13**, 14

Bacon, Edna, plate 28
balance, 9
Basic Mandala Grid (exercise), 159–62, **160**,
    162–63, **239**
Beginning, 26, 83. *See also* Bindu Mandala; Stage
    Four
Bible, 75
Bindu Mandala, 99–100
bird people, **9**
birth, 67, 212. *See also* Rebirthing Mandala; Stage
    Four
Blessing Way, 8
Blessing Words Mandala (exercise), 108–9
Bliss, 26, 57, 58
body, 136, 183–84, 218–19
    and mandala symbolism in Buddhism, **5**
boxes. *See* Nesting Boxes Mandala
brainstorming, 61
"Breath of God" (song), 75, 279
bridge, plate 18

Buddha, 2, 11
Buddha feet in Eastern mandalas, **103**, 104
Buddhism, **5**, 6, 11
Buddhist Wheel of Life, 14, **15**
Burning Wheel Mandala (exercise), 182–83

calendar, **13**. *See also* seasons; *specific stages*
Campbell, Joseph, 2, 42
cancer patients, 23, plate 8
Celtic Spiral Mandala (exercise), 80–81
chalice, 217
chaos. *See* Stage Eleven
Chicago, Judy, 20
children, 83
    mandalas and other art of, **17**
    See also inner child work
Child's Play Mandala (exercise), 61
Child's Pose, 252–53, **253**
Christianity, 6, 10, 14, 86
Circle of Self (exercise), 47
circle paintings
    Joshua Rose on, 18–19
    See also circles
circles, 20–21, plates 2–5, 7
    arm, **259**, 259–60
    completing (*see* stepping to the center)
    concentric, 96, 97, 108, plate 16 (*see also* Stage
        Five)
    intersecting, 163
    See also cycle(s); Family Circle Mandala;
        Qualities of the Circle; Sphere of Influences;
        squaring the circle
clay, 231–32
colors of mandalas, 57, 97, 116, 129, 144, 158, 180,
    196, 213
    using least favorite color, 198–200
    See also mandala templates
consciousness, levels of, 68–70
Cooper, Donald, 19, plate 5
Cornell, Judith, 150–51

Corpse Pose, 276
Craighead, Meinrad, 22–23
Crazy Quilt Mandala (exercise), 203–4
creativity, 150–51
    destruction and, 197–98
crisis, mandala making at times of, 23
Crystallization, 26
crystals, 159
curved vs. straight lines. *See* Stage Seven
cycle(s)
    life, 182
    mandalas and, 12, 14, 16
    See also circles

dance, 9–12
Dancer, 267–68, **268**
Dancing Your Body Mandala (exercise), 218–19
dark night of the soul, 195, 270
darkness, 44, 216. *See also* "In the Darkness Deep";
    Stage Twelve
death, 26, 185–86, 212
deceased persons, 185–86
"Deep in the Song" (song), 152, 283
Defensive Shields Mandala (exercise), **102**, 102–5
dervishes, 9–10, plate 3
destruction, 195
    creativity and, 197–98
    See also Kali; Stage Eleven
dialogue, inner, 34
Discovering the New Mandala (exercise), 88–89
dots, 19
Dragon Fight, 26
Dream Catcher Mandala (exercise), 75–76, **76**
Dream Mandala (exercise), 74–75
dreams of mandalas, 22–23, 74–76

Earth Mandala (exercise), 48–49
Easy Pose, 270, **271**
Ecstatic Mandala (exercise), 215–16
ego, 178, 202, 211
    non-ego and, 224–25
Eight-Pointed Star Mandala (exercise), 164–68
embracing the new. *See* new, embracing the
energy
    sacred, 4, 6

types of, 150
enlightenment, 212
Enso (exercise), 232, **233**
Europe, 10
Exploring Your Opposites (exercise), 225–26

face mask, 187–88
facing things, 186–87
falling apart, 30, 193, 200, 201, 208, 268–70. *See
    also* Stage Eleven
"Falling Apart" (song), 197, 205, 284
Falling Apart Mandala (exercise), 205–6
family, 98. *See also* Ancestors Holding Mandala
Family Circle Mandala (exercise), 100–101
feet, Buddha, **103**, 104
Finger Painting Mandala (exercise), 76–77
five, 143, 145
floating into the light, 27, 55, 64. *See also* Stage
    Two
flowers, 89–90, 108, 170–71
footprints, **103**, 104–5
forms in mandalas, 35
fragmentation, 26, 197, plate 31. *See also* falling
    apart; Stage Eleven
free association, 35
Functioning Ego, 26
functioning in the world, 141, 152. *See also* Stage
    Eight

Gates of Death, 26
gender polarity. *See* masculinity and femininity
Ghost Catcher Mandala (exercise), 183
God, 6, 172, 212. *See also* Higher Power
God's Eye Mandala (exercise), 109–10
grace, opening to, 30, 211, 212, 216, 270. *See also*
    Stage Twelve
"Grace Notes" (song), 89, 279
great round of nature, 14–15
Great Stretch with Wide-Angle Forward Bend,
    265–67, **266**
Gregory, Diana, 41, plates 9, 19, 32
Group Clay Mandala (exercise), 230–32
groups, working with, 286–87
    guidelines, 287–88
guilt, 214

Happy Baby Pose, 253, **254**, 255
hatching, 89
healing, 149–50
healing energies, 23
Henri, Robert, 20
Hero Pose, **257**, 257–59
Higher Power, 172, 214. *See also* God
Hildegard of Bingen, 6
    medieval world view from manuscript of, **7**
Hildegard's Mandala, 97–98
Hip Rotation, 255–57, **256**
"Hope of Sky" (song), 116, 281
Hutton, Patty, 40, 54, 66, 82, 94, 112, 126, 140, 154,
    176, 192, 210, **253–54**, **256**, **258–59**, **261**, **263**,
    265–66, **268–69**, **271**, plates 18, 20, 22, 25, 33

"I Will Let Go" (song), 180, 181, 284
igniting the inner fire, 28, 113, 117. *See also* Stage
    Six
"In the Darkness Deep" (song), 47, 278
individuation, 1, 21–22, 128. *See also* selfhood
inner child work, 83–84, 87–88. *See also* Little Me
    Mandala
intrauterine experience. *See* pregnancy; Stage Two;
    Umbilical Mandala; womb
"It Is Here" (song), 158, 171, 283

Jesus Christ, plate 2
Johnson, Robert, 38
journaling, 35
Jung, Carl Gustav, 18, 179
    mandalas and, 21–24, 26

Kabbalah, diagram inspired by, 8
Kahn, Sue, plates 11, 23, 26
Kali, 179
Kali Yantra (exercise), 188–89
Kast, Verena, 23
Kelahan, Annie, plates 24, 27
Kellogg, Joan, 56, 68, 83, 142, 178, 196
    on Archetypal Stages, 24, **25**, 26
    on boundaries and polarities, 114
    on consciousness, 68

names of stages, 57, 67, 83, 141, 193, 212
    on ritualistic behavior, 96
Kinesthetic Mandala of Letting Go (exercise), 190

Labyrinth, 26, 67, 77. *See also* Stage Three
Labyrinth Mandala (exercise), 77–79
labyrinths, 10, 67, 69
    diagram for drawing, **78**
landscapes, 116
Lerner, Jonathan, 19
"Let go and let God," 196
"Let It Sing" (song), 215, 285
letting go, 29, 177, 268. *See also* Stage Ten
life cycle, 182
light, 132–33, 216
Little Me Mandala, 98–99
Liturgical Year Mandala (exercise), 227
Loopy Thread Mandala (exercise), 71–72

Madonna and Child Mandala (exercise), 86–87
"Make My Way" (song), 110, 280
Mandala cards
    Card One, 51–52
    Card Two, 64
    Card Three, 81
    Card Four, 93
    Card Five, 111
    Card Six, 123–24
    Card Seven, 138–39
    Card Eight, 152–53
    Card Nine, 174
    Card Ten, 191
    Card Eleven, 208
    Card Twelve, 222
mandala exercises, 33–36. *See also specific exer-
    cises*
Mandala for Exploring a Dilemma (exercise),
    120–21
Mandala for Facing It (exercise), 186–87
Mandala for the Lost and Gone (exercise), 185–86
Mandala Gateway to the Worst Thing That Can
    Happen (exercise), 184–85
Mandala Invoking Your Creative Energy (exercise),
    150–51
Mandala Mask (exercise), 189–90

Mandala Mask for Letting Go (exercise), 187–88

Mandala of a Functioning Ego (exercise), 144

Mandala of Abiding Order (exercise), 206–7

Mandala of Abundant Potential (exercise), 63

Mandala of Baby Me (exercise), 87–88

Mandala of Beginning (exercise), 86

Mandala of Bliss (exercise), 58

Mandala of Broken Mirrors (exercise), 204–5

Mandala of Cards (exercise), 229–30

Mandala of Choosing Your Name (exercise), 122–23

Mandala of Crystallization Moments (exercise), 173

Mandala of Firm Foundation (exercise), 130

Mandala of Fragmentation (exercise), 197

Mandala of Igniting the Inner Fire (exercise), 117

Mandala of Letting Go (exercise), 181

Mandala of Light at the Center of Darkness (exercise), 216–17

Mandala of Looking Back (exercise), 224

Mandala of Offering Up (exercise), 214–15

Mandala of People I Dislike (exercise), 202–3

Mandala of Possibilities (exercise), 61–62

Mandala of Receiving Grace (exercise), 214

Mandala of Resting in the Darkness (exercise), 44

Mandala of Sacrifice (exercise), 180–81

Mandala of Taming the Dragon (exercise), 119–20

Mandala of Tearing Apart (exercise), 197–98

Mandala of the Breath of God (exercise), 75

Mandala of the Four Quadrants (exercise), 137–38

Mandala of the Great Round Mandalas (exercise), 224–25

Mandala of the Great Round of the Year (exercise), 226–27

Mandala of the Sacred Chalice (exercise), 217

Mandala of the Sacred Marriage (exercise), 133–34

Mandala of the Shining Star (exercise), 145–47

Mandala of the Twelve Astrological Signs (exercise), 227–28

Mandala of the Winter Solstice (exercise), 219–20

Mandala of Transient Beauty (exercise), 217–18

Mandala of Turning Points (exercise), 73–74

Mandala of Turning Toward the Journey (exercise), 71

Mandala of Welcoming What's Up (exercise), 90

Mandala of Your Higher Power (exercise), 171–72

Mandala of Your Least Favorite Color (exercise), 198–200

Mandala Series for Healing (exercise), 149–50

mandala sites, 2, 4

mandala templates, 235–51

mandala(s)
    ancient, 2, **3**, 4
    creating, 1, 2, 35, 36
    handling, 35
    interpreting, 37–38
    letting go of, 36
    meaning of the term, 1, 12
    nature of, 1
    oldest known ink drawing of a, **5**
    and the sacred, 2, 4, 6, 8
    techniques for relating to, 34–36
    where to keep/store, 36
    witnessing, 1
    See also specific topics

mandalic road, 10

Mandorla Mandala (exercise), 163–64

marriage, sacred, 133–34

masculinity and femininity, 118–19
    balance and integration of, 128–30, 133, 155–56

mask, 187–88

matriarchy, 128, 193

Medicine Wheel, 12

Medicine Wheel Mandala (exercise), 135–36, 228–29

Memory Mandala (exercise), 200–202

Million Star Mandala (exercise), 58

Mind's Eye Mandala (exercise), 220–21

moon. *See* Solar/Lunar Metallic Mandala

mother, 116, 118, 119
    good, 83, 86–87 (*see also* Stage Four)
    See also birth; pregnancy

Mountain Pose, **259**, 259–62, **261**, 264–65, **265**

movement, mandalas and, 8–12

music, 10–11

mystics, 6

names and naming, 122–23

Native Americans, 12. *See also* Navaho

Navaho, 8, **9**

near death experiences, 212
Nesting Boxes Mandala (exercise), 105–6
Nesting Mandala (exercise), 89
Neumann, Eric, 114
new, embracing the, 28, 90, 93, 258. *See also* Stage Four
New Moon Mandala (exercise), 49–50
Norment, Rachel, 23, plate 8
Nowicki, Kaaren, plate 30
Nurturing Flower Mandala (exercise), 89–90

"Soul Awake" (song), 138, 282
oneness. *See* Stage Two; "We Are One"
opening to grace. *See* grace
oral stage, 83. *See also* Stage Four
orgasm, 212

parental archetypes, 117–19
participation mystique, 55
patriarchy, 128
personal growth, 24, 26, 109–10. *See also* inner child work; self-understanding
Personal Shield Mandala (exercise), 134–35
pinwheel, **151**, 151–52, **238**
Pizza Mandala (exercise), 207–8
Plotinus, 10
pregnancy, 67. *See also* Umbilical Mandala; womb
Pregnancy Mandala (exercise), 92
Problem Solving Swastika Mandala (exercise), 148–49
projection, 203
protection. *See* Nesting Boxes Mandala; shields

Qualities of the Circle (exercise), 45–47
quilts, 203–4

reaping rewards, 29, 155, 173, 267. *See also* Stage Nine
Rebirthing Mandala (exercise), 59–60
responsibility, taking, 96
resting in the darkness, 27, 43, 44, 252. *See also* Stage One
rewards. *See* reaping rewards

Reynolds, Annette, plates 12, 14
Roa, Francisco, 19, 20, plate 7
Rose, Joshua, 18–19, plate 4

Sacred Flower Mandala (exercise), 108
sacrifice, 180–81
sand mandalas, 6
Scratch Art Mandala (exercise), 206
seasons, 121–22, 219–20
    four, **9**, 12, 182 (*see also* calendar)
Self, 21–24, 128, 178
self-understanding
    mandalas and, 16–19, 20–21
    See also personal growth
selfhood, claiming, 28, 95, 96, 110, 260. *See also* individuation; Stage Five
sexual orgasm, 212
shadow, 198–200, 202
Shelton, Maureen Jenci, 34, 277–85, plate 16
shields, **102**, 102–5, 134–35
singing. *See* music; songs for the Great Round
sleep, 41
Solar/Lunar Metallic Mandala (exercise), 132–33
Solomon's Seal Mandala (exercise), 169–70, **170**
songs for the Great Round, 277–85. *See also* specific songs
Soothing Mandala (exercise), 62–63
space, sacred, 2, 4
Sphere of Influences (exercise), 106–8
Spider Web Mandala (exercise), 47–48, **48**
spinal flex, upper, 257–58
Spinning Inward Mandala (exercise), 79–80
spirals, 77, 80–81
squaring the circle, 26, 29, 128, 130. *See also* Stage Seven
Squaring the Circle Mandala (exercise), 130–32, **131**, **236**
Stage One, 27, 41–43
    exercises, 44–51
    intentions for, 43
    mandalas, 43–44
    reflecting on, 51–52
    yoga movements, 252–53, **253**, 272
Stage Two, 27, 55–56
    exercises, 57–63
    intentions for, 56

mandalas, 57
reflecting on, 64
yoga movements, 253, **254**, 255, 272
Stage Three, 27–28, 67–69
exercises, 70–81
intentions for, 69–70
mandalas, 70
reflecting on, 81
yoga movements, 255–57, **256**, 272
Stage Four, 28, 83–84
exercises, 85–92
intentions for, 84–85
mandalas, 85
reflecting on, 92–93
yoga movements, 257–58, **258**, 272–73
Stage Five, 28, 95–96
exercises, 96–111
intentions for, 96
mandalas, 97
reflecting on, 110
yoga movements, **259**, 259–60, 273
Stage Six, 28, 113–14
exercises, 116–23
intentions for, 114–15
mandalas, 116
reflecting on, 123–24
yoga movements, 260–62, **261**, 273
Stage Seven, 28–29, 127–28
exercises, 129–38
intentions for, 129
mandalas, 129
reflecting on, 138–39
yoga movements, 262–64, **263**, 274
Stage Eight, 29, 141–42
exercises, 144–52
intentions for, 142–43
mandalas, 143–44
reflecting on, 152–53
yoga movements, 264–65, **265**, 274
Stage Nine, 29, 155–57
exercises, 158–73
intentions for, 157
mandalas, 157–58
reflecting on, 173–74
yoga movements, 265–67, **266**, 274
Stage Ten, 29, 177–79
exercises, 180–90

intentions for, 179
mandalas, 179–80
reflecting on, 191
yoga movements, 267–68, **268**, 275
Stage Eleven, 29–30, 193–95
exercises, 197–208
intentions for, 196
mandalas, 196
reflecting on, 208
yoga movements, 268–70, **269**, 275
Stage Twelve, 30, 211–12, 221
exercises, 213–32
intentions for, 212–13
mandalas, 213
yoga movements, 270, **271**, 275–76
standing, 104–5
Standpoint Mandala (exercise), 104–5
star
eight-pointed, 164–68
five-pointed, 143, 145, **146** (*see also* Stage Eight)
Star Me Mandala (exercise), 147
Star Pose, 264–65, **265**
stepping to the center, 223
exercises, 223–32
stillness. *See* Stage One
straight vs. curved lines. *See* Stage Seven
Sublime Flower Mandala (exercise), 170–71
Sufism. *See* dervishes
Summer Solstice Mandala (exercise), 121–22
sun. *See* Solar/Lunar Metallic Mandala; swastika
surrender. *See* falling apart; letting go
swastika, 143, **148**, 148–49. *See also* Stage Eight

Target, 26, 95. *See also* Stage Five
Target Mandala (exercise), 100
"terrible twos," 95
Thackston, King, 19, plate 6
Things Fall Apart Pose, 268–70
Three-Part Healing Breath, 262–64, **263**
Through the Circle (exercise), 45
Tibetan Buddhist ceremonies, 6, 11
time, counting, 14. *See also* calendar; seasons
titling mandalas, 35
tradition. *See* Ancestors Holding Mandala
Transcendent Ecstasy, 26, 212
transcendent function, 115

transformation, 42, 198
Treasured Body Part Mandala (exercise), 183–84
Tree Mandala (exercise), 136–37
Tucci, Giuseppe, 20
turning toward the journey, 28, 68, 70–72. *See also* Stage Three

umbilical cord, 67, 72–73, 80
Umbilical Mandala (exercise), 72–73
union with God, 212

Void, 26, 41

Water Mandala (exercise), 59
"We Are One" (song), 57, 60, 279
Wheel of Life. *See* Buddhist Wheel of Life
wheels. *See* Burning Wheel Mandala; Medicine Wheel; pinwheel

Whirled Peace Mandala (exercise), **151**, 151–52, **238**
wholeness. *See* individuation
will, 119
Womandala Bag (exercise), **50**, 50–51
Womandala Bag Reprise (exercise), 230
womb, memories of being in, 48, 67. *See also* pregnancy; Umbilical Mandala
women artists, 20
Wosien, Maria-Gabriele, **9**

Yantra Mandala (exercise), 159
yoga, 10
yoga mandala of the Great Round, 271–76
yoga movements, 252
    free form, 268–70, **269**
    See also under specific stages

zodiac, 228–29

About the Author

Susanne F. Fincher, MA, is a Jungian-oriented psychotherapist, licensed professional counselor, and board certified art therapist with a practice in Atlanta, Georgia. She is known internationally as an authority on the spiritual, psychological, and health-enhancing dimensions of creativity as expressed in the drawing and coloring of mandalas. Her five books on mandalas have been translated into numerous languages. *The Journal of Art Therapy* called *Creating Mandalas* "a classic," and described her Coloring Mandalas series as inviting "a deeper understanding of the cycles of psychological life." More information on Susanne can be found at www .creatingmandalas.com.

Also by Susanne F. Fincher

Creating the circular designs called mandalas is a meditative practice, a healing exercise in times of crisis, and a pleasurable act of creativity. As a symbol of the Self, the mandala provides a connection to our innermost being. This series of Coloring Mandalas workbooks offers an opportunity for creativity and self-exploration.

Coloring Mandalas 1: For Insight, Healing, and Self-Expression
Coloring this book from start to finish will carry the reader through a balanced experience of change through twelve archetypal stages, guided by the accompanying text.

Coloring Mandalas 2: For Balance, Harmony, and Spiritual Well-Being
Fincher's second collection of colorable circles focuses on the phase of "crystalization" or completion, and is intended to help us understand ourselves and our place in the greater scheme of things.

Coloring Mandalas 3: Circles of the Sacred Feminine
The mandalas here evoke an encounter with the Divine as a feminine presence and are based on circular imagery of the Goddess from a range of countries and cultures.

Creating Mandalas: For Insight, Healing, and Self-Expression
The traditional designs known as mandalas were recognized by C. G. Jung as symbolic representations of the Self. This book is a practical guide to mandala drawing for personal growth, stress reduction, and creative expression. Fincher introduces the history and ritual use of mandalas in cultures all over the world; offers guidance in choosing art materials, techniques, and colors for the creation of personal mandalas; and discusses the symbolism of shapes, colors, numbers, and motifs, such as birds and flowers, that may appear in mandalas. She also presents several illustrated case histories of people who successfully use her techniques.

Available at bookstores and from www.shambhala.com.

Chris Claassen